Søren Ł

Son of Spinoza

Georg Brandes and
Modern Jewish Cosmopolitanism

Aarhus University Press

Son of Spinoza

© Søren Blak Hjortshøj and Aarhus University Press 2021

Cover, layout and typesetting: Jørgen Sparre

Cover illustration: Georg Brandes, around 1900. Photograph by Strelitsky.

The Portrait Collection, The Royal Danish Library

Publishing editor: Mark Eaton

Excerpts from Brandes translated by: Nancy Aaen

This book is typeset in Warnock Pro and printed on 100g Munken Lynx

Printed by Narayana Press, Denmark

Printed in Denmark 2021

ISBN 978 87 7219 018 1

Aarhus University Press

aarhusuniversitypress.dk

Published with the financial support of

POLITIKEN-**FONDEN**

and Landsdommer V. Gieses Legat

International distributors

Oxbow Books Ltd.

ISD – distributor of scholarly books

PEER REVIEWED

MIX
Paper from responsible sources
FSC
www.fsc.org FSC™ C010651

Table of Contents

Discussion
Brandes' Representation of Jewishness
as a Vital Archive for Today's Cosmopolitanisms | 193

Introduction

Brandes as a Vital Cosmopolitan Archive

In the first years of our current global age, shortly after the collapse of the Eastern European and Soviet communist regimes, Francis Fukuyama's "end of history" thesis seemed for many to be an accurate diagnosis and prognostication of forthcoming world historical events. In the introduction to *The End of History or The Last Man Standing* (1991), which was based on the Hegelian interpretation of the human "desire for recognition" as the key principle for historical development, Fukuyama designated Western liberal democracy as "the end point of mankind's ideological evolution."[1] In explaining why Western liberal democracy applies itself to the human struggle of recognition better than any other state form, Fukuyama writes that:

The inherently unequal recognition of masters and slaves is replaced by universal and reciprocal recognition, where every citizen recognizes the dignity and humanity of every other citizen, and where that dignity is recognized in turn by the state through the granting of rights.[2]

Fukuyama does not reflect much, however, on terms such as "national cultural tradition," "nation state," or "nationalism," except from downgrading the continuing relevance of these terms. Influenced by Fukuyama's "end of history" thesis and similar diagnoses of a global and non-binary world order after the fall of communism, the long-gone field of cosmopolitanism was revitalized in the 1990s. Important cultural thinkers, philosophers, and sociologists such as Julia Kristeva, Homi K. Bhabha, Martha Nussbaum, Jacques Derrida, and Ulrich Beck designated themselves as cosmopolitans in the tradition of Kantian liberal cosmopolitanism. All of these influential scholars wrote essays and books thematizing that the universally shared "cosmopolitan existence" which Immanuel Kant had envisioned in "Idee zu einer allgemeinen Geschichte in weltbürgerlicher Absicht" (1784) would in the succeeding decades replace the dominance of nation states and national cultural traditions.[3] According to Ulrich Beck in *The Cosmopolitan Vision* (2004), in what could be seen as the culminating work in this wave of liberal cosmopolitan optimism of the 1990s, the so-called national outlook and the twentieth-century tendency to observe all historical and political matter through the lenses of national state paradigms had become backwards and outdated.[4] Instead, according to Beck, we should all develop what he calls the cosmopolitan outlook.[5] The increasingly globalized world would thus increasingly develop through borderless, transgressing, and transnational processes. Beck observes how the development from national to cosmopolitan outlook could already be observed in the early 2000s in the way we—as Westerners—semantically represented our global age existence:

A transvaluation of values and words is taking place, symbolized by a veritable flood of words such as "diaspora" and "hybridity" [...]. The experiences of alienation or living in between, the loss of ontological security [...] and existential exclusion, talk of ambivalence [...] even the reproach of "rootlessness", have lost much of their apocalyptic meaning.[6]

Beck refers to a time in history when the concept of "rootlessness" and the "experiences of alienation or living in between", as well as cultural diaspora, had an "apocalyptic meaning" for many, and he seems to be certain that such views now belonged to the past.

Ulrich Beck has been criticized since the publication of *The Cosmopolitan Vision* for not paying enough attention to the unintended consequences of the globalization processes in his cosmopolitan vision of how this bond of cosmopolitan-oriented human beings will gradually—and almost naturally—replace the national outlook.

However, in recent years, it has become clear that many people,

Westerners as well as non-Westerners, do not feel part of a "progressive global age" in which terms such as *cosmopolitanism, strangeness, diaspora, rootlessness,* and *cultural hybridity* have lost their apocalyptic meaning. Right-wing populism is on the rise and many, it seems, do not want to live according to a cosmopolitan outlook. In this context, the constant flow of new "revolutionizing" technologies, the individual flexibility required by an ever more globalized work market, and accelerating information loads are often experienced as difficult challenges, and not only by those usually counted as "Modernisierungsverlierer."[7] Also, recent research documents that some segments benefit more from the positive effects of the globalization processes than others, and have easier access to the advantages of our global age.[8] In fact, more and more people fear the future of our global age, and why would it be any different? A majority of TV series, films, political campaigns, and journalistic breaking news feed us narratives on a daily basis that represent the world we inhabit as overloaded with crises prognosing the future of our present-day global age through various dystopian and catastrophic scenarios (for example in the context of the climate crisis, the Western democracy crisis, pandemic crises, financial crises, migration crises, etc.).

According to the German historiographer Reinhart Koselleck, it is only logical that we can observe this intensification of cultural products, political ideologies, and journalistic breaking news forecasting our future through such dystopian crises and catastrophic scenarios. Hence, according to Koselleck, modern human consciousness is characterized by a temporal distinction between the past and the future, instead of perceiving time mainly as pre-modern and cyclical.[9] In this way, modern consciousness also generates a gap between past experiences and future expectations. This gap amplifies the human utopian and dystopian imagination, which grows still further if the gap between our *Erfahrungsraum* and *Erwartungshorizont* increases. The accelerated social and technological changes of our present-day global age thus leave us with less and less useful *Erfahrungsraum* on which we can built constructive expectations of the future.[10]

Indeed, today, we live in an age of accelerated overheating and unintended crisis consequences of which we cannot rationally predict the outcome. As such, it seems that the type of optimistic cosmopolitanism that Ulrich Beck designated as an ideal for all to follow back in the 2000s has lost its relevance. Following Koselleck's concepts of *Erfahrungsraum* and *Erwartungshorizont*, one could instead ask: Do we have any concrete experiences of cosmopolitanism and global-age processes from which we can learn and build our present-day anticipations of how our global age will develop, so that we do not act in an atmosphere of reckless optimism or, on the other hand, on feelings of anxiety, panic, and crisis?

Recently, in *Once Within Borders: Territories of Power, Wealth and Belonging since 1500* (2016), Charles S. Maier defines the period from the 1970s onwards as the second modern era of intensified globalization in the history of modern Europe.[11] Maier convincingly argues that the fin-de-siècle period, from the 1870s to 1914, should be considered as forming the first wave of accelerated globalization in modern European history.[12] The fin-de-siècle period was thus—like our present-day global age—characterized by continuous upheaval and renewal, which transformed the existing European societies and individual life worlds. In this process, Jews and Jewishness became a focal point in discussions of the dramatic transition from the old world to the liberal democratic and capitalist modern societies of the twentieth century. As such, it was indeed in the fin-de-siècle period that cosmopolitanism and various globalization processes acquired this "apocalyptic meaning" Ulrich Beck speaks of in the passage quoted above. Hence, it was not in Hitler's Nazi Germany of the 1930s that the identity characteristics of cosmopolitanism, alienation/strangeness, rootlessness, in-between-ness, and cultural hybridity became interconnected with Jewishness, and established a dominant cultural code by which the accelerated processes of the first intensified globalization period were discussed and anticipated.[13] Historical research that focuses on the period from when Hitler gained power in Germany as the time when modern antisemitism became a dangerous new form of populism is merely addressing the culmination of a much longer historical course of interconnected events and narratives. According to the already classic studies on modern antisemitism by Reinhard Rürup and Shulamit Volkov, and newer work by Michael Stanislawski and Maurice Samuels, we must go further back, at least to the 1870s. This was the time when modern antisemitism developed into a dominant cultural code that primarily focused on Jews and Jewishness in the context of the unintended consequences of this first period of intensified globalization.

The Goals of the Book

The construction of an almost synonymous relation between Jewishness and cosmopolitanism became the focal point in the modern antisemitic and the later Nazi ideology. As such, Georg Brandes (1842–1927) stands as a key historical actor due to the great influence he exerted as one of the leading European intellectuals in the fin-de-siècle period, not only in the context of the creation of modern antisemitic populism, but also because of his own interconnections of Jewishness and cosmopolitanism. From his earliest writings, Brandes characterized himself as a cosmopolitan, and he defined the cosmopolitan tradition of which he considered himself a part as Jewish-related. Most of Brandes' interconnections of Jewishness and cosmopolitanism were contextually bound to the different ongoing discussions of the so-called Jewish Question in the fin-de-siècle period; his passionate engagement with different topics related to the so-called Jewish Question is evident from the first of his publications in the 1860s to the last four books he published before he died in 1927. Brandes drew from various intellectual sources when he elaborated on the relation between Jewishness and cosmopolitanism in both his early and later writings.[14] He was particularly influenced by other modern European Jewish intellectuals and writers such as Berthold Auerbach, Heinrich Heine, Moritz Lazarus, Benjamin Disraeli, and Ferdinand Lassalle. Doubtlessly, Brandes' greatest inspiration for identifying with the cosmopolitan tradition, which in his early writings he calls "modern Jewishness", was the Dutch Jewish philosopher Baruch Spinoza.[15] In previous (mainly Danish-based) research on Brandes, little attention has been paid to his representations of Jewishness, and none has so far thematized which cosmopolitan tradition Brandes considered himself part of, though the primary identity marker with which most previous research characterizes Brandes is that he first and foremost was a cosmopolitan, in his writings as well as in his practice.[16] As such, this book seeks to contribute to two fields. First, it adds to the existing research on Georg Brandes and the key theme in this literature: Brandes' role in shaping modern Denmark. In this context it also intends to establish more substantial links between Brandes research and the field of Danish Jewish history, as well as to the much larger scholarly field of Jewish Studies. The book's second historiographical goal is to create an awareness of the importance of Georg Brandes' life and work as a cosmopolitan archive in the modern intellectual historical field. Regarding the first goal, in my opinion, the dominant post-WW2 collective memory of the "miracle of '43" vis-à-vis the rescuing of Danish Jews from Nazi concentration camps during WW2 plays an important role when it comes to the lack of existing research on Danish Jewish history, and specifically on the Jewish themes in Brandes' oeuvre. The way this collective memory is usually narrated today reflects a belief that Denmark and Danish history is mainly to be considered an exception in the broader history of antisemitism in modern Europe. However, there are many other important historical events in Danish Jewish history that we can learn from today; the case of Georg Brandes represents rather different perspectives, no less important than the rescuing of the Danish Jews in 1943.

There is no doubt that what happened in 1943 offers a unique historical perspective in the context of the Holocaust. We must never forget that most of the Danish Jews were rescued and sailed to Sweden, and it is natural that the story has become one of the most significant Danish post-WW2 collective memories and as such an important modern Danish nation-building element. This was evident in 2018 when the 75th anniversary celebration of this event at the synagogue in *Krystalgade* in Copenhagen was broadcast live on the national Danish television station, DR. The Danish Prime Minister Lars Løkke Rasmussen gave a speech at the synagogue and the Israeli Foreign Minister also attended the ceremony. Subsequently, as a collective memory, the rescuing of the Danish Jews has come to symbolize that, in 1943, the Danish Jewish minority had become recognized as fully equal Danish co-citizens even though the Danish Jews were a non-Christian minority. As a narrative, this collective memory has come to symbolize that, in the midst of occupying Nazism and the horrors of WW2, democratic co-citizenry had materialized as a crucial nation-building element in Denmark.[17] Fundamentally, Danes trusted and recognized each other as equal citizens no matter what religious and cultural background they came from.

In recent years, important perspectives have been added to how we can narrate this historical memory to younger generations, for example in the education system. The high prices that the fishermen who sailed the Danish Jews to Sweden charged have been scrutinized; recent research furthermore documents that, after the war, many Danish Jewish families returned to Denmark only to find that their houses and apartments were now occupied by Danish co-citizens who refused to move out.[18] The somewhat passive but seemingly calculated role of the German commanding forces in Denmark, particularly the role of *Reichbevollmächtigten* Werner Best, in October 1943 has also been touched upon. Denmark was one of the most important foreign suppliers of agricultural products to Germany and German troops during WW2 and, in 1943, it was more necessary than ever for the Germans to maintain the export of Danish goods.[19] Such perspectives are necessary because of the central role that key collective memories play in our continuing nation-building process; indeed, this was reflected in the way we celebrated the 75th anniversary of the rescuing of the Danish Jews.

The reactions to Georg Brandes' Jewish background in the context of his enterprise as an active public intellectual represent a rather different perspective in Danish Jewish history than the collective memory of the rescuing of the Danish Jews in 1943. Studying Brandes and the modern antisemitic reactions to him and his work presents us with many examples of how the democratic virtue of equality was constantly put to the test in the building of modern Denmark.

The general lack of interest in elements other than the rescuing of the Danish Jews in 1943 in the context of Danish Jewish history is also reflected, as mentioned, in the existing research on Brandes' representations of Jewishness. The scholarly articles and books that have already thematized Brandes' representations of Jewishness certainly present valuable examples, and so does Jørgen Knudsen's monumental biography.[20] However, the main tendency has been to represent Brandes as a so-called "assimilated Jew" who mainly distanced himself from Jewishness. To give an example: Although Jørgen Knudsen's biographical work on Brandes is significant, it fundamentally lacks frameworking analytical concepts and terminology as regards Brandes' representations of Jewishness. Overall, Knudsen represents Jewishness as a fixed identity position, which Brandes himself did not identify with. Following this, at one point, Knudsen even characterizes Brandes as a self-hating Jew;[21] and Knudsen has even previously been accused of being an antisemite.[22] Regarding the academic works that take Brandes' representation of Jewishness as their key topic, Henry J. Gibbons' "The reluctant Jew" (1980) delivers a substantial overview of the complex field of Brandes' representations of Jewishness. However, Gibbons and more recent work such as Tine Bach's *Exodus* (2004) do not really move beyond pointing to Brandes' distancing strategy and to the contradictory and ambivalent nature of his Jewish themes.[23] This has contributed to the more general conception within research on Brandes that his representations of Jewishness are unimportant and not relevant as regards his more famous struggles and writings.

Generally, in the research on Brandes, there has been a tendency to highlight the influence exerted on him particularly by the Danish Protestant-based philosophy of Søren Kierkegaard, rather than more obvious Jewish-related influences. A number of works have been published which emphasize that the most important inspiration for Brandes (as Paul Rubow already stated in his influential 1932 doctoral thesis *Georg Brandes' Briller* (*Georg Brandes' Spectacles*)) was the influence of Kierkegaard.[24] However, it is significant that it was not Søren Kirkegaard but Baruch Spinoza who Brandes himself identifies as his greatest intellectual and spiritual influence, in a key scene from his autobiography *Levned I–III* (*Recollections of my Childhood and Youth I–III*) (1905–08). As such, it is the argument of this book that Spinoza and specifically that a particular depiction of Spinoza as a life example in the literary genre of Spinozism was Brandes' primary intellectual and spiritual guide in life. In this context, Berthold Auerbach's literary biography *Spinoza* plays a key role in Brandes' designation of the cosmopolitan tradition he considered himself part of, and in how Brandes conceived of his in-between position in society in general.

In fact, Brandes' fascination with Spinoza and the Spinozism that Auerbach's novel represents has already been documented in what must be considered one of the most quoted—if not *the* most quoted—works in the research on Brandes, Henning Fenger's *Georg Brandes' Læreår* (*The Formative Years of Georg Brandes*) (1955). However, Fenger's book also seems to have helped instigate the idea fundamental to the previous research on Brandes that Brandes' Jewish themes were unimportant. Hence, Fenger is quite eager to stress that the different Jewish sources that Brandes occupied himself with did not have any substantial influence on him; there is almost no mention of Brandes' Jewish background and the role this played in his *Bildung*, although there is no doubt that Fenger's book is a well-researched piece of work.

According to Fenger, Brandes studied the work of Spinoza thoroughly and from as early as 1861/1862 Brandes called himself a Spinozian materialist and pantheist.[25] Yet, having documented this, Fenger symptomatically highlights Kierkegaard as a greater inspiration for Brandes than Spinoza. Then, having documented Brandes' fascination with Auerbach's work of Spinozism, Fenger goes on to scorn Auerbach's two Jewish-related novels, *Spinoza* and *Dichter und Kaufmann* (1840). First, Fenger determines them to be of poor artistic value; he even calls them "sickly." After this, Fenger claims that the only reason Brandes favors Auerbach's Jewish-related novels is because of the writers' "racial kinship."[26] As can be seen in the following quote, Fenger moreover reproduces the antisemitic stereotype of perceiving Jewish males as feminized and de-masculinized in comparison with Christian-baptized males:

It is difficult to say anything pleasant about Auerbach [...]. His work can in no way be compared to the masculine art of Gottfried Keller. In his Jewish pseudo-historical novels, there is a sickly humanism and tolerance, with which even the most passionate admirer of Lessing and Lessing's *Nathan* will have difficulties. [...] Brandes' admiration should be understood on the basis of the historical context – and the racial kinship.[27]

Surprisingly, given this statement, Fenger's book was in fact written less than ten years after WW2. However, we can observe that antisemitic racial stereotypes continued to play an influential role in the Danish civil sphere after WW2, and as such also after the rescuing of the Danish Jews in 1943. In fact, no one has ever questioned or even brought up Fenger's influential verdict on some of Brandes' most important Jewish influences as being racially disposed and "sickly", even though his book has been quoted and used as a valuable reference in most scholarly work on Brandes since 1955.

The point that I want to make is not that Danish history is a hidden gem of unresolved antisemitism. However, modern Danish history should not be considered as an exception in the history of antisemitism of modern Europe, either. Certainly, antisemitism has been evident in Denmark just at it has all over Europe. In this context, we must not forget that three documented violent pogroms occurred in Denmark in the first half of the nineteenth century.[28] In 1819, the week-long Hep Hep pogrom was a rather savage and violent event in which Danish Jews in several Danish cities were chased and beaten up, and many Danish Jewish properties were wrecked. H. C. Andersen was one of the few to write about the Hep Hep pogrom, in his autobiography *Mit Livs Eventyr* (*The Fairy Tale of my Life*) (1855), since he first arrived in Copenhagen from Odense as a teenager in the midst of it.

In the case of Georg Brandes as a significant historical actor in the building of modern Denmark, this book provides many useful perspectives on the various ways in which the cultural code of modern antisemitism was used to warn against the dystopian dangers of modernity and as such modern rootlessness, alienation, and cultural in-between-ness. As mentioned, in the fin-de-siècle period liberal democracy was materialized and capitalism took its last steps in becoming an all-encompassing structure of society. In general, in Western Europe, the dominant public reaction to these significant changes was initially a liberal optimism, which the visions of Brandes' Modern Breakthrough project incarnated. Yet, as the years went by, particularly from the 1890s onwards, this optimism grew into widespread pessimism. Modern antisemitism became a popular cultural code, not only in Germany, to explain why modernity had become a runaway locomotive. Back then, according to many, not just the antisemites, the spirit of modernity, the dominant *zeitgeist*, was the modern Jewish spirit. As such, this *zeitgeist* was represented by a particular kind of Jewishness: The emancipated bourgeois-influenced Western European Jews, the so-called "assimilated Jews," those individuals who had transgressed and challenged the otherwise fixed categories of class, nation, gender, and religion. For many, in the Christian-based majority societies of Western Europe, these socially mobile individuals of Jewish descent threatened social cohesion and the national order with their willingness to be mobile, their ability to create vivant, transnational networks, their "rootless" freethinking, and their cosmopolitan-oriented, "de-nationalized" ideas.

In a Danish/Scandinavian context, Georg Brandes and his brother Edvard Brandes became the most frequently projected incarnations of this type of Jewishness. Georg Brandes was constantly signified as a subversive "cosmopolitan Jew," who threatened social cohesion and the Danish Protestant-based cultural tradition. He even went into a 5-year exile in Berlin because the stigmatization of him and his Jewish background in Denmark became intolerable after the publication of *Emigrantlitteraturen*. Hence, Brandes' Modern Breakthrough project and the self-confidence with which he had presented these visions in 1871 were increasingly seen as a kind of fatal hubris. Subsequently, Brandes was held responsible by many for how this transition manifested itself in Denmark (although Brandes can in no way be held responsible for any of the unintended consequences of the accelerated capitalistic processes and the industrialization of this period). In a poem written for Brandes' 70th birthday, in 1912, the Danish 1917 Nobel Prize-winning author Henrik Pontoppidan described Brandes' Modern Breakthrough as having turned out to be a "mirage," like spring-smelling hot air, which had seduced the Danes without containing lasting and meaningful substance. Pontoppidan represents Brandes' Modern Breakthrough project as having catalyzed a development, which had resulted in Eve and "the baboons" eating lustfully of the fruits of the tree Brandes had attempted to plant in Danish soil back in 1871 (using the ancient Jewish tale of Adam and Eve as an analogy).[29]

Brandes' Jewish Cosmopolitanism

Still, it makes little sense to contextualize Brandes' representations of Jewishness as only relevant to an isolated version of the national history of Denmark. Throughout his writings, Brandes continuously participated in broader Western European discussions of the so-called Jewish Question. It would be an historical error to perceive these discussions as separated national discussions. Particularly, in Brandes' work there is a noteworthy transnational dialectic, which in some cases is surprising. A good example of this is the significant role he played in the very creation of the ideology of racially based modern antisemitism. In historical research, the *Berliner Antisemitismusstreit* of 1879–81 is generally viewed as the dispute from which racially based modern antisemitism developed.[30] The founders of this ideology are usually understood to be Heinrich von Treitschke, Wilhelm Marr, and Adolf Stoecker. In 1877, the Norwegian bishop J. C. Heuch published an anti-Jewish pamphlet against Georg Brandes that garnered a lot of attention in the Danish civil sphere. A few years later, one of the founding fathers of modern antisemitism, Adolf Stoecker, then used and quoted from Heuch's writing when, in the German *Reichstag*, he warned against the growing Jewish influence. Stoecker put forward Georg Brandes as a primary example of this type of subversive rootless Jewishness,[31] this "kirchenverach-tende moderne Judentum."[32] I will elaborate more on the development of this new form of populism, modern antisemitism, in 1879–81 and on Brandes' role and reaction to Stoecker's attack on him in the following chapters, since the invention of the ideology of modern antisemitism was significant in Brandes' own interpretations of the modern Jewish cosmopolitan tradition of which he considered himself part. But before we come to this, I want to explain in more detail the connections be-tween the reactions to the first period of globalization, the discussions of the so-called Jewish Question, and the role that the kind of Jewish-ness Brandes represented played in these discussions, in order to sup-port the argument that Georg Brandes represents an important archive in the Western intellectual historical field.

Thus, the transition from the old world to a modern world char-acterized by liberal democracy and capitalism took place in a complex globalizing age. The rapid changes of the period had both positive and negative consequences, and it is often difficult to separate the two.[33] In recognizing how this period can give us valuable perspectives for today, it is necessary to acknowledge how deeply intertwined the so-called Jewish Question was with the discussions of this transition. The emancipation and acculturation of the European Jews in many ways became the litmus test for the general emancipation processes of the eighteenth, nineteenth, and early twentieth centuries. Most modern Western constitutions were written in this period and most of these constitutions idealistically proclaimed that all human beings are cre-ated as equals. Accordingly, the struggles of the European Jews reveal the contradictions of how an ideal liberal democratic state and society, with its promises of equal rights and equal individual freedom, can be materialized in a particularistically based modern nation state.

Yet, since the Holocaust, the status and representation of Jews and Jewishness has undergone a transformation in Western societies. Jews and Jewishness are no longer represented in mainly negative terms. On the contrary, the Holocaust has become an immensely influential col-lective memory in the way we, as Europeans, apprehend how the domination over and exclusion of a minority out-group can result in fatal events in a modern nation state. In the fin-de-siècle period, in Denmark as many other places, there was a constant battle about how to signify and hierarchize what Jews and Jewishness denoted. Unlike the Germany and Austria of the 1920s and 1930s, in most of the debates in which Brandes participated, the connotations of the terms of Jews and Jewishness had not yet been fixed and monopolized by specific stereotypical views, although some of these negative views were rather dominant in the earlier decades. At the same time, Brandes himself clearly had mixed emotions regarding what Jewishness and the Jewish tradition meant for him on a personal level. As such, a major inspiration in writing this book has been Michael Stanislawski's *Zionism and the Fin de Siècle* (2001), which sheds light on how the in-between segment to which Brandes belonged were riddled with ambivalence in their understanding of their Jewish background, while simultaneously finding it unjust and bizarre that they were continuously stigmatized and excluded because of it:

Their "identity" as Jews [...] was a complex and often semi-conscious web of actions and inaction, beliefs and feelings, embarrassment and pride, always conditioned and complicated by familial, political and social realities that varied from one individual to the next and from one society to the other.[34]

As Stanislawski demonstrates in his book, this in-between segment's understanding of Jewishness was often closely interrelated with their understanding of cosmopolitanism. It was also linked to their perception of the bourgeois *Bildung* ideal—as it was for the founder of Zionist movement, Theodor Herzl. For many years, in fact, Herzl was editor of the *Feuilleton* part of the Viennese liberal newspaper *Neue Freie Presse*, and Brandes wrote numerous articles for him.

Thus, no matter whether individuals of this segment were "acculturated or assimilated, observant, *Confessionslos*, or baptized,"[35] they existed as an out-group in the Western European national states they had been born into throughout the nineteenth century. Still, this segment of modern cosmopolitan-oriented European Jews was vital for the building of modern Western civilization through their many innovations in the fields of financial entrepreneurship, modern science, journalism, arts, and politics. In this context, Daniel B. Schwartz's *The First Modern Jew: Spinoza and the History of an Image* (2016) has provided me with many useful perspectives not only on Georg Brandes but also on many other "rootless" nineteenth- and early twentieth-century European Jewish intellectuals and writers who used the life example of Baruch Spinoza as a key role model for how they perceived their own identities and roles in society. In the literary genre of Spinozism, Spinoza is as such usually depicted as a character who even in early modern times—back in the seventeenth century—strove to be a free, individualistic modern human being with a rationalist mindset. At the same time, Spinoza did not follow the logic of acculturation of this period in his striving toward living as a "free philosopher," since he refused to convert to Christianity. On the other hand, neither did Spinoza view Orthodox Judaism as embodying absolute truths. Therefore, the meeting with the modern world required a new position in society, at least according to Berthold Auerbach's *Bildungsroman, Spinoza* (1837/56), which particularly influenced Brandes.

By focusing on the role Baruch Spinoza is given as a life example and as the father of modernity in the writings of Brandes,[36] this book demonstrates how Brandes thematizes a specific modern Jewish cosmopolitan tradition in both his early and later writings. This cosmopolitanism emphasizes the Jewish co-construction of European civilization (most often as a reaction to antisemitic rejections of this), and highlights virtues such as universal justice, rational thinking, *Bildung*, cultural flexibility in combination with rootedness and a fundamental focus on combining idealism with practice. Thus, according to Brandes, cosmopolitanism is primarily about the present and not the future—as Kantian cosmopolitanism otherwise tends to imply. As such, this book offers a new and cohesive reading of Brandes' oeuvre, from his first publications in the last part of the 1860s to the last four books written before his death in 1927.

As mentioned, in the blossoming of literature on cosmopolitanism over the past three decades, the historical tradition of interconnecting Jewishness and cosmopolitanism has largely been forgotten, although the construction of a closely connected semantic relation between these two concepts was to become one of the most essential structures of modern antisemitism, for example in the writings of Heinrich von Treitschke, Wilhelm Marr, and Adolf Hitler.[37] In the article "Cosmopolitanisms," Sheldon Pollock, Homi K Bhabha, Carol A. Breckenridge, and Dipesh Chakrabarty have argued along these lines that the present-day field of cosmopolitanism, and more concretely our current global age, has a lot to learn from"past embodiments" of cosmopolitan ideas and cosmopolitan actors.[38] They also emphasize the necessity of finding "cosmopolitan archives" from cosmopolitan traditions other than the historical context of the Greek/Roman-Kantian cosmopolitan tradition:

If it is already clear that cosmopolitanism begins with the Stoics, who invented the term, or with Kant, who reinvented it, then philosophical reflection on these moments is going to enable us always to find what we are looking for. Yet what if we were to try to be archivally cosmopolitan and to say: "Let's simply look at the world across time and space and see how people have thought and acted beyond the local."[39]

Sheldon Pollock et al. make a good point here, since usually Diogenes and/or the Stoics are viewed as the ancient foundation of cosmopolitan thought in the cosmopolitan literature of the last three decades. Moreover, Immanuel Kant is typically put forward as the modern founder and revitalizer of the cosmopolitan tradition in most present-day writings on cosmopolitanism. This can be observed in key cosmopolitan writings by Jacques Derrida, Ulrich Beck, Mary Helen McMurran, and Robert Fine.[40] In their article "Cosmopolitanism: The End of Jewishness?" (2012), Michael Miller and Scott Ury have also raised our awareness of the European Jewish fin-de-siècle tradition of cosmopolitanism as containing many relevant perspectives for writings on cosmopolitanism of the last three decades, particularly in the context of the development of modern antisemitism as an influential political ideology, an anti-elite populism, that led to fatal consequences in modern European history.[41] However, they also elaborate on the lack of scholarly examinations of this archive.[42] In this context, Georg Brandes stands as a key cosmopolitan archive within the tradition of European cosmopolitanism. Thomas Mann, for example, called Brandes' European literary history of the nineteenth century, *Hovedstrømninger i det 19de Aarhundredes Litteratur* (*Main Currents in Nineteenth-Century Literature*), "the Bible of young, intellectual Europe."[43]

The Jewish Question(s)

Besides pointing to the significance of Spinoza and Spinozism, this book argues that most of Brandes' interconnections of Jewishness and cosmopolitanism should be understood as closely contextually bound to the ongoing discussions of the so-called Jewish Question of the period in which Brandes was an active public intellectual. The so-called Jewish Question is however not one but several questions, which arose in the context of the acculturation process experienced by European Jews in the various Western European states in the enlightenment period. It is unclear when the term "the Jewish Question" was first used. However, it seems to go back to the middle of the eighteenth century and some of the earliest modern discussions of whether the Jews in European states should be emancipated.[44] The so-called Jewish Question is thus the question of how the European Jews should be treated, and what the appropriate social and juridical status of the Jews should be in the modern Western European states.[45] These discussions therefore became part of the more general *raison d'état* discussions about how Jews and other out-groups could contribute more substantially to the economy of modern Western European states. Related questions were raised about whether groups of people who were occupied within the agrarian field—peasants and the rural proletariat—should be granted civil equality rights. If we go back to the work which was most influential in initiating the process of emancipation, not only in the German-speaking states but also in Denmark (in this period, Denmark was, culturally and politically, tied to the German-speaking areas of North-ern Europe)[46], namely C. W. Dohm's *Über der bürgerliche Verbesserung der Juden* (1781–83), we can observe that the focal point of the *raison d'état* argument is that European Jews should be granted civil rights, so that they could be transformed into so-called "useful citizens."[47] Hence, Dohm proposes that the various European monarchs and rulers should emancipate the Jews and provide them with equal civil rights. Yet at the same time, his famous "rights for regeneration" argument suggests that Jews were not "useful citizens" in their present condition; hence, Dohm considered most Jews at that time as uncivilized barbarians.[48] Dohm does not propose that monarchs and rulers legally establish specific standards of civilization, which the Jews should live up to; nor does he recommend that Jews should convert to Christianity. Yet he demands that Jews must begin to transform themselves, and that the Christian majority society and its educational institutions assist in educating the Jews on how to become such useful citizens.[49]

Dohm's two-part essay was quite influential, and his "rights for re-generation" argument was also the basis for the emancipation of Dan-ish Jews in 1814, which Brandes, or rather his grandparents' generation, experienced.[50] In Denmark at the end of the eighteenth century, we can furthermore observe the importance of this integration discourse in the fact that Jews living in Copenhagen, such as Naphtali Herz Wessely, be-came a vital part of the North European Jewish *Haskalah* discussions.[51] However, Dohm's ambivalent "rights for regeneration" view on the pro-cess of "civilizing Jews" logically enough gave rise to a large number of varying and contradictory ideas about how this acculturation should take place, who should be the active participants in the process, and what the precise goal was. As Thorsten Wagner describes, in the dec-ades leading up to *Frihedsbrevet* (The Charter of Emancipation), the primary goal of the Danish version of the Jewish Question had already been outlined in 1796:

[The Danish government] not only wants to enforce the civil rights of the Jews, but even to smooth the way for them to amalgam with the older citizens of the country.[52]

The most interesting word, or rather verb, in the citation above is "amalgam," which in Danish, as a reflexive verb, "*at amalgamere sig*," emphasized that the Jews themselves should be active in the acculturation process. Thus, "amalgamation" becomes the defining term used by the Danish king, or his civil servants, to describe the acculturation process in Denmark.[53] Like so many other late eighteenth- and nineteenth-century terms relating to cultural matters, the word "amalgamation" originates in the natural sciences, where it was originally used to describe how metals fuse. In Danish, this term also means "*sammensmeltning*" ("melting together").

Following this legal definition of how Danish Jews should "amalgam" rather than be fully assimilated, the vast majority of Danish Jews continued, after 1814, to be Jews in a religious sense and did not convert. However, since there was no specific and detailed description of how this "amalgamation" should take place, many different variations arose among the Danish Jews (as was the case all over Western Europe).

One of the consequences of the equal civil rights was that a wider range of career opportunities was now available to Jewish populations. However, as David Sorkin documents in *The Transformation of German Jewry* (1987), in a German historical context, the Jewish nineteenth-century bourgeoisie was not really embraced by the majority society bourgeoisie. Correspondingly, in the prose writing of two other influential Danish Jewish writers, M. A. Goldschmidt and Henri Nathansen, it is evident that the Danish Jewish bourgeois-influenced families also existed as a secluded sub-culture alongside the Danish majority society bourgeoisie in the nineteenth century.[54] There was undoubtedly interaction, which grew throughout the nineteenth century and the fin-de-siècle period. However, if an individual of Jewish descent wanted to be recognized and acknowledged for his/her talents and abilities, the best way to ensure this, at least in the first half of the nineteenth century, was to convert to Christianity. This can be seen in the cases of the professor and politician H. N. David, the writer Henrik Hertz and the leading Danish actress from the 1830s to the 1860s Johanne Luise Heiberg. We can also find evidence that Brandes was born into this out-group: In the building in which Brandes lived during his childhood, which was owned by his Danish Jewish merchant grandfather, two thirds of the tenants were fellow Danish Jews.[55] To contextualize: At that time, only 2% of the inhabitants of Copenhagen were of Jewish descent.

Brandes' inner circle of friends and all the allies he trusted the most throughout his life were as such also other individuals of Danish Jewish descent. He never converted to Christianity; as he describes it in his autobiography, faced with his ultimate life crisis, he chose Spinoza and modern Jewishness over the Protestant philosophy of Søren Kierkegaard. Nevertheless, as already mentioned, Brandes has typically been identified as a so-called "assimilated Jew" who mainly distanced himself from Jewishness. Yet if this term is to be applied we must be aware of a decades-long and ongoing debate in Jewish Studies about whether a term such as "Jewish self-hatred" has relevance as regards the segment of so-called "assimilated Jews."[56] These terms—"assimilated Jew" and "self-hating Jew"—have been synonymously applied to Brandes by his leading Danish biographer Jørgen Knudsen, and also by Tine Bach.[57] They seem to have been used for the first time to describe Brandes' relationship to Jewishness by Henri Nathansen in his 1929 biography.[58] The term "self-hating Jew" has been defined by Sander L. Gilman as follows:

"Jewish-Self-Hatred" (a term interchangeable with "Jewish anti-Judaism" or "Jewish anti-Semitism") is valid as a label for a specific mode of self-abnegation [...].

Self-Hatred results from outsiders' acceptance of the mirage of themselves generated by their reference group – that group in society which they see as defining them – as a reality.[59]

Sander L. Gilman's extensive examination of this complex psychological phenomenon clearly offers many valid perspectives, and with regard to a fin-de-siècle intellectual such as Jewish-born Otto Weininger, who became one of the most important early founders of modern antisemitism, it is clearly a relevant term to apply to him and his *Geschlecht und Charakter* (1903). Gilman moreover usefully documents how the phenomenon of the "self-hating Jew" is historically traceable in the way Western European Jews often viewed the more traditional Eastern European Jews, the so-called *Ostjuden*, who migrated to and sought refuge in Western European countries and the United States in great numbers from the late 1870s and up until the 1920s.[60] However, by no means were all of these Western European so-called "assimilated Jews" "self-hating Jews" (according to Gilman's definition). Thus, the term "self-hating Jew" has become a stereotypical and reductive way of viewing these integrationists/"assimilated Jews." Subsequently, in *The Origins of Jewish Self-hatred* (2012), Paul Reitter demonstrated that one of the first writers to use this term was Theodor Lessing in his book *Jewish Self-hatred* (1930). Reitter demonstrates how Lessing, who was an eager supporter of Zionism, consciously framed this term negatively in order to describe Western European Jewish integrationists as "the tragedy of the Jew who tries to flee himself and his Jewishness."[61] Accordingly, since the nineteenth century, there have been heated debates between supporters of the Zionist ideology (e.g. Henri Nathansen) and the integrationists, which counted Georg Brandes among them.

In studies of Brandes' representations of Jewishness, even the most recent work has stated that he internalized civil society's predominantly negative views on Jewishness.[62] However, this book will argue that Brandes' interconnections of Jewishness and cosmopolitanism instead should be viewed as a contextually bound process in which he developed his ideas on Jews and Jewishness. Thus, I wish to avoid terms such as "assimilated Jew" and "Jewish self-hatred" as labels to identify how Brandes represented Jewishness, since they are historically entangled with this unsettled discussion between supporters of Zionism and the integrationists, who believed that their home was in Europe.

Methodological Reflections:
Brandes' Struggles in the Civil Sphere

What initially motivated Brandes to enter the public scene was a desire to start a social movement that would transform Denmark and emancipate the mindsets of the Danish people. Although throughout the next decades he would repeatedly experience that the reception of his campaigning and ideas did not match his own—at times megalomaniac—self-image, Brandes nevertheless continued to struggle for his views and for what he considered to be unjust and reactionary structures and dogma. For example, he was occupied with defending the equality rights of many different European minorities, Jewish and non-Jewish, particularly in his later writings, and one could argue that his many battles within the civil sphere regarding this matter reflected his own struggles to be considered—and have the right to be considered—an equal to Christian-born men.[63]

Yet Brandes' work reflects more than an individual struggle for recognition. It exemplifies social and political structures that many great scientists, intellectuals, politicians, and financial entrepreneurs of Jewish decent fought to change as they strived to be acknowledged as equal individuals. In this context, this book draws particularly on Jeffrey C. Alexander's idea in *The Civil Sphere* (2006) of liberal democratic societies as centered around a communicatively based civil sphere in which a diverse field of actors meet and struggle with each other for dominance in signifying and hierarchizing the social world. Thus, Alexander views the civil sphere of the Western civil societies as a battlefield in which different actors, media, associations, politicians, institutions, and social movement representatives debate, negotiate, and disagree with each other, primarily over questions of how democratic universal justice should be defined and signified (through questions of freedom of speech, racism, gender equality, illiberal elite structures, etc.).[64] The question which we as modern individuals share and which essentially binds us together is what and which "secular faith" we should collectively live by—which standards of equality and individual freedom we all should follow and which opinions and categorizations should be sanctioned from a moral perspective.[65] In this way, any discussion of morality and democratic justice in the civil sphere "must be connected to the discussion of culture and tradition, if only to understand why morality is so often the claims of the strong, so often falsely universal, and so prone to camouflage and cover-up rather than to upholding reciprocity and claims to truth."[66] Thus, in the history of the development of liberal democratic societies in the Western world, this struggle has often led to historical moments when specific views and interpretations have monopolized the civil sphere. In many of these moments, the opposite of justice has occurred as a consequence of such domination. Think only of the history of the United States since the Declaration of Independence in 1776 in relation to its African-American historical perspectives, or the dramatic series of events in the short life of the Weimar Republic.

In fact, in *The Civil Sphere*, Jeffrey C. Alexander views European Jewish history and the so-called Jewish Question as a key case in how these contradictions of modern Western civil societies materialized. For two thousand years, Jews were "constructed as "anti-civil," as the ultimate threat to broad solidarity and the good life."[67] Moreover, with the emancipation of the Western European Jews in the nineteenth century, these contradictions were in many cases and places intensified. Thus, in the different Western modern constitutions and as part of various kinds of emancipation laws, "the universal civil competence of all human beings was proclaimed. [...] At the same time, the civil capacities of various out-groups were continually questioned."[68] Also in Denmark, after *Frihedsbrevet* (The Charter of Emancipation) of 1814, individuals of Jewish descent were still stigmatized; efforts to exclude them were also a consistent part of Brandes' intellectual career, as this book will show.

Thus, in the period between Brandes' first public debate in 1867 and his death in 1927, an open democratic civil sphere was not yet fully developed in Denmark or indeed in the other Western European states. For example, women were not given fully democratic equal rights until 1915 in Denmark, and this happened still later in other Western countries. Accordingly, although all Jewish individuals had been emancipated formally, in many places there still existed specific laws which denied individuals of Jewish descent the same opportunities as individuals of the Christian faith. In many states, non-Christians could not become civil servants of the state by law (they had to be baptized Christians).[69] Indeed, for many decades, Brandes' primary career goal was to become a professor at the University of Copenhagen; he was refused this title several times, and along with it a steady and respected bourgeois position, although he was undoubtedly the most important Danish intellectual in this period. Alexander points out that central actors of the majority group(s) who dominate the civil sphere will often "deny [...] that any such primordial stratification" exists. He also makes it clear that "particular goals and even the most strategic of actions are framed and sometimes bound by commitments to cultural codes [...] to understand it we need to employ semiotic theories of binary codes, literary models of rhetoric and narrative, and anthropological concepts of performance and myth."[70] As such, it is important both to recognize and to examine in more detail the cultural codes with which central actors continuously make an effort to maintain their dominance. It is equally important to examine how out-groups react to these efforts, and one should bear in mind that cultural chauvinism and particularistic self-promoting motives indeed exist and occur on all levels of these discussions.[71] Subsequently, all types of actors will typically make an effort to cover their strategy and goals through various filters of cultural codes. In the historical case of the so-called Jewish Question and particularly in the nineteenth century and fin-de-siècle period, exclusionary cultural codes often developed into rather sophisticated instruments of dominance and control in the civil sphere, as this book will document in the case of the Athens vs. Jerusalem dichotomy and the first professor in Danish literature, Vilhelm Andersen. Many central actors thus framed individuals of Jewish descent typically as "rootless," "strangers," and as "de-nationalized cosmopolitans," whose aim was to subvert the order of society. Accordingly, all the important actors within the civil sphere would know that when Brandes was denoted a "cosmopolitan," "stranger," or "freethinker," or as "rootless" these terms also referred to his Jewish background. These labels connoted a long intellectual tradition, going back hundreds of years; they were often the very same words the feudal authorities and the Christian Church used to describe Baruch Spinoza, when he first argued that the subjugating feudal and clerical dogma and structures of seventeenth-century Europe should be dissolved.

It is not the purpose of this book to trace the cultural code of modern antisemitism all the way back to Spinoza in the seventeenth century (although this could be a very interesting study). At the same time, it is clear that modern antisemitism as a cultural code goes back much earlier than the 1870s. For example, as Maurice Samuels has recently argued in *The Betrayal of the Duchess: The Scandal that Unmade the Bourbon Monarchy and Made France Modern* (2020), the cultural code of modern antisemitism already played a significant exclusionary role in the French civil sphere in the 1830s. The connection of labels such as cosmopolitanism, rootlessness, and stranger with Jews and Jewishness has arguably played an important role in the discussion of the transition from the old world to modern liberal democratic societies for centuries in European history.[72]

Alexander writes in *The Civil Sphere* that—in his view—there is no difference between pre-modern and modern Jew-hatred and this is a view that has become predominant also in recent years' studies of antisemitism. Thus, according to Alexander and many other scholars, no distinctions should be made between "antisemitism" and "anti-Judaism". Alexander argues that from the beginning Christianity incorporated an aggressive opposition toward Judaism, and this became an inherent part of the Christian tradition per se.[73]

In this book, the subject is not whether antisemitism goes all the way back to early Christianity and whether for example the New Testament's key author, Paul, can/should be called an antisemite or whether, as Gavin Langmuir has suggested, "the chimerical irrationality of European Jew-hatred in the twelfth and thirteenth centuries marks a passage from anti-Judaism to anti-Semitism," or even whether—as Peter Schäfer has suggested—antisemitism goes all the way back to ancient Egyptian civilization.[74] Certainly, something more than analytical concepts of civil societal framework is needed to settle the old discussion of whether most anti-Judaism can be called antisemitism. In Reinhard Rürup and Thomas Nipperdey's classic article on the origins of the term "antisemitism," "Antisemitismus – Entstehung, Funktion und Geschichte eines Begriffs" (1975), a more pragmatic approach is suggested, which can serve as a guide for the use of the terms "antisemitism" and "modern antisemitism" in the following chapters.[75] They explain how for most people "antisemitism" has come to signify the same as the more general term *Judenfeindschaft*. Pragmatically speaking, then, "antisemitism" is the most adequate term to use in general because—in accordance with our everyday usage—it denotes a diverse field of negative representations of Jews and Jewishness.

In the analysis of the Jewish-related topics in Brandes' oeuvre, I will not hierarchize the interconnections of Jewishness and cosmopolitanism according to whether they appear in his intellectual biographies, essays, journalistic articles, and so on. Also, I refer primarily to the first editions of Brandes' writings because of the division of his oeuvre into the early and later writings. However, in some cases other versions of the same work will be taken into consideration and compared to the first editions, particularly in Chapter 3, where Brandes' editing process for his collected writings (*Samlede Skrifter* (1899–1910)) is part of the analysis. The division between Brandes' early and later writings is based on his changing view of the concept of race, which has already been observed in earlier research by Paul Rubow.[76] Essentially, I view the rise of race-orientated modern antisemitism as causing Brandes, in the early 1880s, to abandon the concept of race as a central component of his lifelong primary means of understanding cultural matters: the *Volksgeist* concept. In his early writings, race is as such a significant part of Brandes' vocabulary, but his use of it gradually fades in the 1880s (parallel to the rise of modern antisemitism) and, similarly, he discontinues thematizing the racially related concept of modern Jewishness, although his primary frame of reference for understanding cultural matters in his later writings is still the concept of *Volksgeist*.

Methodologically, besides the use of Alexander's framework, this book is structured in a way that is consistent with Reinhart Koselleck's historiographical reflections. However, the following chapters should not be viewed as an example of *Begriffsgeschichte*; rather, the analysis of Brandes' oeuvre follows another aspect of Koselleck's historical thought. As Helge Jordheim has argued,[77] besides constructing a theory on modernity, Koselleck can also be interpreted as proposing a Heidegger-inspired historiographical philosophy of time. Helge Jordheim defines Koselleck's view on history and time as an "attempt to replace the idea of linear, homogeneous time with a more complex, heterogeneous and multilayered notion of temporality."[78] As such, Jordheim shows how Koselleck calls to attention to the fact that "for the Historian [...] the main challenge of analyzing [...] consists in retrieving [...] history's character of *Geschehen*, of something that is taking place."[79] Subsequently, in the interpretation of Koselleck's view on history and time, present time is viewed as a multilayered instance of temporality, where interpretations of both the past and the future merge and become equal parts of the present. An event that took place long ago, like the destruction of the second temple in Jerusalem, or the Modern Breakthrough project, is in this context a continuous *Geschehen* which can influence and become a vital part of the present. According to this view, history has a strong continuous influence on our social world: "There is no 'total otherness of the past' [...] but instead stratum upon stratum of the past flows in and through the present at varying velocities."[80] Consequently, utopian or dystopian visions of the future will also play an important role in how we debate and struggle for dominance in denoting and hierarchizing the social world in the present time. Specific collective memories and interpretations of the past can also majorly influence how we understand the present. By combining Koselleck's view on the present time as "heterogeneous and multilayered" with Alexander's key focus on the struggles within the civil sphere, I view Brandes' representations of Jewishness as consisting equally of grand recreations of the past and transformative visions of the future. However, all the different temporal layers and the semantic content of Brandes' representations of Jewishness must, first and foremost, be seen as directed at his present and the struggles in the civil sphere of which they were part. We will thus see how, in his early writings, Brandes is mainly concerned with interconnecting Jewishness and cosmopolitanism in terms of creating a vision of the future. Here, he dreams of a transformed, emancipated mankind, with the figure of the modern Jew as the primary role model of how to undertake this transformation. In his later writings, Brandes' interconnections of Jewishness and cosmopolitanism reflect the more general tendencies after 1879–81 and the dominance of racially based modern antisemitism as a cultural code within the Western European civil spheres. The antisemitic construction of the Jew as a parasitical stranger in the different histories of the European national traditions becomes an essential element of the ideologies of nationalistic right-wing movements all over Europe. In this period, it is interesting to observe how most of Brandes' interconnections also become focused on creating re-inventions of the past by projecting a different view on the role of Jews in the history of the European civilization than the idea of European Jews as a parasitic element.

The methodological perspective on the multilayered temporal aspects of the present time will frame the discussion section of this book. Here, it will be argued that, today, Brandes is a valuable cosmopolitan archive, and his modern Jewish cosmopolitanism displays innovative perspectives on how to use and think of cosmopolitanism as a constructive term in relation to our present global age. Chapter 1 sheds light on the representations of Jewishness in Brandes' early writings. The main focus is on Brandes' cosmopolitan ideal of the transnational vision and how this ideal is represented through the figures of the modern Jew, the emigrant, and the critic, and through the topos of exile. The chapter argues that Brandes' modern Jew must be seen as an essential but covert and thus far overlooked subtext to his Modern Breakthrough project. Chapter 2 elaborates further on Brandes' figure of the modern Jew and seeks to demonstrate how, through the ideal stranger figure, Brandes was part of an interesting pattern within modern intellectual history at this time when different versions of the Jewish "stranger" were projected as reactions to modern antisemitism. This cosmopolitan archive represents valuable perspectives for today's idealization of strangeness.

The last three chapters focus on the representation of Jewishness in Brandes' later writings. This part includes one more chapter than the first part because, in his later writings, Brandes seems to reflect more substantially on Jewishness and the Jewish tradition. Chapter 3 explores how, in his later writings, Brandes seems to distance himself from Jewishness even more than in his early writings, particularly through the two significant strategies of de-Judaizing and de-cosmopolitanization, which are most evident in the editing process of his *Samlede Skrifter* (*Collected Writings*) (1899–1910) and in his autobiography *Levned I–III* (*Recollections of my Childhood and Youth I–III*) (1905–08). These distancing strategies are viewed as a part of Brandes' reactions to modern antisemitism and as related to his goal of becoming a professor at the University of Copenhagen. Chapter 4 and Chapter 5 show how Brandes continues to accentuate the Jewish co-construction of Western civilization in his later writings. In Chapter 4, the key focus is on Brandes' original re-interpretations of the influential nineteenth-century dichotomy Athens vs. Jerusalem. In this part of his oeuvre, Brandes reconstructs the dichotomy so that Athens vs. Jerusalem becomes Athens *and* Jerusalem. Chapter 5 elaborates further on Brandes' writings on the Old Testament[81] and early Christianity by examining the role Baruch Spinoza is given as the father of modernity. Influenced in particular by Berthold Auerbach's *Bildungsroman Spinoza* (1837/1856), Brandes thematizes a coherent tradition of Jewish secular thought that runs from the Old Testament to modern times.

Chapter 1

Brandes' Early Writings and the Transnational Vision

Introduction

In November 1871 in Copenhagen, the newly appointed Dr. Georg Brandes held a series of lectures titled *Hovedstrømninger i det 19de Aarhundredes Litteratur* (*Main Currents in Nineteenth-Century Literature* hereafter referred to as *Main Currents*). Shaped by the liberal, secular-orientated Danish Jewish bourgeoisie of Copenhagen, these lectures aimed at more than just presenting an insightful overview on the European literary history of the nineteenth century. At that time, Denmark was still dominated by undemocratic authoritarian rule. The leading parts of the Danish bourgeoisie, who had demanded democratic influence more than two decades earlier in 1848–1849, had become reactionary and satisfied with the status quo.[82] However, with these lectures, Brandes demanded that it was time that Denmark finally moved into the modern world.

Ideologically, Brandes was a sworn liberal cosmopolitan, and he considered himself a progressive modern thinker—but he was also an elitist.[83] The purpose of his 1871 academic lectures on European literature history was consequently not to influence and inspire the masses, i.e., servants, craftsmen, and uneducated labourers, but to change the mindsets of the younger generations of the Copenhagen bourgeoisie and to persuade Danish artists to commit themselves to realism and to "debate problems" ("sætte problemer under debat"),[84] rather than continuing to represent a dreamy National Romanticism. The idea was for the younger generations of the Copenhagen bourgeoisie and Danish artists and writers to listen carefully and understand this self-appointed leader's messages, and then to proceed to transform the mindset of the lower classes.

The rest is history, so to speak. Brandes' Modern Breakthrough was to become one of the most significant events in Denmark, if not *the* most important, in the latter half of the nineteenth century, culturally and politically. Over the following decades, Brandes became one of Europe's most important intellectuals, as documented by Stefan Zweig, for example, who credited the writings of Brandes as conveying a "a powerful wind-gust of freer, more spiritual air."[85] Brandes built himself a name due to his literary/aesthetical criticism and political observations in newspapers and magazines such as *Politiken* (*Politics*), *Deutsche Rundschau*, and *Neue Freie Presse*.

Previous research on Brandes has already documented the importance of the Modern Breakthrough.[86] This chapter intends to show that Brandes' interconnections of Jewishness and cosmopolitanism were a crucial part of this social movement. Works otherwise considered peripheral and of much less importance than, for example, *Emigrantlitteraturen*, in fact put forward the idea that the so-called modern Jew must be considered a natural leader in the development of the modern world (and hence a movement such as the Modern Breakthrough). Furthermore, Brandes promotes the idea that the modern Jew is to be seen as a role model for all human beings in transforming themselves into modern, cosmopolitan-oriented individuals. His modern Jew must be seen as an essential but also somewhat disguised topos in several of his early writings; he provides a fragmented representation of the modern Jew throughout various texts, though he never presents it as a key topic in any of them. As such, I suggest that the ambivalent nature of Brandes' representation of the modern Jew should be viewed as an example of what Moshe Rosman called a counter-reaction to the typical image of Western European Jews—but, in Brandes' case, this should be considered a disguised counter-reaction to early modern antisemitism.[87]

In treating Brandes' modern Jew figure as a reaction to modern antisemitism, it is important to understand what Brandes was struggling with in the civil sphere, and why it was crucial to him to react to the antisemitic stereotype of the bourgeois-influenced Western European Jew as a non-contributive stranger. Indeed, Brandes seems to have had enough personally motivated reasons to take a stand on this aspect of the so-called Jewish Question around 1870. His earliest experience of participating in a debate in the civil sphere saw his opponents immediately linking his ideas to his Jewish background.[88] In particular, this pattern became visible with the publication of *Emigrantlitteraturen* in 1872, which, along with the Modern Breakthrough, led Danish bourgeois newspapers and magazines to claim that Brandes' fundamental criticism of Danish culture and society revealed him as a typical non-contributive Jew. For example, his writings' "puzzling lack of originality" was identified, thus establishing a negative discourse portraying "the Jew" Brandes as unable to understand the deeper meanings of Danish culture.[89] However, this pattern of accusing Brandes of being an "alien Jew" goes back to 1867, when he participated in a public debate for the first time, namely *Tro og Viden Debatten* (The Debate on Faith and Science). The leading writer in Norway at the time, Bjørnstjerne Bjørnson, criticized Brandes for even participating in this otherwise open public debate because of his lack of Danish consciousness, as a non-Christian.[90] In his early writings, Brandes' primary public reaction to this standard accusation would be to invoke the figure of the modern Jew. This response was somewhat disguised and fragmented, in all probability was due to the ideological climate and accepted forms of antisemitism within the Danish/Western European civil spheres at that time. Brandes' goal from the beginning was to become a professor at the University of Copenhagen. When he initially began to reflect loosely on what he called "modern Jewishness," his thoughts were soon after considered provocative and subversive, with leading Danish bourgeois newspapers claiming in 1872 that they were a direct threat to Denmark as a nation.[91] Thus, already at the earliest stages of Brandes' career, Brandes surmised that his interconnected thoughts on Jewishness and cosmopolitanism would be perceived as inflammatory and would obstruct his efforts to achieve his goal of becoming a professor.

The nature of the attacks on Brandes, linking his ideas with his Jewish background, was by no means exceptional. Rudolf Schmidt's notion in 1872 that Brandes' writings fundamentally lacked "originality" because of his Jewish descent (a notion leading Danish bourgeois writers and newspapers frequently repeated in the following decades) mimicked the dominant discourses witnessed across contemporary Western Europe. This discourse depicted the bourgeois-influenced Western European Jew as a "cold, [...] hostile onlooker,"[92] as an individual who was perhaps educated but who was not really capable of understanding the deeper layers of the various different European cultural traditions. This stereotype became more and more prevalent in the latter half of the nineteenth century.[93] In a Danish cultural context, it was visible in the civil sphere already in 1848–1849, when Pastor N. F. S. Grundtvig, who is today considered a Danish national father figure, used it in a public polemic against Danish Jewish prose writer Meir Aaron Goldschmidt. Grundtvig wrote:

Well then! I indeed contend that Danishness and Norwegianness, like any genuine folksiness, has its secrets (mysteries) and its altars, which the stranger may well consider and hold in esteem, but whose true fervor he cannot feel because he does not belong to this congregation of people, has neither the spirit nor the heart in common with it.[94]

Grundtvig uses the term "stranger" to denote Goldschmidt; this discourse of representing the acculturated Western European Jew as a non-contributive stranger was already a widespread topos at the time. One of the most influential texts advocating it in a trans-European context was Richard Wagner's essay "Das Judentum in der Musik" (1850), a diatribe against two of Wagner's fiercest rivals, the German Jewish classical composers Giacomo Meyerbeer and Felix Mendelssohn. Wagner's criticism of Meyerbeer and Mendelssohn was both a normative description and a warning against the new type of Jewishness, i.e., the acculturated Western European Jew, who could no longer be recognized by his accent or his appearance, unlike the traditional Jew. Wagner instead pointed to less obvious elements such as blood or specific linguistic discourses to identify this new type of Jew. Along these lines, Sander L. Gilman, among others, pinpoints "Das Judentum in der Musik" as one of the most influential works in the shaping of modern antisemitism.[95] Wagner writes:

In the first place, then, the general circumstance that the Jew speaks the modern European languages merely as learnt, and not as mother tongues, must necessarily debar him from all capability of therein expressing himself idiomatically, independently, and comfortably to his nature in any higher sense. A language with its expression and its evolution, is not the work of scattered units, but of an historical community; only he who has unconsciously grown up within the bond of his community, takes also any share in its creation. But the Jew has stood outside the pale of any such community, stood solitary with his Jehova in a splintered, soilless stock to which all self-sprung evolution must stay denied [...]. Now to make poetry in a foreign tongue has hitherto been impossible, even to geniuses of highest rank. Our whole European Art and civilization, however, have remained to the Jew a foreign tongue; for just as he has taken no part in the evolution of the one, so has he taken none in that of the other; but at most the homeless person has been a cold, nay more, a hostile onlooker. In his speech, his art, the Jew can only mimic and mock – not truly make a poem of his words, an artwork of his doings.[96]

Wagner here argues that specific internal Jewish traits do not disappear regardless of how much the educated and acculturated European Jew tries to blend in—no matter how hard he tries to adjust to the majority group of society. Well-educated Jews are, according to Wagner, forever marked by the homeless, rootless Jewish *Volksgeist* which has followed the Jewish people throughout the ages. As a result, they lack the basic ability to understand the deeper layers of European national cultures, and are therefore unable to produce any original work comparable to that of inborn, so-called native (or rather, Christian-born) geniuses, because they do not have the capacity to take root in these traditions.[97] The educated and acculturated Jew would therefore never be anything more than a "cold, [...] hostile onlooker," a destabilizing element within the national cultures.[98]

Like Wagner, Brandes uses the Herderian concept of *Volksgeist* in his early writings to determine deep-rooted Jewish traits that still influence what he calls "modern Jews." However, in contrast to Wagner's negative view of Jewish *Volksgeist* traits, Brandes argues that the Jewish *Volksgeist* heritage is positive and constructive. In fact, Brandes advocates for modern Jews as among the most innovative individuals in the various nineteenth-century European national cultures. He did not accept the claim that individuals of Jewish descent do not have the capacity to connect to the deeper layers of significance in the various European cultural traditions. In addition, he clearly thinks of himself as an incarnation of this contributive and innovative modern Jew. With Stephen Greenblatt's concept of "self-fashioning,"[99] one could argue that Brandes is also portraying himself when, in several biographies, he describes the great achievements of different nineteenth-century personalities of Jewish descent such as Ferdinand Lassalle, Benjamin Disraeli, and Heinrich Heine—a characteristic which his own brother, the politician and for many years leading editor of *Politiken* Edvard Brandes, also noticed early on. [100]

This chapter will show that: 1) Brandes' cosmopolitan ideal of the transnational vision represents the idea of a socio-cultural identity in which the individual acts in a national culture but at the same time does not feel bound to its tradition by any special devotion, thus allowing them to innovate more freely; and 2) Brandes projects his cosmopolitan ideal as a universal one, which he represents through the topos of exile and the figures of the modern Jew, the emigrant, and the critic in his early writings. Still, as a result of Jewish racial *Volksgeist* heritage, Brandes claims that the modern Jew takes precedence in the development of the transnational vision and argues that the modern Jew is the most innovative individual at that time in history.

Brandes' Seemingly Predestined Academic Path

During the 1860s, Georg Brandes followed a clear and designated path toward an impressive academic career. For example, in 1872, the professor of Aesthetics Carsten Hauch declared on his deathbed that the candidate most suited to follow him was Georg Brandes.[101]

Back then, before the modernization and democratization of the university as a state institution, one or more patriarchal "protectors" were needed for a young man to build an academic career.[102] Accordingly, besides Carsten Hauch, Hans Brøchner also recognized Brandes' academic talent early on, and Brandes became his promising intellectual protégé.[103] Brøchner became Brandes' private teacher, tutoring him in particular on the German philosophical tradition.[104] Brøchner's greatest and most substantial influence on Brandes, however, was in the context of Spinoza and Spinozism, as has been described in previous research.[105] For many years, Brøchner himself had also been categorized as a "freethinker" and as a Spinozist materialist; this categorization had affected his academic career negatively, although his reputation was gradually rehabilitated during the 1860s in the then reactionary academic milieu of Copenhagen.[106] It was through Brøchner that Brandes began to read Spinoza's own work and works of Spinozism.

In 1870, Brøchner was made a professor. Accordingly, with his elder's "protection" and advice, step by step, Brandes achieved the goals that would normally have defined the beginning of a life-long academic career at this time in history. He won the gold medal of the University in Copenhagen in 1863. The first time he applied for the prestigious Smith's Scholarship (*Smiths Legat*) he was granted it, and he successfully submitted his doctoral thesis on Hippolyte Taine in 1869.[107] Soon after, Brandes began a fully funded *Bildungsreise* in 1870–71, as this was seen as a necessary experience for any young man embarking on an academic career. When he returned, he brought with him great plans of leading a social movement, which would develop Denmark into a modern society. The first step was to deliver lectures which inspired and transformed the mindsets of the younger generations of the Copenhagen bourgeoisie. Hans Brøchner liked Brandes' plan and he even advised him to alter the original idea he had for the topic of these lectures, so that they could truly win Brandes a broader name as an insightful and innovative young scholar.[108] The self-confident Brandes followed Brøchner's advice and changed the topic of his lectures. Instead of focusing only on the French early Romantic literary reactions to the French Revolution, Brandes now aimed to give a lecture series that explained the main patterns of European literary history in the nineteenth century. The lectures emphasized that the strongest force within the literary innovations of this period had been due to the cosmopolitan "stranger" outlook of French émigré writers on French culture. Brandes wanted to create a subtext within these lectures, by way of an analogy with Denmark and Danish society. It was implicitly argued that for Denmark to have a chance of developing into a genuine modern society, it must be on the basis of similar critical thinking and practice; in the spirit of Spinoza, Brandes aimed at dissolving remaining dogmatic thought and structures by urging the younger generations to "debate problems" and thus to combine idealism with action and struggles in the civil sphere. It was emphasized that cosmopolitan "alienated" outlooks on Danish culture were particularly valuable in pointing out the inherited prejudices that meant most Danes resisted liberal progressive development. This ideal of the transnational vision would forever change Brandes' otherwise seemingly pre-destined career in the academic world, in an incident we will examine more closely later, particularly in Chapter 3.

Brandes' Conception of the Modern Jew in his Early Writings

Brandes' first presentation of the Modern Breakthrough ideal of a cosmopolitan outlook was not, however, in *Emigrantlitteraturen*. Already in texts from 1867 and 1869, Brandes had put together the first building blocks of the transnational vision by reflecting on the figure of the modern Jew. This figure took precedency in the development of the transnational vision; in Brandes' early writings, alongside the Modern Breakthrough, he continuously reflected and built on this notion of the modern Jew. His primary source for his idea of the *Volksgeist* and the race concept was the French historian and aesthetician theorist Hippolyte Taine, about whom he wrote his doctoral thesis in the late 1860s. According to Taine, race is a fundamental part of the *Volksgeist* in which every individual is born. J. G. Herder's "*Volksgeist*" was the most common nineteenth-century term applied to gain an understanding of cultural heritage, and in Taine's interpretation environment, race and moment (the time in history) form the constituents of the people's spirit.[109] Taine believed every *Volksgeist* comprised various layers, among which environmental influence represented the random and most recent layers. According to Taine and to Brandes in his early writings, race is the deepest layer of the *Volksgeist* influence (in this context, we must remember that Brandes' use of the race concept occurred before 1879–81, before the *Berliner Antisemitismusstreit* and before the race concept was monopolized by the antisemites; I will also return to this in Chapter 3).[110]

The race concept influenced Brandes the most in the late 1860s and the 1870s, as is clearly evidenced by his essayistic text "Shakespeare: 'Kjøbmanden i Venedig'" ("Shakespeare: 'The Merchant of Venice'") (1867),[111] in which reflections on Shakespeare's *Merchant of Venice* develop into contemplations on Jewish racial traits. In the essay, Brandes recognizes that certain negatively drawn racial elements in Shylock's character capture some of the more undesirable elements of his Jewish racial heritage; he acknowledges, for example, Shakespeare's conception of Shylock's sense of justice as a fossilized relic of the biblical "eye for an eye".[112] Fenger believes that Brandes' thoughts on what Fenger also calls "modern Jewishness" must be Brandes' own personally developed reflections.[113] These reflections represent the first time that Brandes publicly contemplates what may comprise Jewish racial heritage. As will be demonstrated in this chapter's analysis of "Shakespeare: 'Kjøbmanden i Venedig,'" Brandes maintains that flexibility (*smidighed*) is a central positive element in Jewish racial heritage.

Brandes' essay on M. A. Goldschmidt first appeared in the newspaper *Illustreret Tidende* (*Illustrated News*) in 1869,[114] and the following year it became part of *Kritiker og Portraiter* (*Critique and Portrayals*)

(1870), as did "Shakespeare: 'Kjøbmanden i Venedig.'" When commenting on this essay, previous research on Brandes primarily tends to criticize him for his treatment of Goldschmidt as a writer and as a person.[115] It is true that Brandes' personal opinion is clear in the essay, which comments on Goldschmidt as a person and as a writer, occasionally rather harshly, especially in the first edition.[116] However, the relationship between these two distinguished nineteenth-century Danish Jewish intellectuals and writers was problematic from the beginning of their acquaintance, and holding Brandes sole responsibility for this would be narrow-minded. According to Brandes, Goldschmidt initiated their relationship by telling him that he was going to emigrate to England in order to get Brandes—who was a young but fast-rising Copenhagen literary critic in the late 1860s—to write a positive, sentimental preface to his collected works.[117]

In addition, the two men belonged to two different generations of Danish Jews. According to Brandes, Goldschmidt belonged to the generation before him:

His Jewish birth was of decisive importance to him, as it was at that time for most German and English writers of the same descent. With all of them, one feels that the civilized world had opened its doors to them recently: as children they still heard the gates of the ghettoes clanging shut behind them.[118]

With his partly bourgeois, partly Jewish traditional/religious "ghetto" appearance and with his appraisal of certain mystical elements in the Jewish religious tradition, Goldschmidt was a symbol of precisely those elements that the modern Jew ought to move away from, according to Brandes. Nevertheless, while Brandes negatively criticizes certain aspects of Goldschmidt's work and his personality, there are also clear signs of identification with him in the essay. This is evident, for example, through an ambiguous blending of comments on themes in Goldschmidt's prose, which resembles Brandes' own biographical experiences as a Jewish child attending a Christian school.[119] In the characterization of the figure of the modern Jew, "M. Goldschmidt" then develops into a sort of manifest and essayistic reflection on what Brandes calls "the task of the Jew in modern culture."[120]

In 1874–75, Brandes published four sequential articles entitled "Ferdinand Lassalle" in the progressive-liberal magazine *Det nittende Aarhundrede* (*The Nineteenth Century*), edited by Georg and Edvard Brandes. Overall, these four articles show that Lassalle, the founder of social democratic ideology, was one of Brandes' personal heroes at that time. Jointly, the four articles formed the structure of an intellectual biography when they came out in book form in German in 1877 (a re-worked version was published for the Danish market in 1881).[121] Like his biography *Benjamin Disraeli* (1878) and to the typical nineteenth-century biography genre in general, the Lassalle biography has the structure of a *Bildungsroman*. The first article provides the most important childhood and family background information, including Lassalle's primary Jewish racial characteristics. Next is a description of the most significant events of Lassalle's *Lehrjahre* as a young man.[122] In this part, Brandes heavily emphasizes Lassalle's efforts to be included and accepted as an equal bourgeois male within Christian society. It is the experience of being treated as a no-good "Jew boy" that first inspires the young Lassalle to pursue an energetic and dynamic lifelong political and judicial struggle for universal justice.[123] However, Brandes equally underlines Lassalle's German *Bildung*, arguing that Lassalle was deeply rooted in the German bourgeois tradition. He explains, for instance, that intellectually Lassalle was a pupil of Hegel.[124] Furthermore, through a description of the increasingly close relationship between Bismarck and Lassalle, Brandes stresses that Bismarck was the political figure who most closely resembled Lassalle in character (and Bismarck himself testified to this).[125] Through accentuating both Jewish-related racial characteristics and influences (in particular of Heinrich Heine)[126] while at the same time emphasizing the essential input Lassalle received from the (Christian-based) German *Bildung*, Brandes represents Lassalle's innovative achievements, in particular his founding of social democratic ideology, as a result of his German Jewish in-between position.

Brandes' biography *Benjamin Disraeli* (1878) and his article "Bevægelsen mod jøderne i Tyskland" ("The movement against the Jews in Germany") (1881) were specifically written in the context of the so-called Jewish Question, the biography mainly in relation to the Danish/ Scandinavian Jewish Question and the article in relation to the German Jewish Question. However, it seems that, in the 1870s and the early 1880s, the Danish/Scandinavian and the German Jewish Questions were closely linked to each other, and that Brandes specifically played a big part in this dialectic. Initially, August Rohling's *Der Talmudjude* (1871) was a central work in developing this dialectic relationship. A part of this influential work was translated into Danish and published in *Dansk Kirketidende* (*Danish Church News*) in 1877, inflaming the anti-Jewish side in the debate on the Danish/Scandinavian Jewish Question, as did J. C. Heuch's pamphlet written directly against "the Jew" Brandes that same year.[127] Inspired by Rohling's work and others, the third part of Bishop H. L. Martensen's *Den Christelige Ethik* (*Christian Ethics*) (1878) became another influential text in this period in the Danish/Scandinavian context. In this book Martensen, the most influential Danish theologian at the time, raged against "the ruling Jewish regime," thus indirectly commenting on Brandes and his ideas.[128] Brandes' *Benjamin Disraeli*, which was then published in December 1878, is a retort against the accusations of negative Jewish influence and the personal attacks on him. In the final pages, he projects the figure of the modern Jew as a constructive and progressive individual who is both European and Jewish, and who co-constructs European civilization.

Brandes then wrote the article "Bevægelsen mod jøderne i Tyskland" in January 1881 as a reaction to particular German discussions of the so-called Jewish Question. To begin, Brandes mentions Adolf Stoecker's personal attack on him in the German Reichstag in December 1880 and also historian Heinrich von Treitschke's antisemitic articles of the *Berliner Antisemitismusstreit* as motivations for him to write the article.[129] Regarding the interconnections between the Danish/Scandinavian and the German Jewish Questions of the 1870s and the beginning of the 1880s, Stoecker's antisemitic attack on Brandes in the German Reichstag in 1880 was, as mentioned, based on a German translation of Heuch's 1877 pamphlet against Brandes. Stoecker uses direct quotes from the pamphlet in his speech, in which he warns against the Jewish influence and specifically Georg Brandes' negative influence.[130] In "Bevægelsen mod jøderne i Tyskland," Brandes then defies these antisemitic accusations of negative Jewish influential dominance in German politics and journalism, and condemns Stoecker's attack on him. Brandes ends his article by urging West European Jews to continue the liberal, secularly orientated, bourgeois *Bildung* begun in the late Enlightenment so that antisemitic stereotypes will die away.[131]

My analysis of the figure of the modern Jew in Brandes' early writings also covers the preface to *Heinrich Heine* (1897), where he expresses his idea, one last time, of a particular Jewish racial heritage that makes the modern Jew more likely to develop the transnational vision than anyone else.

The Figure of the Modern Jew

When identifying the constituent elements of the positive Jewish racial heritage, Brandes refers to three different eras in Jewish history. Some of the racial elements he characterizes can be traced back to the Jewish Semitic people of the ancient world, and as such they correlate with Jewish history before the destruction of the second temple in AD 70. Brandes also views the bourgeois *Bildung* acculturation of North European Jews as another important environmental influence, which in the merging with what he describes as the Jewish Semitic trait of *chutspe*, as is the case with Lassalle and also Disraeli, according to Brandes, has formed impressive modern Jewish individuals.[132] However, as we will see next, most of the qualities of the modern Jew relate to the period of the European diaspora.

The next section presents the three most important and iterative traits, which are essential for understanding Brandes' idea about the modern Jew as the most innovative individual in the transition to the modern world: flexibility, a love of universal justice, and a critical view.

Flexibility

In "Shakespeare: 'Kjøbmanden i Venedig,'" Brandes asks what the most significant quality of the Jewish race is, across all time periods. He wonders which racial element represents the connecting factor behind the achievements of various great Jewish individuals such as "King David, Spinoza and Heinrich Heine."[133] His aim is to identify the shared racial element that has made these great men of Jewish descent able to produce innovative ideas and practice within such varied fields as politics, philosophy, and literature, from the ancient world to the nineteenth century. Subsequently, Brandes answers his own question with an essayistic reflection on the topic:

If the Jewish character is the most persistent, it is, on the other hand, also one of the most flexible: In times of antiquity bearer of the most exclusive principle of nationality and through it the Weltanschauung of monotheism, yet fragmenting in recent times into various modern tribes and becoming one with them without losing its stamp or gaining new traits, being sometimes Romanic, sometimes Germanic; then in recent times, within one and the same tribe, as within the German people, joining and often leading national, liberal movements, be it in a cosmopolitan fashion like Heine, or be it like Auerbach, so consumed by national sentiment that he, a Jew, was the one to give Germany the peasant novels and village stories emulated by almost every other country [...]. What contradictions within such a small tribe![134]

Here, Brandes initially observes that some of these innovative achievements seem almost contradictory. Berthold Auerbach's National Romantic stories of rustic peasant life appear to be the quintessential counterpart to Heine's cosmopolitanism. However, Brandes identifies flexibility (*smidighed*) as their shared racial trait. Further on in the essay, he explains that this trait has mainly been noticeable during the European diaspora.[135] Consequently, Brandes' positive accentuation of the Jews' ability to adjust themselves to new cultures through the European diaspora goes against the typically negative depiction of the flexible Jewish nature that dominated the representation of Jewishness in the bourgeois public sphere at the time. In "Das Judentum in der Musik", Wagner claims, as noted above, that the Jewish trait of flexibility is yet another sign of the alienated, rootless Jewish spirit. The Jew, according to Wagner, may be able to copy European tradition but he will never be able to create the original, innovative work of which native European "geniuses" are capable.[136] This view on Jewishness, as mentioned earlier, was also perpetuated by N. F. S. Grundtvig, the Danish national cultural father figure, who stated that Goldschmidt might very well have been able to write in a seemingly educated and cultivated way, but the meaning of his writings would always be that of a stranger and therefore would fail to contribute positively to Danish culture. Brandes delivers a solid counter-narrative to this negative view of Jewish flexibility by providing the indisputable proof of the innovative achievements of Spinoza, Heine and Auerbach. Furthermore, Brandes' essay on Goldschmidt, written two years after the Shakespeare essay, contains in its very last sentences a striking metaphor that could be seen as a direct response to the hegemonic idea of the bourgeois Jew as influenced by the rootless Jewish *Volksgeist* that prevents any positive cultural contribution beyond mimicry and copying. The essay contends that:

When faced with a nature and enterprise such as that of Goldschmidt, the reluctant observer is inclined to use the word "rootless," yet this epithet does not fit. If one were to compare this writer to a tree, he would not be a rootless tree, but a transplanted and grafted tree whose trunk does not grow tall but whose branches spread far and wide, and whose smooth-skinned fruits have a subtle and complex flavor.[137]

In another part of this essay, Brandes argues that a modern Jew such as Goldschmidt possesses traits demonstrating that Jews took root in every one of the various cultures during the diaspora. Goldschmidt's prose thus comprises racial "essences", as Brandes calls it, from cultures as varied as the Jewish Semitic, Arabic, Portuguese, Spanish, German and Danish cultural traditions.[138] Interestingly, Brandes' essay on Goldschmidt also uses Giacomo Meyerbeer and Felix Mendelssohn, the main targets of Wagner's negative image of the bourgeois assimilated Jew, as primary examples of this type of innovative nineteenth-century modern Jew. Whether or not Brandes was familiar with or had read Wagner's essay at this time is uncertain. However, Wagner's essay was republished in 1869, causing a much greater stir than it had initially. Brandes' later text "Raceteorier" ("Racial Theories") (1913) clearly indicates a familiarity with "Das Judenthum in der Musik."[139]

Universal Justice as a Primary Virtue

In his early writings, Brandes makes a point that is particularly relevant to a view of the fin-de-siècle period as a globalization period and a transition phase. He emphasizes a racial trait that allows the modern Jew to be a natural born leader in the struggle to establish a progressive modern world, namely an inherent, deep-seated contempt toward all forms of suppression and inequality, as a result of the many hundred years of unjustified repression the Jews had experienced during their diaspora. According to Brandes, one of the most significant characteristics of the modern Jew is the consideration of universal justice as a primary virtue. At the close of *Benjamin Disraeli* he explicitly states:

If the Jews are the most eager to preach to the world that they are by no means God's chosen people [...] might not the source of this be honesty and altruism and self-abnegation rather than base motives? [...] When in 1848 Jews everywhere led the revolt against outdated tradition and entrenched injustice [...] could they not have acted out of a love of liberty, which goes hand in hand with a love of truth? And if Jews, finally rich and wealthy men, [...] should have ushered in, if not the Communist, then the Socialist movement in Europe in our age [...] could they not be motivated by a noble and passionate love for mankind, a philanthropy, which far-removed from any claims for their race to the rank of 'the natural aristocracy', is steeped in a genuine, human aversion to aristocracy by birth and thus applies its vigor to leading democratic ideas forth to victory directly and without further ado?[140]

Leading up to this passage, Brandes summarizes Disraeli's idea of the modern Jew as a descendant of the Jewish aristocratic race, and as such the first in line to fight against the liberal, democratic attempts to subvert the meaningful structures of the old world.[141] He calls Disraeli's idea of the Jews as a conservative aristocratic race "the Semitic principle."[142] According to him, *Lord George Bentinck* (1852), in particular, displays Disraeli's Semitic principle as the idea that the Jewish Semitic civilization and religion of the ancient world are the foundation of Western civilization.

The passage quoted above expresses a strong opposition to Disraeli's Semitic principle. Brandes argues that the modern Jew is an individual whose most significant racial trait is an inherited hatred toward all forms of suppression and inequality. Following this, he describes the modern Jew as the most eager representative of the fight to eliminate the structures of the old world, "leading democratic ideas forth." Moreover he does not identify the Jewish race or people as God's chosen people. Instead, the modern Jew is against all forms of "entrenched injustice," and thus Brandes strongly opposes the idea of the existence of a race or people as a natural blood aristocracy.

The idea that universal justice is a key Jewish virtue is also present in "Ferdinand Lassalle" and "M. Goldschmidt," where it is associated with experiences of the European diaspora.[143] In "Ferdinand Lassalle," Brandes calls Lassalle's innovative creation of the social democratic ideology a result of the diaspora heritage, which "gave him centuries of constraint and centuries of injustice to avenge his maternal heritage."[144]

A notable contradiction, however, is detectable in the passage from *Benjamin Disraeli* cited at the beginning of this section. Brandes condemns Disraeli's Semitic principle and the idea that the Jewish race represents a natural blood aristocracy in Western civilization; nevertheless, by canonizing this particular Jewish racial trait concerning an intrinsic loathing of subjugation and inequality, Brandes projects an idea of Jewish superiority that is in fact very similar to Disraeli's Semitic principle. For example, Brandes maintains that Jews are "leading" the rebellion against the structures of the old world due to their racial heritage. Like Disraeli, he therefore proposes that the modern Jew is a natural born leader, but differs in his stance in that the modern Jew is leading the development of the modern world, not the preservation of old world structures. As will be shown in Chapter 4, on Brandes' re-interpretations of the Athens vs. Jerusalem dichotomy, and also in Chapter 5, Brandes was apparently consistently influenced by Disraeli's Semitic principle, though he also seems to reflect more substantially on the Jewish trait of holding universal justice as a primary virtue. But for now let us concentrate on Brandes' early writings and the third important characteristic of the figure of the modern Jew.

The Critical View

Being critical, or naturally in opposition, is the final crucial aspect proposed here for understanding Brandes' idea of the modern Jew as the most innovative individual in the transition to the modern world. In "Ferdinand Lassalle," Brandes identifies Lassalle's natural critical reason as related to the Jewish "chutspe" characteristic (I use Brandes' spelling of the term, which is more likely to be known as "chutzpa"); in fact, he proclaims that it is the most significant element of Lassalle's personality.[145] According to Brandes, chutspe denotes that someone is impudent (fræk), but it also has connotations of boldness, recklessness, presence of mind, pushiness, and a sense of humor.[146] He claims that before the emancipation of the Jews, this Jewish characteristic most often showed itself in uncivilized behavior.[147] However, he explains that chutspe underwent a positive development after the emancipation of the Jews due to the positive influence of the *Bildung* ideal.[148] Brandes finishes his reflection on Lassalle's chutspe by laying out what he understands as the essence of this trait, which was often used (by others) to describe Brandes:[149]

It was an enterprise which sought resistance and lived and breathed only in opposition [...], in other words, an undertaking which sought out impediments and overcame impediments [...].[150]

Brandes believed that Lassalle thrived on the political battles in which he took part, because they provided a forum for Lassalle's impudence and boldness, allowing him to speak against the authoritarian patriarchal political and clerical powers of Germany in the 1850s and 1860s in a manner no one else dared to, or indeed had the ingenuity for.

In "M. Goldschmidt" and *Benjamin Disraeli*, Brandes reiterates that one of the central Jewish characteristics is taking a critical view, or naturally being in opposition. The essay on Goldschmidt also describes this trait as related to Jews' European diaspora experiences—the experience of living between cultures:

Yet the Jewish mind is already free at birth, the Romanic and anti-Romanic culture [...] Catholicism and Protestantism, Classical and Romantic civilization, for him they are all equally familiar and equally remote. He is the son of Spinoza. Hence, he is from birth polemically opposed to any European narrow-mindedness, he is oppositional, free-born and emancipated, both as scientific observer and as poetic reproducer.[151]

Several times in "M. Goldschmidt," Brandes refers to the free, critical outlook of the European Jews and how their peripheral position during the diaspora created "an equally familiar and equally remote" relation to Christian-based European traditions. The modern Jew is thus presented as occupying a position that is simultaneously inside and outside the various European societies. It is interesting that Brandes refers to Baruch Spinoza by calling the modern Jew "the son of Spinoza." In referring to Spinoza's life example in this way—rather than to his philosophy—Brandes seems to follow a particular branch of Spinozism in which Spinoza is depicted as highly influenced by his Iberian Sephardic Jewish immigrant background. Similarly, the above-quoted passage describes how experiencing and living in the periphery of a variety of cultures allowed European Jews to grow accustomed to having an "equally near and equally remote" outlook, and this ultimately enabled them to perceive these cultures more objectively than monocultural individuals. This sociocultural position also permitted them to escape the constraint of just one cultural tradition, thus providing enough distance to view cultural traditions critically. Along these lines, in *Benjamin Disraeli*, Brandes concludes that:

> Seen in this light, the genius of the Jewish race shows a different physiognomy, bright and open, it is a critical and questioning, an undogmatic spirit.[152]

Brandes indisputably has a point when he identifies a critical outlook as a particularly valuable modern virtue. One of the most important elements in the development of the modern mindset is the ability to question and analyze the dogma and inherited authoritarian structures of the old world. In particular, a methodical, reasoned approach is considered an asset in the Spinozian Enlightenment tradition, of which Brandes considered himself a successor. From the early stages of the early modern Enlightenment tradition in Amsterdam in the seventeenth century, one of the dominant characteristics was an oppositional curiosity toward the so-called absolute truths and norms that had a hegemonic status then. For early radical writers and thinkers such as Uriel da Costa and Baruch Spinoza—and in the depictions of them as life examples in the literature of Karl Gutzkow and Berthold Auerbach—the primary approach was systematically questioning the legitimacy of the ruling feudal authoritarian structures, particularly clerical ones.[153]

The Transnational Vision

Brandes idealizes the characteristic of having a free and unprejudiced outlook on the different traditions and values that constitute a culture. His essay "M. Goldschmidt" expresses the point most significantly as follows:

> The modern Jew [...] has the advantage of being at an Archimedean point away from the innate boundaries of the Arian peoples, looking on with an unrestricted view from a high vantage point. In this, there is something fortunate. On the other hand, the modern Jew—who, as soon as his nature begins to express itself, feels like the black sheep of the flock, being neither of the same

religion nor of the same temperament as the people in whose midst he lives and, owing to his temperament, not sharing with them common opinions or feeling the same ancestral spirit stirring within him—surely feels more spiritually homeless than any other. In this, there is something truly tragic.[154]

Brandes acknowledges aspects of the hegemonic discourse on the acculturated modern Jew dominant in the civil sphere at that time. Wagner's essay "Das Judentum in der Musik" also points out that because of this Jewish characteristic, the educated and acculturated Jew stands alone, without a community, whereas the European native is born into a meaningful, rooted *Volksgeist*; loneliness and individualism become part of a pathology with which the acculturated modern Jew is forever cursed to be homeless and alienated. Brandes, however, having similarly identified loneliness and individualism as central traits of the modern Jew, ambivalently connects this "tragic" position with the positive quality of having a free and critical outlook that enables modern Jews to create far more innovative works of art than monocultural Europeans can. In the dominant discourses of the civil sphere, the individualistic position of the modern Jew most often became a sign of the Jew as a cold, "hostile onlooker," whereas Brandes turned it into a constructive feature.

One could view the critical outlook and flexibility of the modern Jew as predisposing them for success in the modern world. The flexibility trait fosters the ability to blend various aspects of European and Jewish traditions, whereas the critical outlook bestows a capacity to eliminate unconstructive, dogmatic elements of a tradition and to point out the most beneficial ones. The dialectic between these two characteristics of being flexible and being critical constitute what I call the transnational vision, which represents the idea of a socio-cultural identity in which the individual acts within a national culture but at the same time does not feel bound to its tradition by any special devotion. This individual can then innovate more easily. In his early writings, Brandes idealizes individuals who experience and perceive the world from a socio-cultural inside-outside position, and he holds this identity higher than that of the monocultural natives whose horizon is obstructed by the dogmatic traditions and prejudices of the cultural tradition into which they are born and/or which influences them most. Additionally, as will be shown, the transnational vision is a universal cosmopolitan ideal promoted by Brandes as a model anyone can use to transform themselves, in order to take part in the development of the modern world. His early writings thus indicate that he was a liberal cosmopolitan utopian, since he believed —like so many other nineteenth-century bourgeois-influenced Western European Jews[155]—in the transformation of all human beings according to these liberal Enlightenment ideals.[156] It could even be said that the young Brandes was a believer in Jewish assimilation. Though, as a liberal utopian—a *citoyen*, which is how Harald Rue and Svend Møller Kristensen describe him—Brandes was of the opinion that all Jews, all Danes, and all Europeans had to assimilate and transform themselves according to the universal liberal Enlightenment ideals.[157] He did not, for example, embrace the notion that all others had to adjust to the norms and traditions of a particular European national tradition.[158] Rather, he envisioned that Jewish particularism, along with all other forms of religious and cultural particularisms, would eventually fade in the transformed and universally oriented modern world (and as such it was an unrealistic vision).

In relation to Brandes' utopian transformation of all of humankind in his early writings, it is furthermore important to note that he did not believe that all European Jews of his time had developed the transnational vision. Brandes is critical of M. A. Goldschmidt, for example, because, with his appraisal of certain mystical elements in the Jewish religious tradition, Goldschmidt was a symbol of those elements that the modern Jew ought to move away from, according to Brandes. Thus, in his essay on Goldschmidt, he writes that: "Goldschmidt owes most of his merits to his Jewish nationality, his original Jewish piousness he perhaps owes first and foremost to his weakness."[159] This demonstrates that Brandes does not identify the traditional Jewish religion and its customs as part of the constructive Jewish heritage that the modern Jew should appreciate and cultivate. Goldschmidt was not an ideal modern

Jew, since he still believed in core elements of the Jewish religious tradition.[160] With his criticism of Jewish religion and tradition, Brandes identifies what he perceives to be a negative Jewish heritage as not racially conditioned, since each modern Jew is free to choose whether he, to paraphrase Brandes, will let himself be suppressed and brought to heel by clericalized Judaism or, by conversion, to institutionalized Christianity—or whether he will embrace the transnational vision.

Interestingly, in his early writings Brandes rejected the label of atheist,[161] preferring instead to be called a Spinozian pantheist and materialist.[162] Accordingly, like Spinoza's biographical struggles and the depiction of these in Auerbach's novel *Spinoza*, it was above all the structural power that the different religious institutions still enjoyed that Brandes opposed more than anything. He was a firm opponent of clericalism, Christian or Jewish, and this is consistent throughout his oeuvre. He believed that it was forms of dogmatic authoritarian power that kept pre-modern mindsets and medieval societal structures alive. In texts such as "Bevægelsen mod jøderne i Tyskland" and "Jøderne i Finland" ("The Jews in Finland") (1908), Brandes demonstrates that he instead favors the environmental effect of the liberal, secularly orientated, bourgeois *Bildung*. Subsequently, in these texts, he advocated that modern Jews should recognize the bourgeois *Bildung* as their guideline in life, rather than following the dogma of institutionalized religion.[163]

The Exile

For Brandes, it was not only modern Jews who had the ability to develop the transnational vision. In his early writings, he presents exile as a topos denoting an individual process by which all people can develop the transnational vision. As such, he argues that individuals who are not born into a cultural in-between position can still transform themselves to exist and perceive the world according to a free, critical, and flexible outlook through either an internal or external exile. *Emigrantlitteraturen* (1872) describes how spending an extended amount of time in the Italian culture and nature enabled Brandes himself to distance himself critically from the Danish and North European aesthetic traditions, putting him in a better position to assess certain aspects of Shakespeare's drama:

He who has not painstakingly labored to understand the point of view of an entirely alien race does not know how difficult it is in this respect to shake off innate tribal prejudices. To do this, it is necessary to breathe in the same air, to live for considerable time in the same surroundings as the alien race. If it were not for the journeys which Mme de Stäel was obliged to undertake upon being exiled, she could not have expanded her intelligence. I believe, in all modesty, that I am in a position to speak from experience. I dare say that it was only during solitary walks in the region of Sorrento that I succeeded in seeing Shakespeare at such a distance that I could grasp him and truly understand him and consequently his antithesis [...]. It was dusk, Venus shone brilliantly and the rugged mountainsides and rock faces gradually assumed the fantastic features which darkness imparts. But the scene was not what we Northerners would call romantic [...]. I understood how natural it is that a country like this should not have produced a Shakespeare or needed a Shakespeare, since nature has taken upon itself the task which in the North falls to the poets.[164]

Brandes here describes how he gained a deeper insight into Shakespearian drama as a product of attaining a critical and flexible outlook. His Italian exile allowed him to achieve this outlook, freeing him from the confines of the prejudices and given truths of Northern European cultural tradition. Berthelsen and Egebjerg describe Brandes' conception of the exile topos as a "painful and laborious process of spiritual emancipation."[165] Brandes had already proclaimed, in his doctoral thesis of 1869, that any ambitious artist or scientist whose goal is to create innovative, original work should live through one or several exiles. Here we can again observe that the key cosmopolitan ideal of the Modern Breakthrough—the figure of the emigrant—in fact had already been thematized in works of the late 1860s.[166]

The following two sections present the figures of the emigrant and the critic and explore the idea found in Brandes' early writings that any individual can transform themselves through either an external, physical exile or an internal one.

Brandes' Figure of the Emigrant

Brandes defines the figure of the emigrant in *Emigrantlitteraturen* (1872). In particular, it was the liberal cosmopolitanism idealism represented by this figure that roused the reactionary Copenhagen bourgeoisie; the reviews of the book in 1872 in leading Danish bourgeois newspapers testify to this.[167] In much the same fashion as was the case with the figure of the modern Jew, Brandes idealizes the in-between and out-group position of the emigrant. He claims that the experiences of leading French writers living as emigrants were the catalyst to a new, innovative type of literature, the literature of what Brandes calls "the reaction," in the beginning of the nineteenth century:

But those most profoundly influenced by foreign surroundings, however, were those for whom these great events meant a permanent life-long exile from their homeland […]. The French emigrant was obliged to acquire a more than superficial knowledge of foreign tongues, if for no other reason, in order to be able to give French lessons in the foreign country. A new spirit was diffused by intelligent French emigrants throughout France, and thus it was that the literature of the new century in this country began as Emigrant Literature.[168]

As with the figure of the modern Jew, Brandes argues that an additional effect resulting from the distance of physical exile from one's native cultural tradition is the development of a critical outlook toward that maternal cultural tradition, and thus an ability to create an overview of it and to distinguish its different elements more clearly.[169]

As regards Brandes' construction of the ideal of the emigrant, it is furthermore important to remember that it serves an aesthetic and also an ideological purpose, namely that of representing liberal cosmopolitanism. However, as already mentioned, Brandes' liberal cosmopolitan world view was also elitist. His aim is not to describe the contemporary sociological reality of the typical emigrant; his models are not Eastern

European Jews fleeing suppression, poverty, and violence in Russia, or the deprived Scandinavian proletariat peasants who settled in North America in great numbers in the latter part of the nineteenth century. On the contrary, the models for the figure in *Emigrantlitteraturen* are privileged bourgeois/aristocratic writers such as Mdm. De Stäel, Chateaubriand, Voltaire, and Byron. Emigrants of this type may also have fled their native country because they felt pressured to do so. However, this pressure was political and intellectual, rather than socioeconomic; they were not fleeing famine or social deprivation. Correspondingly, the emigrant's development of the transnational vision is constructive in a broader context than the emigrants themselves and their aesthetic production. Such emigrants provide innovative contributions to their native cultural tradition:[170]

One single grand notion poses the greatest threat of all to the despotism of every society's established beliefs and rules. Not the notion of the logical [...], nay! What arouses and astonishes the masses more than anything else, provided one is able to put it into perspective for them, is the fact that an ideal which they assume to be universally recognized is regarded as an ideal only by so many concurring minds, while other peoples [...] have an entirely different concept of what is fitting and beautiful [...]. Thus, were I to characterize what Mme de Stäel gained from French society, culture and literature, [...] I would put it like this: In her two major works 'Corinne' and 'De l'Allemagne' in particular, she put the human and literary beliefs and opinions in France, England, Germany, and Italy into perspective for the inhabitants of the various countries.[171]

In current theories of cosmopolitanism, a common dichotomy is between strong and weak cosmopolitanism, where a thinker or theory is categorized based on the emphasis accorded to the cosmopolitan outlook and/or the national outlook.[172] Weak cosmopolitan theory emphasizes that structures of the national outlook and framework, e.g. the national state, are still valuable and necessary even though the cosmopolitanization of our present-day individual life-worlds is growing.[173] Brandes' transnational vision represents the opposite of a weak cosmopolitanism. Like Ulrich Beck's ideal of the cosmopolitan outlook, Brandes' opinion is that individuals can free themselves from being caught in the confines of the national cultural tradition they have been brought up in through the experience of living in the periphery of one or several other cultures. Yet, notably, this strong cosmopolitanism in Brandes' early writings did not aim to develop a form of transnational identity that was not rooted in any cultural tradition.[174] In the above-quoted passage, the most important reason for developing the transnational vision is the contribution that individuals with such vision give back to the cultural tradition (or rather, the *Volksgeist*) they are brought up in and feel most rooted in through their innovative achievements. It is crucial to understand that while Brandes was a strong cosmopolitan in his early writings, his preferred concept for understanding cultural matters was, throughout his oeuvre, that of *Volksgeist*. He was convinced that all individuals had resilient ties to the *Volksgeist(ern)* in which they were born. Thus, even when Brandes is mostly oriented towards well-developed cosmopolitan outlooks, as is the case in his early writings, he does not ignore the strong and continuous influence of the national outlook (as Beck seemingly does in *The Cosmopolitan Vision*).

The Figure of the Critic

Besides the physical exile the emigrant undergoes, Brandes also sees an exile of introversion as a way of developing the transnational vision. Occasionally, *Emigrantlitteraturen* merges the figure of the emigrant and the critic.[175] As the following excerpt from the introductory chapter of *Den Romantiske Skole i Tydskland* (*The Romantic School in Germany*) (1873) indicates, a similar blending occurs between the figure of the critic and the figure of the stranger:

Finally, there is one element which the stranger discerns more easily than the native; it is the racial distinction, the feature of the German writer which characterizes him as a German. For the native observer, being German and being human becomes all too easily indistinguishable, since he is generally accustomed, whenever dealing with a person, to dealing with a German. The stranger whose singularity the native overlooks because he is accustomed to seeing it, and above all because he possesses it himself or is it himself, is very striking.[176]

In this chapter, Brandes reflects on what he, as a non-native German critic, has to offer to the already extensive writings on the German Romantic tradition by German critics. He writes that native German critics have superior knowledge compared to him due to their familiarity with the central texts and sources of the German Romantic tradition, since the native German develops an acquaintance with these sources and texts at German educational institutions throughout childhood and youth.[177] Brandes then describes the advantage "a stranger" has in assessing the German Romantic tradition. The non-native critic's lack of influence from the dense German scholarly tradition and consequently also his lack of bias is simultaneously his advantage.

In addition, Brandes' doctoral thesis on Hippolyte Taine describes the ideal of the transnational vision as a form of individual identity that any serious-minded critic must develop before being fully capable of delivering work worthy of examination by others. The following passage illustrates Brandes' notion that whereas the emigrant must endure an outer, physical exile, the critic must undergo an internal, intellectual exile to develop the transnational vision:

He [the critic] must add to his national and natural spirit five to six artificial, acquired spirits in order to call forth in himself extinct sentiments from the past or contemporary alien sentiments. The greatest result from his action is perhaps the fact that it detaches him from himself, compels him to calculate the influence of the environment in which he is embedded, teaches him to distinguish objects from the transient hue which his person and his era impart to them [...]. We discover that the hue is not in the thing itself but in ourselves, we forgive our neighbors for seeing differently from us and recognize that they must see as blue what appears to us as yellow [...]. We can see how the critic, who is so certain of the natural limitation of the minds of others, is so self-assured about being able to transcend his own. He sees how the others are tethered and believes he can loosen his own tether.[178]

Brandes elaborates on how an intellectual inner exile allows the critic to achieve a higher mental stage that permits objective reading and analysis. His fragmentary thematization of the critic makes it difficult to ascertain whether Brandes believed that a higher mental state of pure critical reason was possible (this would be another parallel to Spinoza's philosophy). However, it is clear that he believed it was possible to acquire a more objective outlook if people allowed themselves to be transformed by an inner exile. Accordingly, Brandes' early writings apply a scientific method, comparative literature, to substantiate the ideal of an inner exile. Brandes' inaugural lecture in 1871 on French emigrant literature, from the series which caused such a big stir, begins by demonstrating the utility of this underlying literary method, which he describes as being based on adopting a "stranger's" perspective:

The response which literature of the nineteenth century in the first decades showed toward eighteenth-century literature and the overcoming of this reaction: This historical event is European in essence and can only be understood through a comparative examination of literature. [...] The comparative examination of literature has a dual nature; it brings us closer to that which is foreign so that we may adapt it, and it distances us from that which is our own so that we may gain a clear view of it [...]. We must use it to correct the illusions created by our natural vision.[179]

Conclusion

Brandes' figure of the modern Jew is a strong reaction to the otherwise negative representation of the emancipated and acculturated Western European Jew in the second half of the nineteenth century, touting the modern Jew's ability to co-construct and be part of Western civilization. In fact, Brandes announces that this segment of modern Jews not only co-constructs Western civilization but also comprises the most innovative individuals in his time, if the transnational vision is adopted.

Three racial characteristics—flexibility, holding universal justice as a primary virtue, and taking a critical view—are specifically used by Brandes to represent the modern Jew as potentially the most innovative individual of his time. His preface to *Heinrich Heine* (1897) represents the idea of the modern Jew one last time:

He [Heinrich Heine] depicts, as do later Disraeli in England, Lassalle in Germany, and possibly Gambetta in France, the clash during which the character of his race crackled and flared when modern culture assailed it, like flint striking steel.[180]

Brandes believed that the modern Jew must make an individual choice about whether or not to develop the transnational vision. Instead of the Jewish religion, in his early writings, Brandes proposes that the liberal secular-orientated bourgeois *Bildung* should be the primary existential guideline for European Jews. As we will see in Chapters 4 and 5 of the book, Brandes nuances his view of the Jewish religious tradition in his later writings, while also pointing to a specific tradition for secular thought within the tradition of Judaism.

The young Brandes believed that the modern Jew should serve as a role model for all human beings, and as this chapter has demonstrated he also projects the figures of the emigrant and the critic as related role models. The transnational vision thus stands as a universal ideal. Similar to the modern Jew's societal inside–outside position, a cultural or an inner intellectual exile can transform any individual, according to Brandes. Through the process of exile and the development of the transnational vision, all individuals can free themselves from the narrow horizon of the primary cultural context into which they were born. Additionally, Brandes understands this transformation as a necessary self-emancipatory project for every modern individual.

As mentioned, it was not the first time Brandes presented the cosmopolitan ideal of the transnational vision when he made it the key focus of *Emigrantlitteraturen*. Already in texts of 1867 and 1869, he had begun reflecting on the figure of the modern Jew. Furthermore, before his lectures of 1871, Brandes had been following an almost pre-destined path toward a promising academic career for many years. He had completed all the expected rites: He had won the gold medal of the University of Copenhagen, he had been awarded Smith's Scholarship (*Smiths Legat*), and after his doctoral thesis he had taken a classical *Bildungsreise* to France and Italy. However, he was not appointed professor in the 1870s, even though the former professor in Aesthetics Carsten Hauch had recommended it on his deathbed. In comparison to the treatment of Christian freethinkers—for example, that of his mentor Hans Brøchner, who became a professor at the University of Copenhagen—it does seem that Brandes' Jewish background was the decisive factor as regards the harsh and stigmatizing treatment he received after his 1871 lectures.[181] The negative effects of the stigmatization of Brandes from 1871/1872 as being simultaneously a Jew, an atheist/Spinozist materialist, a freethinker and a cosmopolitan were thus rather severe. One result of this exclusion was that it became difficult for Brandes simply to earn a living after 1872.[182] Consequently, he came to outlive his own personal exile; he moved to Berlin and lived there from 1877 to 1883. He eventually returned to Copenhagen, and as we will see in Chapter 3, it continued to be his primary goal to be appointed professor at the University of Copenhagen and to achieve this final visible sign of inclusion into the Danish-Christian core group of the bourgeoisie.

Before ending this chapter, and as a prelude to the next chapter, I would like to suggest that Brandes' modern Jew should be seen as a predecessor to Georg Simmel's figure the stranger, as portrayed in the 1908 essay "Exkurs über den Fremden." Today, Simmel's construction of this figure stands as the progenitor of the widespread use of the term the stranger in academia.[183] Yet, with the figure of the stranger, Simmel constructs a figure that shares the same fundamental, constructive qualities as Brandes' modern Jew. Simmel's stranger is also defined by being simultaneously inside and outside a cultural tradition. Thus, Simmel describes the stranger through a "characteristic of objectivity," as he calls it that resembles the description of the free, critical position of the modern Jew[184]:

Objectivity can also be defined as freedom. The objective man is not bound by ties which could prejudice his perception, his understanding, and his assessment of data. This freedom, which permits the stranger to experience and treat even his close relationships as though from a bird's-eye view (...) he is the freer man, practically and theoretically; he examines conditions with less prejudice; he assess them against standards that are more general and more objective; and his actions are not confined by custom, piety, or precedent.[185]

Simmel's essay also states that these strangers would typically be appointed judges because their characteristic of objectivity was recognized. Simmel does not project his figure as particularly Jewish–his Jewish references are quite discrete–but at the same time he also states that Jewish history provides the best examples of how this ideal stranger type has been a consistent part of European history.[186] Also, as Amos Morris-Reich has pointed out, it is more likely the bourgeois-influenced Western European Jews Simmel has thought of than the more traditional Orthodox Eastern European Jews when he composed this essay (notice this sentence, for example: "(...) his actions are not confined by custom, piety, or precedent").[187] In other words, Simmel, like Brandes, does not comment on the contributions of the deprived Eastern European Jews migrating to, for example, Germany at this time in history. Instead, Simmel offers an analogy to the contributions of resourceful bourgeois-influenced Western European Jews like himself or Brandes. Both figures, Brandes' modern Jew and Simmel's the stranger, are nevertheless to be seen as somewhat disguised counter reactions to the dominantly negative discourses on these Western European bourgeois-influenced Jews. This term "disguised counter reaction" is chosen to show that Simmel and Brandes lifelong actively struggled to be included in the Christian-based core group bourgeoisie, since they both struggled to get tenured academic positions at universities. Accordingly, their high evaluation of the Jewish contribution to Western civilization is somewhat hidden; it is revealed "between the lines" and the positive representation of Jewish-related strangeness typically appeared in the margin of their oeuvre to avoid risking too much in their civil lives, where they did not occupy a firm bourgeois position. With regard to Brandes, this assumption is bolstered by the fact that his boldest and most explicit representation of his idea of the modern Jew appeared in the Goldschmidt-essay, published before he truly became a public figure in 1871-1872. After that, he never portrayed the modern Jew as daring again. Simmel's and Brandes' disguised counter reactions, however, denote that they both felt provoked by the dominant negative representation of the acculturated and well-educated bourgeois-influenced European Jews as not being able to produce original work because this was an attack on how they fundamentally understood and defined themselves as scientists and writers, whose goal was to produce innovative work in letters and sociology.

Chapter 2

The Stranger as Ideal in the Fin-De-Siècle Period

Introduction

This chapter will continue the focus on Georg Brandes' early writings, and particularly on the figure of the modern Jew. However, we will also see how Brandes used this figure to contribute to a broader intellectual current. He was far from the only one to define such a figure prior to Simmel, and the main purpose in what follows is to examine the ideal stranger as a well-known Jewish-related topos prior to Simmel's essay, even while Simmel stands as the founder of the term in academia today.[188] Different versions of the Jewish-related ideal stranger were put forward as counter-reactions to modern antisemitism's depiction of the emancipated and acculturated Western European Jew as a negative alien who was a non-contributive and parasitic element. This chapter suggests that, rather than viewing Georg Simmel's "Exkurs über den Fremden" (1908) as the founding text for the concept of the stranger in academia,[189] it should be seen as the culmination of an ideal that had been gestating for a long time. This argument continues the presentation of Brandes' oeuvre as a valuable cosmopolitan archive for present studies of intellectual history, and particularly of cosmopolitanism.

In order to demonstrate that the stranger concept originated from a more general fin-de-siècle representation of the Jew as the stranger par excellence, the most relevant historical sources must be presented. Thus, apart from Brandes' "M. Goldschmidt" and Georg Simmel's "Exkurs über den Fremden," this chapter will include analyses of Henrik Pontoppidan's *Lykke-Per* (1898/1904/05) and Moritz Lazarus' *Was heisst national?* Pontoppidan and Lazarus and their texts have primarily been chosen due to the interrelations and interactions they had with Brandes and Simmel. The leader of the *Wissenschaft des Judentums* association in Berlin and a professor at the University of Berlin, Moritz Lazarus was an intellectual mentor for Simmel during the latter's student years. As has been documented for example by Egbert Klautke and Amos Morris-Reich, many of Simmel's central concepts seem to be derived from Lazarus and his writings on *Völkerpsychologie*.[190] However, no examinations have been conducted on the possible links between the ideal stranger figure of "Exkurs über den Fremden" and the representation of Jewishness in Lazarus' *Was heisst national?* Lazarus is also an interesting historical character in the context of the this book's main focus on Georg Brandes because the two were acquainted from the early 1870s. It seemed likely that these two prominent European Jewish intellectuals would have developed interrelated ideas on Jewishness through their discussions.

The Danish writer and Nobel Prize Winner of 1917 Henrik Pontoppidan has been chosen as a central source in this chapter because in his nineteenth-century writings he was deeply inspired by Brandes and his Modern Breakthrough movement. Documented particularly by Elias Bredsdorff, in *Lykke-Per*, Pontoppidan discusses and presents a processed view of Brandes' ideal of modern Jewishness, which adds to the valuable perspectives of the fin-de-siècle representation of Jewish strangeness for intellectual history studies and Jewish Studies.[191]

As mentioned above, similar cosmopolitan ideals and projections of ideal strangeness have been put forward again by many prominent scholars in recent decades. The topos of the ideal stranger is a key focus in works by Julia Kristeva, Homi K. Bhabha, Jacques Derrida, Zygmunt Bauman, and Ulrich Beck, for example.[192] Accordingly, the thematization of this ideal type of the stranger has led to a variety of interesting ideas on cultural pluralism, integration vs. assimilation, antisemitism, and national culture vs. globalization in the twentieth century. A good part of the intellectual historical context of the ideal stranger figure has been documented by Amos Morris-Reich in *The Quest for Jewish Assimilation in Modern Social Sciences* (2008). Morris-Reich mainly concentrates on the vast impact Simmel's stranger figure has had on American academia, for example, through Robert Ezra Park's topos of the marginal man in American sociology/anthropology.[193] In a European context, however, Simmel's depiction of the ideal stranger must also be viewed as the primary inspiration for Julia Kristeva's concept of the stranger in her well-acclaimed *Strangers to Ourselves* from 1991.[194] "Exkurs über den Fremden" is also the primary inspiration for Zygmunt Bauman's description of his version of the stranger figure and the circumstances of nineteenth-century German Jews in *Modernity and Ambivalence* (1991).[195] In these books, Kristeva and Bauman both also create intellectual ideals for our present modern world, which they base on Simmel's stranger character. They both focus on trait Simmel calls the "characteristic of objectivity." In *Strangers to Ourselves*, Kristeva describes how a similarly estranged and objective outlook forms the basis of an ideal identity for present-day artists and intellectuals.[196] In *Modernity and Ambivalence*, Bauman presents a parallel intellectual ideal that he calls the modern intellectual; this intellectual role model is also a critically aware stranger who has a more objective outlook on the world.[197] Moreover, I would argue that Ulrich Beck's more recent ideal of the cosmopolitan outlook in *The Cosmopolitan Vision* (2004) is influenced by Simmel's stranger figure in that Beck projects a true cosmopolitan as someone who has emancipated himself from what he calls the national outlook.[198] Following this, according to Beck, a true cosmopolitan is able to clarify more objectively what the important elements in our cultural tradition are, as well as being better able to determine questions of ethical matters.[199]

Nevertheless, this chapter will show that the idealized objective outlook of the stranger that Kristeva, Bauman, and Beck all present as the key trait of their intellectual role models in fact stems from a rather elitist and also somewhat utopian aspect of Simmel's original description of the stranger figure. Thus, when Simmel describes and determines what the characteristic of objectivity implies, it denotes an individual who is devoid of particularity. This chapter will show that this somewhat utopian aspect of his original depiction of the stranger can be explained as a logical trait when viewing his essay as a counter-reaction to modern antisemitism in the fin-de-siècle period. On reading other versions of the ideal stranger produced prior to Simmel, for example Brandes' modern Jew, we can see that this Jewish-related ideal stranger existed in multiple forms in the fin-de-siècle period. In other words, different actors, both Jewish and non-Jewish, discussed "the scandal of Jewish particularity."

Before we turn to the analysis of these earlier presentations of the ideal stranger, I will give a critical reading of Simmel's 1908 essay with the help of some of the most central post-WW2 revitalizations of his stranger character in a European context. This critical reading will be used to demonstrate that what appear first to be ambivalences within Simmel's 1908 essay can in fact be logically deduced when interpreting the essay as a reaction to modern antisemitism.

A Critical Reading of Simmel's "Exkurs über den Fremden"

As touched upon in the final section of Chapter 1, Simmel constructed an individual socio-cultural identity that shares the same fundamental qualities as Brandes' modern Jew. Simmel's stranger is thus defined by being simultaneously inside and outside of a cultural tradition. On this basis, he describes the stranger with a "characteristic of objectivity,"[200] which resembles the description of the flexible and critically aware outlook of Brandes' modern Jew. Consequently, Simmel also projects the ideal stranger as having a freer outlook on the norms, taboos, and customs of the group/community of which he stands in the periphery. Simmel writes:

Objectivity could also be defined as freedom. The objective man is not bound by ties which could prejudice his perception, his understanding, and his assessment of data. [...] He is the freer man, practically and theoretically; he examines conditions with less prejudice; he assesses them against standards that are more general and more objective; and his actions are not confined by custom, piety, or precedent.[201]

According to Simmel, the stranger must be conceived as valuable with regard to the group and cultural tradition of which he stands in the periphery because he has a more objective outlook than so-called natives of this group. The stranger is thus also capable of identifying the most constructive elements of the tradition in question, and at the same time eliminating unfertile and dogmatic elements. Simmel also writes that historically this type of stranger and his abilities have been recognized by the group among which he was perceived as a stranger.[202]

It is not Brandes' modern Jew or his emigrant figure but Simmel's stranger ideal that has had an immense influence on post-WW2 academic discussions on topics such as cultural pluralism and assimilation vs. integration, and on defining central traits of our late modern age. In the post-WW2 realizations of the importance of Simmel's stranger figure, it is unlikely to be a coincidence that this ideal of cultural pluralism, originally created by a German Jewish avant-garde sociologist of the fin-de-siècle period, established itself as a significant antipode to a rather different conception of cultural encounters: Samuel Huntington's clash of civilizations thesis. While Huntington perceives cultural encounters mainly as ridden with conflict, Simmel's stranger figure sees them as highly productive and beneficial for the group and cultural traditions in question.

It is also unlikely to be a coincidence that Simmel's depiction of the stranger was first proposed after the Second World War and then further developed by highly acclaimed Western thinkers of Jewish descent such as Hannah Arendt and Zygmunt Bauman, and that both of these writers—unlike Georg Simmel—emphasized particularistic Jewish characteristics of the stranger.

Arendt and Bauman use the European Jews/German Jews as their primary historical case when they determine characteristics of this type of stranger. They also both thematize how the cultural encounter between the Jewish stranger and the European Christian majority groups has not been as friction-free as Georg Simmel originally thematized it in 1908. In this context, one could say these writers indirectly point to what could initially be determined as a contradictory ambivalence in

Simmel's "Exkurs über den Fremden." Thus, Simmel defines the socio-cultural position of the stranger in an ambiguous way when he states that the stranger is "an element of the group itself" while at the same time stating that the stranger is not fully assimilated into this group.[203] It is this unique inside-outside position, "composed of remoteness and nearness," which creates the stranger's characteristic of objectivity, according to Simmel.[204]

Yet, as Bauman reflects in *Modernity and Ambivalence*, a position that is both inside and outside a cultural tradition will always create tension within the group in question. The observations of the stranger, delivered without "piety," can easily be interpreted as an attack on the fundamental norms of social cohesion within the group. For instance, the stranger can unintendedly touch upon taboos. Bauman in fact states that it is the unease that the free outlook of the Jewish stranger produces among the so-called "natives" that is the primary source of modern antisemitism: "the objectivistic (rootless, cosmopolitan or downright alien) bias of the stranger is the most serious of charges the native community holds against him."[205]

When Bauman looks at the historical case of the German Jews, he shows how the interaction between the Jewish strangers and the German Christian core group was never as positive as Simmel originally proposed the cultural encounter between the stranger and the primary group would be.[206] Bauman describes how this population came to occupy a position in between the religiously and traditionally based Jewish community and the German Christian-based bourgeoisie. The outlook of this type of Jewish stranger was moreover often perceived as an aggressive intrusion among the members of the Christian-based core group. Typically, German Jewish observations were conceived as an assault on the German Christian cultural heritage.[207] In "Exkurs über den Fremden," Simmel only momentarily thematizes the stir the free "rootless" gaze of the stranger creates among the members of this group. He writes that:

From earliest times, in uprisings of all sorts the attacked party has claimed that there has been incitement from the outside, by foreign emissaries and agitators. Insofar as this has happened, it represents an exaggeration of the specific role of the stranger.[208]

As the last sentence of this quotation demonstrates, Simmel is quick to downplay the negative reactions the interaction between the stranger and the group can create.

However, in the first edition of "Exkurs über den Fremden" Simmel lists another type of stranger, "the barbarian."[209] Yet he denies that there is any meaningful comparison to be made between the barbarian and his ideal type of the stranger.[210] He reasons that the two types of strangers cannot be compared because the barbarian is entirely different from the highly contributive stranger figure he sets out to describe. As a result, the barbarian is not relevant to his study.[211] When Simmel sets out to explain why the barbarian is a different type of stranger, he gives as reason that the barbarian is not an included part of the core group in question. Unlike the stranger, the barbarian is not "a member of the group."[212] According to Simmel, the barbarian is always outside the group in question, separated and excluded from it. The barbarian will always be conceived as a negative alien element, as a subversive intruder, by the group.

In this context, one may suggest that Bauman, in *Modernity and Ambivalence*, merges both of these strangers into one, when he describes the typical historical reactions to the German Jews. By contrast, Simmel presents the two types of strangers as wholly different from one another. I will briefly digress here, to provide an explanation of the background to Simmel's approach.

Simmel's Universal Stranger Figure

When considering Simmel's overtly positive view on the impact of and reactions to the specific stranger type he focuses on in "Exkurs über den Fremden," it is important to be aware of the fact that Simmel—unlike Bauman in *Modernity and Ambivalence*—nowhere in his essay writes that this figure must first and foremost be conceived as Jewish. Accordingly, since he does not tie the figure to a specific, historically particularistic group of strangers (although he does mention the relevance of "European Jews" in this context[213]), he makes it theoretically possible for this stranger to be conceived as a universal sociological type. The universality of his stranger left a creative space open for the aforementioned acclaimed post-WW2 scholars to develop his figure further. Under names such as "the modern intellectual" and "the cosmopolitan", parallel universal role models have been created with Georg Simmel's ideal stranger as a primary inspiration. Julia Kristeva, Zygmunt Bauman, and Ulrich Beck all idealize this critically aware stranger, who is inside and outside traditions and normative systems, without being devoted to or rooted in any of them.

Still, Bauman, Kristeva, and Beck—unlike Simmel—all emphasize that while the stranger position is an ideal one when observing and evaluating the transformations of our modern world, it is also a challenging position for an individual. In *Strangers to Ourselves*, Kristeva explains why this position is so tormenting:

One who is happy being a cosmopolitan shelters a shattered origin in the night of his wanderings. It irradiates his memories that are made up of ambivalences and divided values. That whirlwind translates into shrill laughter. It dries up once the tears of exile and exile following exile, without any stability, transmutes into games what for some is a misfortune and for others an untouchable void.[214]

According to Kristeva, this type of stranger is never fully rooted in any community, whether in a family or a culturally/religiously based community/civil society, and such an existence will wear out any individual, suffering "exile following exile, without any stability." Similarly, in his rendering of what the cosmopolitan outlook implies, Ulrich Beck is also intent on making his readers understand that being a true cosmopolitan in our global age is demanding and burdensome. Still, according to Beck, everyone should pursue a cosmopolitan outlook.[215]

Again, one could argue that these post-WW2 academic writers

point to another self-contradictory aspect of Simmel's description of the stranger: the lack of attention paid to the challenging individual implications of existing in the stranger position. Nowhere in his essay does Simmel mention whether the stranger feels lonely in his exile, or whether he experiences the values of his background culture clashing with the cultural tradition of which he now stands in the periphery. Theoretically, in this proto-sociological text, Simmel does not have to include such perspectives, since what he sets out to describe is a socially produced type. The internal and psychological life of the stranger is of no concern to his analysis.

However, by describing the observations of the stranger as more objective than the observations of a native, Simmel does reveal parts of the inner life of the stranger. The same applies when he writes that the observations of the stranger are delivered without "piety:" again he unintendedly characterizes a significant trait of the inner life of the stranger, while at the same time he also constructs a somewhat utopian figure.

It is common sense that all individuals are somehow formed and influenced by the cultural traditions and normative system within which they are raised. Even the ideal type of stranger, which Simmel sets out to describe, has been born somewhere and brought up by parents who belong to a particular community/ society. Yet when Simmel writes that the observations of the stranger will always be more objective and that they will be delivered without "piety," he implicitly constructs an identity which will never experience the normative values and traditions of its maternal culture clashing with the values and customs of the culture of which it now stands in the periphery. In this way, Simmel's stranger ideal is an utopian identity, or at least a rather elitist role model, more than it is a description of a sociological type that could be found and identified in great numbers.

At the same time, one could define the ambivalences within Simmel's description of the type of the stranger as logical, inherent contradictions when interpreting "Exkurs über den Fremden" as a reaction to modern antisemitism. As classic works in Jewish Studies by David Sorkin and Shulamit Volkov have demonstrated, acculturated bourgeois Western European Jews often came to exist as a subculture of the core group bourgeoisie in different Western societies, particularly in the first half of the nineteenth century, where they lived as a secluded bourgeois sub-class.[216] Moshe Rosman has subsequently shown how this isolated milieu produced a particular minority discourse through which the Jewish co-construction of Western civilization was accentuated.[217] Often, individuals in this population shared the tendency to conceive themselves as not being particularly "Jewish" any more. Instead, many of them came to view themselves as somewhat avant-garde modern human beings.[218] In his autobiography *Levned*, Brandes, for example, wrote that most Danes could learn how to transform into a modern human being from him; he thus incarnated this self-understanding.[219] As Pierre Birnbaum has recently argued, individuals from this population stand behind some of the greatest innovations of the nineteenth and early twentieth centuries in Europe in financial entrepreneurship, art, politics, and science.[220] Yet at the same time, and parallel to Simmel's description of the stranger, the surrounding (Christian-based) European societies mostly did not see this Jewish-identified sub-class, the group which Brandes called modern Jews, as more objective or more innovative than individuals of Christian descent. Rather, in the fin-de-siècle period, antisemitic resentments and movements grew all over Europe.

The Historical Context of Simmel's Essay

Following the identification of Simmel's co-constructive stranger with the self-understanding of this specific sociocultural demographic, we will move on to demonstrate that the two ambivalences in the essay were typical of the self-image of the bourgeois-influenced modern Jews. Thus, one might interpret both of these ambiguous traits as logical omissions when reading "Exkurs über den Fremden" as a reaction to modern antisemitism. In Chapter 1, Simmel's ideal stranger and Brandes' modern Jew were explained as disguised counter-reactions to modern antisemitism, because neither are loud or excessive figures. Instead, as counter-reactions, they are disguised, and they appear in the margins of these two writers' oeuvres, because although both writers felt provoked by the continuous antisemitic attacks on them, neither could risk too much in their civil lives, where they both strived for respectable bourgeois positions at the university.

One could argue that these counter-reactions to modern antisemitism were also part of the continuous struggles for equality that Western European Jews endured. While most Jews in the Western European states had been granted emancipation at this time, specific laws still existed in many states which banned Jews from occupying, for example, tenured university positions (in many places, in the latter half of the nineteenth century, it was still a law that tenured faculty had to be baptized Christians).[221] In this way, Simmel and Brandes (along with other writers of Jewish descent who presented versions of the ideal Jewish-related stranger figure) constructed their versions of the stranger to create awareness of the useful abilities and contributions of ideal strangers such as themselves—and to counter the many negative stereotypes that were so prevalent in the civil sphere. Yet they also worded their arguments so that their texts could be sent out into the civil sphere without being stigmatized as being too "Jewish," or too provocative.

Of course, we find a rich diversity within the demographic in question, where some still wholly or partly followed the Jewish religion and many still viewed specific parts of the experiences of Jewish history as advantages in the modern world. It has also been documented in the biographical writings of Kristian Hvidt and Jørgen Knudsen how Georg Brandes' mother, Emilie Brandes, strove to give all three of her sons an upbringing incorporating elements of the *Bildung* ideal.[222] Still, the three Brandes brothers, Georg, Ernst, and Edvard, all had bar mitzvahs, and even as adults, although they did not follow the traditional Sabbath customs, they would still gather together in their childhood home on the same day each weekend, when their mother would serve slow-cooked *Cholent* (Georg Brandes' favorite dish).[223] In this context, Georg Simmel represents a different case than Georg Brandes. Simmel was in fact a second-generation Protestant of Jewish descent; his parents had converted to Protestantism. He had thus moved even further away from the Jewish tradition than Brandes, and his references to Jewish history and the Jewish tradition are also more subtle in "Exkurs über den Fremden" than, for example, Brandes' in "M. Goldschmidt." Nevertheless, one could argue that both texts were produced in order to stress that it continued to be an important matter that the equality rights of Jews be acknowledged appropriately.

In both Simmel's 1908 essay and Brandes' "M. Goldschmidt," there are also textual traces of both of these writings' active contributions to the ongoing discussion of the so-called Jewish Question. We can observe specific vocabulary, for example, that refers to the most common discourses of the so-called Jewish Question at that time.

Both Simmel and Brandes add specific references to the central topic of whether a Jew is rootless or not, and whether this rootlessness is a negative or positive characteristic. Simmel writes that "The stranger is by nature no 'owner of soil' not only in the physical, but also in the figurative sense of a life-substance which is not fixed."[224] He states that the Jewish-related stranger is rootless and, a few lines later, more explicitly explains that this is "because he is not bound by roots."[225] Simmel cleverly turns around one of the most central antisemitic stereotypes, since he does not describe this rootlessness as threatening social cohesion. Instead, the rootlessness of the stranger becomes a positive attribute, providing a freer, less prejudiced outlook than that of the mono-cultural individual.

As we will see later in the chapter, this metaphor of rootless/rootlessness became an intertextual frame of reference, on which the different writers, Jewish and non-Jewish, often developed their individual stance when they presented different versions of the Jewish-related stranger. The form of this metaphor seems to have been central to how they intended their views on the so-called Jewish Question in general to be perceived. For example, one writer might argue that the acculturated Western European Jew was "a smooth-skinned fruit with a subtle and complex flavor,"[226] and at the other end of the scale another writer, most likely non-Jewish, might argue that the rootless Western European Jew degenerated the European national cultures from within.

An introduction to this metaphor of rootlessness and its semantic context of organicist imagery will be given in what follows, before an analysis of texts that rely heavily on it.

The Jewish Stranger and Nineteenth-Century Organicist Metaphors

Sociologically speaking, at no other time prior to the fin-de-siècle period did as many Western European Jews live in between religious Jewish traditions and the different European Christian-based majority societies.[227] In this context, one of the commonest antisemitic stereotypes in this period was the metaphor of the Jew as rootless, as a result of both the European diaspora and the modern European Jewish acculturation process.

Whether Jews could be said to be rooted or not is a discussion that grew out of the increasing focus on the *Volksgeist* of the different Western European national cultures; it was a discussion that went back to the last decades of the eighteenth century. The pioneers of the definition of the European national traditions emphasized that cultural particularism was a constitutional and essential part of every human being, which could not die out. One may view this emphasis on the particularistic *Volksgeist* as a reaction to the Enlightenment's campaigning for abstract universal values. Herder had originally spiced his *Volksgeist* perception with alluring metaphors of the recognizable organic physical world.[228] One of the strongest rhetorical instruments used by Herder and like-minded early Romantics was to depict the *Volksgeist* as an indispensable and almost physical part of the human being (and the nation). One typical root metaphor compared the lifecycle of a tree with the lifecycle of a human being (birth, childhood, youth, maturity, old age, death). As a kind of ecohumanism, like a plant or a tree, any human being and any people of a particular nation would degenerate and die out if they were uprooted or removed from their natural soil and transplanted to an alien climate.

The polemic between the Danish Jewish prose writer M. A. Gold-schmidt and the Danish theologian Grundtvig in 1848–49 (mentioned earlier in Chapter 1) shows that it was not uncommon for dominant actors in the nineteenth-century Western European civil spheres to view the Jewish *Volksgeist* as being essentially homeless and rootless. In the polemic, Grundtvig first identified Goldschmidt as a Jew and therefore not a Dane. Even though he was born and raised in Denmark, Goldschmidt was thus labeled a stranger with regard to understanding the core of the Danish national tradition. Yet, like many others who investigated the traits of the particularistic European cultural traditions, Grundtvig did not perceive the *Volksgeist* as a closed and static container. Cultivation of the Danish *Volksgeist* was indeed one of his prime concerns; his innovative focus on educating "the people" vis-à-vis the Danish peasantry at *højskoler* (folk high schools) was to become one of most important nation-building elements in the development of liberal democracy in Denmark. However, in this specific polemic, Grundtvig seems to have held the rather common view that some cultures lacked essential positive and constructive characteristics that would allow their followers to be merged into a European national *Volksgeist*. The Jewish *Volksgeist*'s key trait of rootlessness was typically associated with the historical uprooting of the Jews from their so-called natural soil in the Middle East.

Georg Brandes' Modern Jew as an Ideal Stranger

While Brandes was a publicly active intellectual, the most persistent antisemitic stereotype applied to him was indeed to label him rootless, and thus unable to contribute anything original or constructive to Danish culture. Brandes' counter-reaction, in portrayals of the modern Jew in writings such as "M. Goldschmidt" and *Benjamin Disraeli*, was to argue that the modern Jew had a freer and more objective outlook on European traditions than monocultural Christian Europeans.

Brandes seems to have been one of the prime actors in creating the counter narrative of the Jewish-related ideal stranger in the second half of the nineteenth century in a European intellectual context. However, he was also part of a fertile cosmopolitan network; his most trusted allies at the time included the German Jews Berthold Auerbach, Moritz Lazarus, and Paul Heyse. Moritz Lazarus is particularly interesting in this context because he was Georg Simmel's intellectual mentor when the latter was a young man. In the 1870s and 1880s, Brandes was engaged in a lively correspondence with Lazarus, and visited him at his private residence.

Let us begin this section by briefly recapitulating Brandes' characterization of the Jewish-related ideal stranger, the modern Jew. The essay "M. Goldschmidt" is the earliest substantial example of his reaction to the hegemonic perception of the rootless Jew in the civil sphere. In it, Brandes argues that modern Jews such as Goldschmidt possess traits showing that European Jews have historically taken root in all the various cultures they lived in the periphery of during their diaspora. Goldschmidt's prose comprises racial "essences," as Brandes calls it, from cultures including the Jewish Semitic, Arabic, Portuguese, Spanish, German, and Danish traditions.[229] Brandes opposes the idea of the Jew as being rootless without belonging to a meaningful *Volksgeist*; rather, for him the modern Jew potentially possesses several *Volksgeistern* at the same time, some inherited from his Jewish forefathers. It is this culturally pluralistic basis of the modern Jew that makes him indispensable with regard to further developing and creating the modern world. In the "M. Goldschmidt" essay, Brandes identifies the inside-outside position of the modern Jew as affording him a more objective outlook on the different European traditions of which he has lived in the periphery. In this context, it seems likely that Brandes was influenced by earlier depictions of the Jewish-related ideal stranger figure that can be found in the literary genre of so-called Spinozism. Works by both Berthold Auerbach and Karl Gutzkow published as early as the 1830s and 1840s emphasized the difficulty of existing in the ideal stranger position; these were among Brandes' most favored writings, as Henning Fenger and Brandes himself attest.[230] Later, Chapter 4 will trace the influence of the particular branch of Spinozism represented by these two works. For now, I will briefly point particularly to Berthold Auerbach's *Bildungs-*

roman Spinoza (1837/1856) as an essential inspiration for Brandes' modern Jew in the way that Auerbach portrays Spinoza as the first modern man, but also the first modern Jew. At the end of the novel Auerbach's Spinoza has shaped himself independently as a product of secular-orientated Jewish religious sources and rational philosophy. The novel also suggests that after his excommunication, Spinoza lived as a stranger in the periphery of Dutch Christian society. His refusal to convert to Christianity is a recurring motif; he insists on living as a "free philosopher" after he is excommunicated, and it is from this inside-outside position, "composed of remoteness and nearness" as Simmel writes in "Exkurs über den Fremden," that Spinoza produces his innovative philosophy, according to Auerbach's novel.[231]

In Karl Gutzkow's drama *Uriel Acosta* (1846), which Brandes praises in the final volume of his *Main Currents* series on the European literary history of the nineteenth century, *Det Unge Tyskland* (*The Young Germany*) (1890), we follow a historical forerunner to Baruch Spinoza in the Jewish Sephardic community of Amsterdam.[232] As a young man, Uriel Acosta also rebels against the dogma of Orthodox Judaism, and Gutzkow focuses on Acosta's critical outlook on the traditional community. With this outlook, however, come challenges. Not only is Acosta stigmatized as subversive and violently punished by the Jewish Orthodox clerical powers; Acosta himself mourns the loss of his ability to comply with the norms and idiosyncrasies of the community of which he is part.[233] He feels an uncontrollable instinct to criticize and deconstruct this community. Rather than presenting Acosta's role as exciting and intellectually stimulating, Gutzkow instead points to the fact that it is painful to exist in such a marginalized outsider position, and to be a genuine critical stranger. Acosta commits suicide at the end of the drama.

Both of these writings of Spinozism detail how an individual who begins to question the validity and origins of the norms and hierarchies of the community/society they have been brought up in is more likely to encounter social exclusion—and even violent punishment—than appreciation of their critical observations. Brandes similarly describes how the modern Jew's existence is a painful one, accompanied by feelings of exclusion and loneliness.

Henrik Pontoppidan and Georg Brandes

Apart from being a relevant source for examining how the Jewish-related ideal stranger figure became a widespread topos in modern European intellectual history in this period, Brandes' ideas on modern Jewishness also had an enormous influence on Danish and Scandinavian cultural and political developments, particularly in the 1870s, 1880s, and 1890s. His advice to focus on the social world and to engage in "debating problems" was a major inspiration for many younger writers and artists. Many followed this advice, and just as many reacted against it (particularly in the 1890s). One of the writers who became fascinated with Brandes' early inflammatory works was Henrik Pontoppidan. Pontoppidan, especially in his nineteenth-century writings, was deeply inspired by Brandes and his Modern Breakthrough ideas. As has been documented, for example, by Elias Bredsdorff and Klaus P. Mortensen, it is primarily because of Brandes that Pontoppidan denotes the modern spirit as "Jewish" in *Lykke-Per*.[234]

From the beginning, Henrik Pontoppidan was focused on describing the social and psychological consequences of the transition from the old world to the modern liberal democratic and capitalistic society, as well as the difficulty of finding true evidence of progress among the lower classes in Denmark. Pontoppidan addressed the ambivalences of this transition, shedding light on both the advantages and the disadvantages of the rapid changes. In his most nuanced writings, including *Det Forjættede Land* (*The Promised Land*) (1891–98), it is significant that Pontoppidan is uncertain about how this transition should be represented normatively. Later in his career, Pontoppidan grew more pessimistic with regard to this transition, and he would come to reject Brandes' early Modern Breakthrough visions unambiguously.

One could say that *Lykke-Per* presents two possible futures, one dystopian and one utopian, and both are inspired by Georg Brandes' representation of Jewishness in his early writings. They may be seen as

Pontoppidan's interpretation of the legacy of Georg Brandes as a Danish Jewish intellectual. In the character of Dr. Nathan and other modern Jewish characters in his novel, Pontoppidan indirectly discusses whether Brandes' contributions to the Danish cultural tradition were constructive and useful—or whether they were non-contributive, un-Danish products. *Lykke-Per* wavers undecidedly between two possible futures through its visions of how the modern world will materialize in Denmark, and between these possible scenarios stands Brandes' idea of modern Jewishness and Pontoppidan's interpretations of Brandes' role as a national educator. The novel also draws on and reproduces many antisemitic stereotypes, though these stereotypes are used in the delineation of his characters' psychological maturation. For example, the main character, Per Sidenius, initially views Jews through the lens of his provincially inherited prejudices against Jews and Jewishness; later on he develops a more nuanced view on the modern Jews in Copenhagen (at the end of the novel, however, he has also transformed some of these older stereotypes into modern antisemitic variations). Furthermore, as Stefanie von Schnurbein has pointed out, a good part of the male Jewish characters are versions of negative stereotypes, while the female Jewish characters are complex figures, such as Jakobe Salomon.[235]

The "Plan" of Lykke-Per

Elias Bredsdorff, among others, has proposed that in the first two decades of his writing career Henrik Pontoppidan was strongly influenced by Georg Brandes.[236] In fact, one could say that Pontoppidan expands Brandes' earlier descriptions of the modern Jew and links it to a more specific sociological and historical context in his novel *Lykke-Per*. Pontoppidan connects Brandes' Modern Breakthrough ideas with the way the modern world materialized in Denmark. Thus, the novel covers the period from the early 1870s to the turn of the century, which, as earlier mentioned, was a key period in the building of modern Denmark—the population of Copenhagen doubled almost three times in the period from 1870 to 1910—as well as focusing on the sociological, cultural, and political aspects of this transformation of Copenhagen and Denmark in general.

In an interview given after Brandes' death in 1927, Pontoppidan explained that "the plan of the novel" was to describe how two fundamentally different cultures were struggling to become dominant in this period.[237] These two cultures were that of traditional Danish Protestantism on the one hand and modern Jewish liberal cosmopolitanism on the other.[238] Accordingly, the novel portrays the modern Jewish spirit as a civilization that already had spread out and become dominant throughout Western Europe.[239] Pontoppidan thought of this spirit as the European spirit, though *Lykke-Per* perceives it as a somewhat alien element in Denmark.[240] Pontoppidan simultaneously views the modern Jewish culture as a sign of the times he lived in. In other words, he saw it as an unstoppable *zeitgeist*. In *Lykke-Per*, Pontoppidan, like many others writers and thinkers of his time, identified the interconnected characteristics of the modern world—capitalism, the rational scientific mindset, urban culture, individualism, alienation, liberal freethinking—as key parts of the modern Jewish culture. *Lykke-Per* questions whether this rapid transformation of Denmark would come to erode social cohesion and shared moral ground, although Pontoppidan was also highly critical about the moral standards of the old world.

In *Lykke-Per*, Pontoppidan presents the new industries of the modern world, such as capitalism, politics, free artisanship, and journalism, as dominated by Jews; this is similar to Heinrich von Treitschke's approach in "Unsere Aussichten," as we will see in a short while. Yet rather than turning this typical identification of fin-de-siècle modernity with Jewishness into one-dimensional antisemitism, Pontoppidan maintains an ambivalent view on the effects of the transformation. One important aspect of this is that Pontoppidan is not nostalgic with regard to the culture the modern Jewish spirit seems to replace. Thus, not only in *Lykke-Per* but throughout his oeuvre, Pontoppidan criticizes the traditional Danish Protestant culture for resting on a functional but static principle of exploitation of a large majority of the population—the rural and urban proletariat, and the agrarian smallholders. According to Pontoppidan, the social cohesive norms and laws of the traditional, feudal Danish society had developed into nothing more than principles which served to keep the religious and political leaders at the top of society and the growing bourgeoisie satisfied. Specifically, in *Lykke-Per* Pontoppidan shows that the majority of the suppressed part of the population had remained caught in an apathetic state of mind for hundreds of years, comparing them to the princess in Sleeping Beauty, who slept for a hundred years before a prince woke her.[241]

Pontoppidan weaves some of the most famous Scandinavian folk tales into the story and plot of *Lykke-Per*, as arabesque analogies to the story and the time in history when the novel is set. The most important question of the novel is thus whether the main character Per Sidenius will become the prince who wakes and liberates the Sleeping Beauty: the Danish people.

Per and Jakobe

The main character, Per Sidenius, is born into a Protestant Pietist-influenced milieu in provincial Denmark as the son of a pastor in Randers, Jutland, just as Henrik Pontoppidan himself was. From a young age, Per is rebellious toward the environment he is being brought up in, and as a teenager he sets himself a personal goal to defeat the suppressed and guilt-ridden part of the Danish *Volksgeist*. Thus, as a young man, in an act deliberately intended to displease his patriarchal father, Per leaves provincial Randers and heads off to Copenhagen to realize his dreams of becoming an engineer educated at the Polytechnic Institute in the Danish capital; at night, Per begins work on a project that will help him achieve his dream. He plans to be the head engineer on a project establishing prosperous trade routes to English cities and the USA from Jutland. This project involves building numerous new dams, which will link the small rivers of Jutland and connect them to a great new harbor city built on the coast of the North Sea.[242] From this new metropolis of Jutland, ships and cargo vessels would then head out to fertile destinations such as America.[243]

Per is inspired to this work by the writings of the Danish Jewish intellectual Dr. Nathan, a name with obvious links to E. G. Lessing's noble Jew Nathan der Wiese. In an interview, Pontoppidan also admitted that Dr. Nathan was a portrayal of Georg Brandes.[244]

In *Lykke-Per*, Dr. Nathan is described as having established himself as the leader of a liberal movement in Denmark, supported and admired as he is by much of Copenhagen's liberal bourgeoisie. Yet Per's primary inspiration is not so much Dr. Nathan as a person as it is his writings. In these aesthetically orientated writings, Dr. Nathan criticizes contemporary Danish art and literature for being anachronistic and lacking contextual focus. For example, most Danish writers still practised the Romantic dogma of celebrating art as "a second world." It had thus become Romantic escapism, which ignored the social reality in Denmark and the lives and rights of poor and underprivileged men and women. Dr. Nathan also attacks the political system in Denmark, demanding that the illiberal demagogues in power should let democracy materialize. Thus, Dr. Nathan's writings are, like Brandes' *Emigrantlitteraturen*, characterized by the liberal cosmopolitan enlightenment spirit.

Per meets Dr. Nathan several times in the novel and at first he is full of admiration. However, it is through Per's acquaintance with the bourgeois Danish Jewish family the Salomons that he familiarizes himself with the modern Jewish spirit. As such, *Lykke-Per* is one of the most comprehensive descriptions of the unique North European urban demographic of modern Jews in European literature of this period, which, in most of these countries, would disappear completely a few decades later. Gradually, Per falls in love with the elder sister of the family, Jakobe Salomon, who embodies certain positive aspects of the modern Jewish spirit. She is a secularly orientated intellectual who increasingly focuses on universal social questions and the necessity of combining idealism with practice.[245] She is also described as being intellectually equal to the many men in high positions who attend social gatherings and discuss politics and cultural matters in the Salomon family's residences.[246]

Opposing the ideal Jewish stranger figure of Jakobe, there are then several male Jewish characters that are variations of negative Jewish stereotypes. For example, Jakobe's German Jewish uncle Heinrich Delft ruthlessly views everything around him as potential financial matters from which he can profit. His de-nationalized language is Danish filled with German and Yiddish phrases.[247] Jakobe's brother Ivan is mainly a variation of another negative Jewish stereotype; he is thin, short, and nervous, with a feminine, shrill voice, and chats constantly. With regard to the new capitalistic spirit, another Jewish character, Max Bernhard, exemplifies all the negative aspects of the new type of economy, pitiless and amoral as he is.[248]

The Metaphor of Jewish Rootlessness

The metaphor of the rootless Jew is used several times in the novel by the narrator to define this demographic of bourgeois-influenced modern Jews. On the one hand, the rootlessness of these Jews means that there is no solid ground under the modern Jewish civilization. On the other, Pontoppidan identifies it as highly positive that they are not stuck in the narrowmindedness of traditional Danish norms and dogma, which otherwise grips the country. The character Pontoppidan uses to represent the positive aspects of Jewish rootlessness most directly is—besides Jakobe Salomon—Dr. Nathan. Pontoppidan almost mimics Brandes' earlier description of the modern Jew in "M. Goldschmidt" when he characterizes Dr. Nathan thus:

He had never doubted his right to speak. He had very early felt himself called upon to play a special role in the nation and that, precisely on the grounds of his origin as an outsider, allowed him to observe the life of his country from a distance and judge it without prejudice.[249]

Inevitably, this statement also anticipates Simmel's 1908 description of the stranger. Dr. Nathan's work is viewed as important by the narrator for this reason. Parallel to the question of Per's role in the beginning of *Lykke-Per*, it could be said that the novel thus casts Dr. Nathan as the prince who wakes the Danes from their apathetic Sleeping Beauty state of mind. As Elias Bredsdorff writes:

Nathan contrasts the quick pace, enterprising spirit, bustle and energy in countries abroad with the sluggishness, torpor and stagnation of the Danes. In contrast to active and revolutionary Europe, Denmark, in Nathan's eyes, is a 'supernatural realm of dreams' – it is the realm of Sleeping Beauty, where time stood still and the pale roses of dreams and tough, thorny stems of speculation deceptively concealed the inner decay [...] (Nathan) had the courage to penetrate and tear asunder the tough web of dreams, the hard, hairy cocoon in which the spirit of the nation had enveloped itself.[250]

Still, all in all, the novel represents an ambivalent view of Jews and Jewishness generally, and of Dr. Nathan specifically. For instance, while the novel appraises Dr. Nathan's positive aspects, it simultaneously recalls the typical Jewish stereotype Richard Wagner defines in "Das Judentum in der Musik." None of the writings of Dr. Nathan are *"originale."*[251] His enterprise is instead described as a disruptive criticism of the Danish tradition; it points to what this cultural tradition lacks compared to greater and more substantial cultural traditions. According to the novel, Dr. Nathan will thus never be able to create genuine and meaningful contributions to the Danish tradition like those by Christian-born Danish geniuses such as Søren Kierkegaard and the aforementioned Danish national father figure, Grundtvig.[252] In the key portrait of Dr. Nathan we also find a variation of the metaphor of Jewish rootlessness, which is used to show that his innovative abilities are too exotic, too alien, for them to be absorbed constructively into the Danish tradition. Dr. Nathan is compared to a cactus, a plant that cannot take root in Danish soil. Cacti require a much warmer climate, like that of the Middle East:

So excessively rich was the essential nature of this man of the capital, born in the heart of the city, growing up on its sidewalks and, like the southern cactus, flaming into bloom out of the rocky ground.[253]

The Ambivalence of Lykke-Per

Still, *Lykke-Per* stands as one of the greatest novels of the fin-de-siècle period because at this time Pontoppidan had not yet become wholly pessimistic as regards modernity and the many fundamental changes that were happening around him. As an author, he still doubts the argument that history is progress and whether great modern-minded male and female political leaders and role models would truly emancipate the Danes and humanity in general. *Lykke-Per* represents modernity as consisting of both negative and positive elements, and wavers undecidedly between two possible futures. Its stance is more similar to Georg Simmel's view on modernity than that of his two intellectual mentors, Georg Brandes and Moritz Lazarus. As we will see in the next chapter, Simmel was in many ways inspired by Lazarus and his representation of Jewishness in *Was heisst national?* However, in his general view on modernity, Simmel does not mimic Lazarus' typical German Jewish nineteenth-century liberal optimistic idea of history as progress.[254] In an essay such as "Die Grossstädte und das Geistesleben" (1903), Simmel observes more negative than positive aspects of modernity, and he also focuses on the accelerating changes as bewildering most people.[255] However, he also points out positive aspects with regard to modernity, particularly the gradually rising standards of universal individual freedom.[256]

Similarly, in the first two decades of his writings, Pontoppidan was highly influenced by Brandes in seeing the alterations modernity was making to the old world as denoting progress. However, after the turn of the century, he grew increasingly pessimistic with regards to this view and to the optimistic liberal enlightenment visions of Brandes' early writings in general. [257] We find this ambivalence everywhere in *Lykke-Per*, for instance in the context of the two different paths of his main characters. With regard to the overall "plan of the novel," the turbulent love affair between Danish Protestant-born Per and Danish Jewish Jakobe ends when they finally agree to end their engagement. At this point, Per has also given up on his great dream of modernizing Denmark. He has moved back to Jutland, and even given up becoming an engineer. Throughout the rest of the novel we mainly follow Per in his other attempts to create a synthesis between traditional Danish culture and the modern world. For example, he marries a daughter of a reform pastor, who has created a new interpretation of the Protestant religion that shares obvious resemblances with Grundtvig's theology.[258] Per's father-in-law sums up Christianity as a fundamental love of humanity and this patriarchal pastor spends much time composing psalms so that his congregation and the common man can more easily understand the true messages of Christianity (as explained by him).[259] Yet Per does not feel that he has become fully himself in this marriage, and he ends up choosing to live a life of solitude in a small village on the coast of the North Sea, working as a Civil Road Inspector and writing short texts in a notebook. These short texts seems to be highly influenced by Friedrich Nietzsche's visions of a solitary aristocratic individualism.

Still, we have another main character in the novel, Jakobe Salomon; it is she who comes to represent a constructive transition to the modern world. Thus, at the end of the novel, she has founded a progressive new school in a working-class area of Copenhagen, where all children are educated for free. Girls and boys are treated as equals and the school's teachings are based on the rational principles of the secular-oriented humanitarian sciences.[260] Teachings on religion have been replaced by a vast scope encompassing health, nutrition, activities in the fresh air, and classes in natural science incorporating the latest scientific research.[261] It is expected that these boys and girls will be role models for everyone, children as well as adults, in this working-class area of Copenhagen.[262] Thus, in many ways, Jakobe Salomon and her school envisage the prototype of an ideal modern welfare state. On the other hand, Per might very well have "become himself" living his life of Nietzschean solitude close to nature. This is an open question, but his secluded life by the North Sea is not a constructive synthesis between the modern world and the old one.

Moritz Lazarus: A German Jew from Posen

Georg Brandes became acquainted with Moritz Lazarus in the early 1870s. Usually, when Brandes struck up a new acquaintance or initiated a friendship, he would consider himself the higher spirit. Within academic and biographical writings on Brandes, there are several firsthand recollections of how he was always the most, if not even the only, talkative party in a relationship.[263] However, when Brandes met Moritz Lazarus, he humbly acknowledged that he had met his intellectual superior. Thus, in a letter to another of his personal heroes, Hippolyte Taine, during the early stages of his acquaintance with Lazarus, Brandes wrote (on 27 September 1874): "This Nathan the Wise of our time, one of the 10 or 11 noble men of Europe who are endlessly superior to me."[264] Around the same time, in a letter to one of his closest personal friends, Emil Petersen, Brandes affirmed that: "I truly have not learnt so much in conversation since I spent time in the company of Stuart Mill and Taine in 1870."[265]

Born into a German Jewish Orthodox lower middle-class family in Filehne (Wielen) in Posen in 1824, Moritz Lazarus grew up in empirical nineteenth-century Central Europe. At that time, Posen was a cluster of different cultures and religions living side by side, but still rather divided. Three different ethnic and religious groups made up the inhabitants of Filehne in Lazarus' childhood and youth: Protestant Germans, Catholic Poles, and Orthodox Jews. It was through trading and commerce in particular that the groups interacted, and Lazarus also went through a practically orientated merchant education before he left Filehne and began to study at the university in Berlin. As Egbert Klautke points out, "Moritz Lazarus used the opportunities that opened up in higher education for Jews to leave the traditional environment of his parents' generation behind."[266]

While attending the Gymnasium, Lazarus experienced a crisis of identity when he broke with the Orthodox Jewish faith of his family and became politically a national liberal.[267] However, he never abandoned Judaism. He became one of the leading figures in the second half of the nineteenth century in further developing the reform work of the *Wissenschaft des Judentums* in Berlin. Accordingly, he never supported a full assimilation of the German Jews. Instead, as we will see, he insisted that the ideal position of the German Jews within the German national cultural tradition was to remain an independent German Jewish minority. Yet it was not until 1879–80 that Lazarus fully developed this view.

Before this and for many years, Lazarus had held the view—together with his trusted intellectual companion Heymann Steinthal—that national culture should be based on the language of the majority group in society. Thus Lazarus and Steinthal were highly influenced by Herder and Herderian thinking on cultural matters, which held that the language of a people constitutes all other aspects of their cultural tradition.

In fact, Lazarus and Steinthal had developed a whole new science, the *Völkerpsychologie*, which in the 1860s, 1870s, and 1880s was a serious competitor to other new sciences in Germany, such as sociology and anthropology.[268] They were inspired by fellow *Volkskunde* German Jewish scientists such as Friedrich Salomon Krauss and Georg Minden.[269] Decades later, German national socialist scholars took over the field of *Volkskunde* science and developed it in an entirely different direction, where it became part of their racial framework. However, originally, it was particularly German Jewish scholars who founded the various *Volkskunde* theories in the latter part of the nineteenth century, with intentions that were not *völkisch* and nationalistic but rather liberal and ecohumanistic.[270]

Besides Herderian thinking, Lazarus and Steinthal's original perception of the *Völkerpsychologie* also included elements of Hegel's philosophy. Thus, in the *Zeitschrift für Völkerpsychologie und Sprachwissenschaft* (*ZfVS*),[271] they define the human being as primarily a product of a national culture. However, unlike Herder, they did not consider *Völkerpsychologie* an immanent essence, which should be excavated from, for example, 500-year-old sagas and folk tales. In adopting some of Hegel's central terms, they were more interested in examining the *Völkerpsychologie* as a visible and rationally traceable "objective spirit," which could be observed through the customs and actions of the people.[272] In this way, each *Völkerpsychologie* differed from the next; it was also not given that it would progress historically. It was just as likely that a *Völkerpsychologie* would decline through specific actions of its people. For example, losing a war might not only reduce the territory of a national state; it could also have an effect on the mutually shared *Völkerpsychologie*, which in the end might lose its cohesive bonds.[273]

As mentioned above, in the first two decades of defining and constructing the *Völkerpsychologie*, Lazarus and Steinthal were not specifically focused on the German Jews or whether this minority had a particular role to play in the German national cultural tradition. Instead, they described the German *Völkerpsychologie* as one homogenic entity.[274] Thus, the German Jews had become part of the German *Volk*, according to Lazarus and Steinthal's scientific logic in the 1860s and 1870s, first and foremost by adopting the German language. The event that came to alter Lazarus and Steinthal's view and made them fundamentally change the definition of national culture was modern antisemitism, and particularly Herman von Treitschke's text "Unsere Aussichten."

The Berliner Antisemitismusstreit and Moritz Lazarus' Was heisst national?

Heinrich von Treitschke was in fact a well-respected historian in German intellectual circles when he published "Unsere Aussichten," and at least prior to *die Gründer-Krise* in 1873–74, he had been a German national liberal of the 1848 spirit. Yet the hasty sociological transformations of Germany in the 1860s and 1870s combined with political changes and the negative financial developments of the 1870s had made Treitschke and other national liberals grow increasingly pessimistic toward the belief that modernity would inevitably lead to an improved version of Germany.[275] Like many others within the Christian-based German civil society, Treitschke had come to believe that it was particularly the German Jews and their negative societal influence that had caused Germany's downfall.

Treitschke's text "Unsere Aussichten" is a typical work of nationalistic antisemitism, which is different from racial antisemitism, since Treitschke does not present all German Jews as (biologically disposed to be) subversive.[276] The text has become famous for the sentence in which Treitschke calls all the German Jews *"unser Unglück"* ("our misfortune"). However, as Marcel Stoetzler documents in his article "Cultural difference in the national state: from trouser-selling Jews to unbridled multiculturalism" (2008), Treitschke is primarily discussing a specific group among the German Jews. This group, according to Treitschke, insisted on creating their own subversive *"Mischcultur"* ("mixed culture").[277] In Treitschke's opinion, not all German Jews strived for full assimilation and thus represented a threat to German social cohesion; it was one specific group, who insisted on being Jewish and German at the same time.[278] He was mainly targeting the seemingly acculturated bourgeois German Jews, no matter whether they were "acculturated or assimilated, observant, *Confessionslos*, or baptized."[279] Treitschke also mentions the many Eastern European Jews who were fleeing the pogroms in Russia and Poland and coming to Germany as problematic elements. Still, his main concern was how a specific group of German Jews had dominated some of society's leading institutions and industries as prominent scientists and intellectuals, as well as, due to their involvement in politics, the financial markets and the newspapers.[280] In "Unsere Aussichten," Treitschke claimed that this German Jewish *"Mischcultur"* destroyed the German culture from within.[281] He believed that the *"Mischcultur"* was particularly dangerous in these years, after 1871, as many Germans were still asking themselves what a unified German nation, and as such cultural tradition, should look like, and which unifying values Germans should consider the most important.[282]

Moritz Lazarus' Reaction to Treitschke's Attack

Although Theodor Mommsen's defense of the German Jews is today the most recognized response to Treitschke's "Unsere Aussichten," Moritz Lazarus' *Was heisst national?* is also a substantial answer to Treitschke's attack.[283] *Was heisst national?* has not received the attention it deserves over the years. Nevertheless, as documented by Egbert Klautke, much of Ernest Renan's famous and widespread definition of the nation in the text *Qu'est-ce qu'une Nation?*—which was delivered in 1882 at the Sorbonne—seems to have been copied from Lazarus' *Was heisst national?*[284] Lazarus himself documents the creative borrowing of Renan in his autobiography.[285]

In *Was heisst national?* Lazarus departs from his former idea of national culture as a monocultural entity. Instead, he perceives the ideal national culture as consisting of many different "tribes," as Klautke perceives:

Rather Lazarus argued they, the Jews, were one of the *Stämme* that made up the German nation: as a religion, Judaism had to be viewed as one of several confessions that coexisted within the German nation.[286]

In arguing that the German Jews can be perceived as Germans without converting or leaving Judaism/Jewishness, Lazarus defined the healthiest and most progressive national cultures as those that were diverse:

Every nation which is to reach a high level of development must be equipped with a great variety of conditions and aspirations. The differences between coastal and inland areas, between mineral-bearing mountains and fertile valleys and plains, must be matched by a variety of spiritual gifts.[287]

As seen here, Lazarus frequently uses organicist imagery to illustrate his view of national culture as complex and varied in this text. Thus, just as Germany in its nature and geography is a rich and varied country with mountains areas, coastlines, and endless fertile fields, so must the German national culture also be diverse and wide-ranging. The German Jewish tribe is just one among many different tribes in Germany, and united they all form the German national culture, according to Lazarus.

Within the German nation, however, the German Jews had a unique role to play, as they had in any European national culture where they lived as a minority:

The Jews no longer have a nationality of their own; there is simply no longer a Jew who only has a Jewish spirit. Therefore they necessarily draw from all the Volkgeistern of which they have become part and which have an effect on them; even in their original and most peculiar way, in their religion itself, they are essentially individualized according to the nations in which they live, and can therefore [...] more energetically transform their receptive participation in culture into a productive one. Philo wrote in Greek, Maimonides in Arabic, Spinoza in Latin, Mendelssohn in German.[288]

Lazarus' idea of the Jewish contribution to the different European cultural traditions is thus similar to Georg Brandes' view in, for example, "M. Goldschmidt." According to Lazarus, the loss of a Jewish nation and the subsequent diaspora had finally included the European Jews in all the different cultures their forefathers had lived on the peripheries of during the European diaspora. Again like Brandes', Lazarus describes the German Jews as having made numerous indispensable contributions to European civilization, since their particular historical experiences had enabled them to combine elements of all the different cultures of which they had been part: "Therefore they necessarily draw from all the Volkgeistern of which they have become part and which have an effect on them." The key argument of *Was heisst national?* is that the German Jews should continue to occupy this specific cultural position. As the last sentence of the passage quoted above demonstrates, Lazarus believes that it was this position which led the greatest European Jewish thinkers to create their innovative work: "Philo wrote in Greek, Maimonides in Arabic, Spinoza in Latin, Mendelssohn in German."

Furthermore, Lazarus' definition of the sociocultural position of the German Jews in the new united German state of 1871 also resembles Georg Simmel's ambivalent definition of the sociocultural position of the stranger in "Exkurs über den Fremden." As pointed out earlier, Simmel writes that the stranger is both "a member of the group" and not fully assimilated into it.[289] In *Was heisst national?*, Lazarus denies that the German Jews are *"fremden"* (strangers), but following this denial, suggests that the innovative work of German Jews stems from an outlook characterized as both equally near to and equally remote from the German tradition:

This power of appropriation and adaption, the nourishment of one's own mind by what is foreign, is certainly an excellent move.[290]

Another similarity between Simmel's and Lazarus' texts is a rather friction-free description of how the innovativeness of the European Jews has been received historically by the European Christian core groups. For example, when Lazarus highlights Moses Mendelssohn's and Baruch Spinoza's co-construction of modern European civilization, he neglects to tell his readers that the most typical reaction to these men's writings was suspicion, exclusion, and stigmatization. A good example of this is that soon after the publication of the *Tractatus Theologico-Politico*, in the latter part of the seventeenth century, Baruch Spinoza was identified throughout Western Europe as the most subversive thinker on the continent by the leading powers of the European states and the Christian Church.

Another interesting aspect of Lazarus' text with similarities to Simmel's essay (if we see Simmel's stranger as an analogy for the German Jewish minority in the-fin-de-siècle period) is that the statement that German Jews and European Jews more generally have a unique and indispensable role to play at this moment in history. Like Brandes in his later writings, as we will see in Chapter 4 and 5, Lazarus points out that the Jews inherited a tradition of secular thought through Judaism. As such, according to him, the European Jews had for centuries held the virtues of equality and universal justice as the core values of Judaism. Lazarus writes that the modern Jews are already familar

with the principles of the new society and the modern state [...] because, already in the teachings of the prophets, the unity of the human race, the equality of all before the law, the equality of all in duties and rights [...] as well as the complete freedom of the individual in his religious conviction and the confession of the same are principles to follow."[291]

As Egbert Klautke writes, "In Lazarus' view the Jews appeared as special Germans whose secular ethics had made them the foremost bearers of humanitarian progress."[292] Lazarus ultimately presents the German Jews as the most important minority in the building of modern Germany due to their unique inside-outside societal position.

Georg Simmel's Idea of a "Third Nation"

I have previously argued that Simmel's stranger figure, like Brandes' modern Jew, should first and foremost be interpreted as a reaction to modern antisemitism. Similarly, Amos Morris-Reich has stated that Simmel's specific definition of the socio-cultural position of the stranger resembles the so-called "assimilated Jews" rather than the traditional Orthodox Jew:

"The stranger is an element of the group itself," Simmel observes, "an element whose membership within the group involves both being outside it and confronting it." In all these senses, the Jewish stranger approximates more the assimilated Jew than the pre-modern Jew of the ghetto.[293]

It is also striking that Simmel's intellectual mentor Moritz Lazarus, in *Was heisst national?*, similarly focuses on a specific group of German bourgeois-influenced modern Jews and not, for example, on traditional Orthodox Jews, who numbered his own parents among them. Lazarus gives examples of the innovativeness only of acculturated bourgeois-influenced German Jews, who work at the juridical courts, in the political parliaments, and within science:

That [...] we German Jews already are allowed to take part in every sense and in full measure is for us a proud awareness, an incomparable liberation. Alongside, we have fought in the wars, sat in the parliaments [...] on the communal council chairs, worked in the laboratories, healed and cared for in the hospitals, taught from the catheters.[294]

When reading *Was heisst national?*, one therefore notices the contradiction between Lazarus on the one hand telling us that the aim of the text is to describe how the German nation is founded on and has always benefited from cultural pluralism, while, on the other hand, him narrowing down the description of the advantages of cultural pluralism by focusing on one specific group of a particular minority, namely the acculturated bourgeois-influenced German Jews. Undeniably, he has a good reason for this, given Heinrich von Treitschke's attack accusing this group of creating a subversive "*Mischcultur*". Still, Lazarus does not choose to declare *Was heisst national?* a discussion of the minority role of acculturated bourgeois-influenced Western European Jews. He presents the text as a reflection on building modern Germany as a culturally plural, national state.

In this context, a parallel could also be drawn between Lazarus' text and Pontoppidan's *Lykke-Per*. While Pontoppidan's "plan of the novel" seems to dissolve the constructive synthesis of traditional Danish and modern Jewish civilizations, Lazarus' plan was to present its possibility. The synthesis between bourgeois-influenced modern Jewish and traditional German cultures is the most fertile soil in which modern Germany could grow, according to Lazarus.

In conclusion, there are several semantic links between Simmel's stranger character and Lazarus' representation of Jewishness, as well as between these texts and Brandes' and Pontoppidan's Jewish-related stranger figures. Both Simmel and Lazarus along with Brandes and Pontoppidan thus discuss whether the European Christian-based majority group cultures would benefit from a fusion with the modern Jewish spirit. With regard to the cultural backgrounds of Simmel and Lazarus, one could—in a strictly German historical context—counterfactually ask: How would the synthesis have materialized, had the traditional German cultural tradition and the cosmopolitan-orientated modern Jewish civilization merged more substantially over a longer period of time? It seems that the one of the two German Jewish writers, who distanced himself the most from Jewishness, delivered the most substantial answer. Thus, in a letter written in 1902, Georg Simmel refers to the synthesis as not only a possible but a realistic futuristic vision of modern Germany.[295] He writes that those (German Jews) who believe that the particular German Jewish culture would be fully assimilated and absorbed into the Christian-based German culture were far too pessimistic. Instead, modern Germany would become a "third nation." In the 1902 letter, this third nation would be a hybrid culture of the modern secularly orientated Jewish culture and the German Christian-based culture:

It is not a question of dissolution (*Aufgehen*) but of fusion (*Verschmelzung*) with the other and in the course of such a fusion of two nations a third nation emerges in which neither of the two nations has disappeared without leaving a trace, a new nation that bears the elements of both nations alike. Haven't the Germans already acquired many Jewish elements and isn't that because the Jews are participating in the cultural life in Germany? The Jews are also taking on numerous elements of the German spirit [...]. I am surprised by this fear of death that is currently seizing the Jews even while their influence is increasing among all European peoples. The risk of dissolution does not at all threaten the Jews; on the contrary, they are at the stage of the Judaization of Europe [...] and this Judaization of Europe is taking place at the same time as the Europeaniza-tion of the Jews. The more the Jews become assimilated, the more they assimi-late themselves and the moment of their utmost assimilation will correspond to that of their greatest psychic influence. It is for this reason that I do not think it is right to say that I am pessimistic. I think it is those who are of the opinion that Judaism can be saved only by isolating it, by shutting it up in a distant cage, located on the other side of the sea, against which no one can launch an attack and that would be brought from time to time to Europe as a rare and peculiar thing so that Europe would not forget its anti-Semitism – I think those are the ones who are the most affected by pessimism. But all dreams are vain. The Europeans and the Jews are firmly held in solid cultural embrace.[296]

This "third nation" is a hybrid of German Jewish minority and Ger-man majority culture. As we all know, history followed quite a different course in the following decades. In the years when Simmel wrote this letter and the *Exkurs*, modern antisemitism was growing to become an increasingly dominant cultural code.[297] However, in this context, Simmel's *Exkurs*, Lazarus' *Was heist national?* and Brandes' "M. Gold-schmidt" essays should be viewed as valuable examples of how these key historical actors of Jewish descent actively opposed the idea of the European Jews as *"unser Unglück."*

Conclusion

Through the analysis and comparisons of Georg Simmel's, Henrik Pontoppidan's, and Moritz Lazarus' representations of the Jewish stranger figure, we have seen that Georg Brandes was far from the only one to project the Jewish-related ideal stranger type prior to Simmel. The Jewish stranger figure was a prevalent aspect of the so-called Jewish Question in the fin-de-siècle period. We have also seen that it was a topos dated back to writings of Spinozism, and that Brandes was most likely inspired by work of this genre.

By including non-Jewish actors such as Henrik Pontoppidan and Heinrich von Treitschke, this chapter has documented that the question of whether the Jewish-related stranger represented positive or negative traits was a heated topic in the fin-de-siècle period. We have also seen that these non-Jewish writers viewed the interaction between the Jewish minority and the rest of civil society differently than Simmel, in his essayistic description of the interaction. For example, Henrik Pontoppidan's *Lykke-Per* represents an ambivalent view; still, his most nuanced and accomplished character, Jakobe Salomon, is Danish Jewish, and at the end of the novel she has in fact initiated a constructive social and political change in Denmark. Her progressive school in the middle of the working-class area of Copenhagen is in many ways a prototype of how an ideal democratic modern welfare state should function. Like Treitschke, Pontoppidan simultaneously offers many examples of negative Jewish strangeness, which are represented as "polluting" the transition from the old world to a modern liberal democratic society. At the same time, it is difficult to deduce whether Pontoppidan (and Treitschke) wrote specifically about Jews or whether it is primarily modernity they are criticizing. The representation of Jewishness certainly seems to have become increasingly synonymous with concepts such as rootlessness, liberal freethinking, de-nationalized cosmopolitanism, modern alienation, and the general accelerated processes of social, political, and economical change in this period. As a result, it is almost impossible to describe a Danish Jewish character in *Lykke-Per* without also discussing the novel's view of the consequences of modernity and the transition to the modern world.

Instead of wavering undecidedly between a utopian and a dystopian modern world, Simmel chose to focus mainly on the constructive abilities of the stranger in his 1908 essay. In this chapter, both Brandes' modern Jew and Simmel's essay have been viewed as defences of bourgeois-influenced modern Jews and arguments that they should be considered equals to Christian-born men.

It is worth noting that it is not Brandes' modern Jew or Lazarus' *Was heisst national?* to which most present-day idealizations of strangeness refer. Scholars such as Zygmunt Bauman and Kristeva suggest Georg Simmel's 1908 essay as the original source of this ideal stranger type. As a perspective on the revitalized idealizations of Simmel's stranger figure in the last three decades, it could however be argued that when leading scholars represent this ideal stranger type as an universal role model today—and, as Ulrich Beck does, urge everyone to adopt a cosmopolitan outlook—it is important to remember that Simmel's stranger is an elitist and utopian ideal. Once we add particularity to the equation, then, as seen through the examples of this chapter, the ideal stranger is no longer necessarily understood as "more objective." This is observed, for example, through the reception of Brandes' modern Jew figure, which in the following decades was repeatedly used against him.

I will return to how this fin-de-siècle archive of different Jewish-related strangers adds valuable perspectives to the present idealization of strangeness and cosmopolitanism in the discussion section of this book. In the next chapters, we will see that Brandes abandoned the ideal of the modern Jew in his later writings because of modern antisemitism. However, at the same time, through other aspects of the so-called Jewish Question, he continued to argue that European Jews were an indispensable part of Western civilization, since the Jewish religion and culture had in fact founded this civilization.

An Introduction to the Representation
of Jewishness in Brandes' Later Writings

In previous research on Brandes, scholars such as Sven Møller Kristensen and Paul Rubow have convincingly argued that the primary
pattern of his later writings is a shift of focus to "great men" as vital
forces in shaping history.[298] The most typical depictions of this phase
have resulted in an image of Brandes as somewhat disillusioned, ceas-
ing to fight for the Modern Breakthrough project, and, as a key part of
this withdrawal process, turning his attention to geniuses.[299] Friedrich
Nietzsche is often identified as the catalyst for Brandes' interest in these
"great men" in his later writings; it was particularly after his 1889 introductory essay on Nietzsche that Brandes wrote his many books on
geniuses. Nevertheless, it could also be argued that in fact Nietzsche
revitalized Brandes' existing admiration of "great men," which was already evident in his doctoral thesis and in his intellectual biographies of
Benjamin Disraeli and Ferdinand Lassalle, for example. Still, Brandes'
essential role in Friedrich Nietzsche's rise to fame is important to document. The Dane was a key actor in introducing Nietzsche to the elites
and in-groups of European intellectual and artistic circles in 1889–1890.
[300] In a wider European intellectual context, during the 1870s and 1880s
Brandes had gradually earned himself a reputation in Germany, Austria-
Hungary, France, the rest of Scandinavia, and even Poland and Russia
as a leading arbiter of taste. Brandes' friends, allies, and acquaintances
included John Stuart Mill, Henrik Ibsen, Ernest Renan, Georges Clem-
enceau, Moritz Lazarus, Hippolyte Taine, August Strindberg, Berthold
Auerbach, Paul Heyse, Stefan Zweig, Arthur Schnitzler, and Otto von
Hoffmanstahl. Brandes vividly engaged in trans-European, cosmopoli-
tan networks at the same time as writing about the specific modern
Jewish cosmopolitan tradition of which he considered himself part.

By way of characterizing Brandes as an intellectual in his later writings, in the last part of this book, I will address Brandes' representation
of this modern Jewish cosmopolitanism as a no less important pattern
in Brandes' later writings. In my last three chapters, there is a continued

focus on the interconnections between cosmopolitanism and Jewishness.

However, in this part of career, Brandes also re-directs his appraisal of the Jewish co-construction of European civilization. He looks back at the early stages of the development of Western civilization to argue that the Jewish civilization, along with the Greek and Roman cultural traditions, formed its basis. Countering the way Jews and Jewishness were identified by modern antisemitism and in the different European nationalistic ideologies that were gaining traction in the fin-de-siècle period, in several works on the Old Testament and on early Christianity, Brandes demonstrates how the Jewish co-construction of European civilization has been evident for the last two thousand years. Baruch Spinoza again comes to play a central role as the link between the premodern and the modern world, and as such the father of European modernity.

As we will see in Chapter 3, it is also in this part of his career that Brandes distances himself most from Jewishness. Nevertheless, I will argue that this distancing and his theory of the Jewish co-construction of Western civilization should be viewed as related contextual reactions to growing antisemitism in this period.

However, when examining Brandes' representation of Jewishness in his later writings, one important modifying aspect of Chapters 3, 4, and 5 will be to demonstrate how Brandes does not merely grow inward and remove himself from the world concentrating on "great men." Thus, it seems that the primary motivation behind most of his representations of Jewishness in this period is to react to the growing nationalism and antisemitism in this period. One of the more significant examples of this may be found in Brandes' last four books, where he interprets the Athens vs. Jerusalem dichotomy and reflects on how the ancient and modern Jewish civilization shaped European civilization. These books were written in the 1920s, a time when Jews were stereotyped all over Europe, not only in Austria and Germany, as negative alien elements that had historically played a parasitical role in European national histories. Brandes' passionate occupation with ancient Judaism and early

Christianity in his later writings is thus an important and so far unexamined factor in understanding his oeuvre as a whole.

Chapter 3 will shed light on Brandes' strategy of distancing himself from Jewishness in his later writings, which is seen as related to his ultimate career goal of becoming a professor at the University of Copenhagen (the only university in Denmark at the time). In Chapters 4 and 5, this distancing strategy is shown to be far from the only interesting aspect of his later writings on representations of Jewishness since he also shifts his focus to the historical role of Jews and Jewishness in both the origins and the modern shaping of European civilization. Still, Brandes primarily uses these interpretations of the past as means to advance his struggles in the present, often as contributions to ongoing discussions of the so-called Jewish Question. In other words, he continued to be an active and observant public intellectual in his later writings.[301]

Chapter 3

Brandes' Distancing Strategies of De-Judaizing and De-Cosmopolitanization in his Later Writings

Introduction

In the previous research on Brandes, it has been documented that he distances himself even more from Jewishness in his later writings. Based on text material primarily from this period Jørgen Knudsen, Henri Nathansen, and Tine Bach go as far as saying Brandes exhibited Jewish self-hatred.[302] However, as elaborated on in the Introduction, this term—Jewish self-hatred—has been used as an overly reductive categorization in the context of the group of so-called integrationists, the majority of Western European Jews, who each struggled individually to be recognized as equal citizens in the European national states they were born and raised in, and who believed that their home was Europe.

The most pressing research question as regards Brandes' later writings could be formulated in this way: How and why does Brandes distance himself even more from Jewishness in his later writings while simultaneously developing—more substantially than in his early writings—this modern Jewish cosmopolitan tradition of which he considers himself a part?

It is difficult today to grasp just how stigmatizing antisemitism was for individuals of Jewish descent in the fin-de-siècle period. For Brandes, the stigmatization of him as a typical "subversive Jew" began immediately after the publication of *Emigrantlitteraturen* in 1872, and it never ceased. Undoubtedly, the main personal consequence for Brandes was that it made it impossible for him to pursue the promising academic career he had initiated in the 1860s. One can count no less than seven episodes between 1871/1872–1901/1902 in which central actors of the institution of the University of Copenhagen, different Danish ministers of government and politicians, and even the leading Danish theologian and the king himself discussed and opposed Brandes' distinction and worthiness of being appointed as a professor at the University of Copenhagen.[303] The absurdity and the antisemitic sub-text of the decades-long struggles of Brandes to become a professor makes this historical case the Danish equivalent of the French Dreyfus Affair, which over a period of 10 or more years disclosed how the leading French state institutions and a good part of the French population were pervaded by stereotyped antisemitic thinking on Jews and reactionary national conservative views. However, as we will see, the saga of Brandes' several attempts to become a professor also illustrates that this was a period of transition.

On two occasions (one of these occurring on his deathbed in 1872), the former professor in Aesthetics Carsten Hauch declared that the only candidate who was gifted enough to succeed him was Georg Brandes. In research on Brandes, it has been argued that he was not appointed as a professor in the 1870s because his scientific work was not substantial enough.[304] However, one could just as easily argue that his 1871 lectures made no difference. Thus, being of Jewish descent, Brandes would never have been made a professor, at least in the 1870s and the 1880s, no matter what books he had published and whatever their quality was. A strong indication of the truth of this is that the first non-converted Danish Jew to be made a professor at the University of Copenhagen, J. A. Fridericia, was not appointed until 1899—almost 30 years after Brandes' first efforts.[305] Like his brother Edvard Brandes' advances in Danish politics, Georg Brandes was a first mover in many areas. And like many other Danish Jews, Brandes and his brother Edvard were aware that a glass ceiling existed, although *Grundloven* of 1849 stated otherwise.

Usually, Brandes' return to Copenhagen after his years of "exile" in Berlin is viewed as initiating the new direction of his later writings. It should be noted that Brandes finally returned from this "exile" of 1877–83 because a group of men of private wealth (among them many other

Danish Jews) offered him a monthly salary if he would come back to Denmark. He accepted, and in his response he wrote that he would now finally be able to live as a "Danish scientist" in Copenhagen.[306] However, this provision of an unofficial equal status with genuinely appointed professors at the University of Copenhagen never proved to be enough for Brandes. After his return in 1883, he continued to pursue his goal of becoming a professor at the University in Copenhagen until he was appointed in 1901–1902.

In this chapter, Brandes' increased effort to distance himself from Jewishness in his later writings will be historically contextualized with his ongoing battle to be made a professor. This battle represents his ultimate struggle to be accepted by the Danish bourgeoisie. As we saw in Chapter 1, Brandes' boldest and most explicit representation of the modern Jew occurred before 1871 in the "M. Goldschmidt" essay, and thus before he experienced stigmatization as a subversive Jew, a denationalized cosmopolitan, and a Spinozist materialist/atheist negatively influencing his intellectual career. In his later writings, Brandes then went to greater lengths to distance himself from Jewishness by abandoning the racially based modern Jew figure, and later by adopting two significant de-Judaizing and de-cosmopolitanization strategies.

I will first examine Brandes' changed view of the concept of race in his later writings as related to the rise of modern antisemitism, following the observation Paul Rubow made in his article "Georg Brandes' forhold til Taine og Sainte-Beuve" ("Georg Brandes' Relations to Taine and Sainte-Beuve"). As early as the 1920s, Rubow linked Brandes' abandonment of the race concept to the rise of racially based modern antisemitism.[307] We will also see how Brandes' increased distance from Jewishness is particularly observable at the time when he was finally appointed as a professor. Thus, in works such as *Julius Lange* (1898), *Samlede Skrifter*, and *Levned I–III*, Brandes erases references to both Jewish and cosmopolitan characteristics while editing past work for his *Samlede Skrifter*. It will be argued that both of these strategies, of de-cosmopolitanization and de-Judaizing, seem to be related to Brandes' goal to become a professor at the University of Copenhagen, and as such they led to him finally and visibly being included in the Danish bourgeoisie.

Brandes' Changed View on Race

In his later writings, Brandes stopped thematizing the particular Jewish racial heritage, and the concept of race also fades from his vocabulary.[308] However, it is also evident that the Herderian *Volksgeist* and reflections on cultural matters continue to be a key element in his writings. For example, in *Indtryk fra Polen* (*Impressions from Poland*) (1886) and *Indtryk fra Rusland* (*Impressions from Russia*) (1888), Brandes appears in disguise as the travelling narrator *"den fremmede,"* "the stranger," who observes particularistic Polish and Russian characteristics. One could argue that he continues to intersect the figure of the stranger with himself, as a less prejudiced and more objective modern Jewish observer. Still, not once in the almost 600 pages of the two books does he use the word "race." The fact that he maintains a focus on particular cultural matters without mentioning race can also be observed in his two famous 1890 essays "Om Nationalfølelse" ("Concerning National Sentiment") (1894) and "Danskheden i Sønderjylland" ("Danishness in Southern Denmark") (1899), in which he ponders particular Danish cultural traits. In these essays, he is concerned with keeping the constructive and meaningful parts of Danish culture alive, which illustrates his now weaker cosmopolitanism.[309] As we will see in Chapters 4 and 5, Brandes is still a sworn cosmopolitan and he still practices a cosmopolitan outlook in his later writings, but there is now a new emphasis on the importance of national culture.[310]

Another departure from his former ideas on particular Jewish racial traits is found in his division of the European Jewry into two different peoples. In the article "Sionismen" (1901), for example, he characterizes the European Jewry as consisting of two basically different races/peoples, namely the Eastern European and Russian Jews, the so-called *Ostjuden*, and the Western European Jews. Brandes goes even further in atomizing his former idea by claiming that any European Jew, Western or Eastern, is of mixed race and is thus in no way a direct descendant of the ancient Jewish Semitic people.[311] Following Ernest Renan, among others, he explains that the Western European Jewish race is more influenced by Frankish blood than by the ancient Jewish Semitic traits.[312] Similarly, Brandes' new arguments rely on the idea that the Eastern European and Russian Jews are descendants of the medieval Khazar people—a Turkish Russian people who, according to Brandes, converted to Judaism in the 9th century AD.[313]

Brandes' division of so-called *Ostjuden* and Western European Jews was not unique in the fin-de-siècle period. It was a widespread strategy with which many writers of Western European Jewish descent distanced themselves from the more traditional Eastern European and Russian Jews who migrated west in vast numbers, especially in the period from 1880 to the 1920s. The dichotomy is also observable in a work such as Stefan Zweig's *Die Welt von Gestern* (1942).[314] In Brandes' oeuvre, the article "Paa den schlessiske Banegaard" (1884) is the first example of his encounter with the so-called *Ostjuden*. It is clear that Brandes already feels distanced from and spiritually unrelated to the so-called *Ostjuden*, although the article is full of sympathy for the immigrant situation of the Eastern European Jews. One could thus see his later racial distinction between Eastern European Jews and Western European Jews as an elaboration of his first, distanced characterization of migrating Eastern European and Russian Jews in 1884.

However, although Brandes clearly distanced himself from the Eastern European Jews after the turn of the century, he also collaborated with the Danish Head Rabbi, David Simonsen, and wrote several articles that were published all over Europe and the USA in which he defended the rights of the Eastern European Jews.[315] He was also one of the very few Western European intellectuals during the First World War to raise an awareness of what was going on in Eastern Europe, when the Russian and Polish pogroms had become more brutal than ever.[316]

Moreover, one could interpret Brandes' attempts to split the European Jews into two different yet both still mixed races as an effort to oppose and defy antisemitism. In the text "Raceteorier" (1913), in which Brandes reacts to the Danish writer Jakob Knudsen's claim that "the

Jewish stranger" Brandes was attempting to destroy the Danish cultural tradition,[317] Brandes answers back by explaining to Knudsen that the very idea that there exists racially or nationally "purified" Jews, Danes, or Germans is an illusion.[318] In other words, not only the European Jews, but all modern Europeans, including all Danes, were of mixed race, according to Brandes.[319] In this article, he particularly mocks the antisemitic idealization of the pure Aryan race since, as he writes, there could be no human beings left in Europe who were the biological product of a line of pure Aryan blood. The notion of an authentic Aryan race is also an illusion, according to Brandes.[320] He also ridicules Richard Wagner for warning against Jewish influence on the Aryan European musical tradition (in "Das Judentum in der Musik"), since Wagner might very well have had a Jewish father and thus himself could be of mixed race.[321]

Modern Antisemitism

Particularly in the editing of texts for *Samlede Skrifter*, and in Brandes' autobiography *Levned* (1905–1908), we can observe a pattern where it becomes important for Brandes to distance himself not only from his former idealizing idea of Jewish racial features, but also from being labeled a "Jewish cosmopolitan." From 1879–81 and after the *Berliner Antisemitismusstreit*, racially focused modern antisemitism became an increasingly influential ideology throughout Western Europe. The focal point in modern antisemitism can be viewed as an extension and further development of the "clash of races" thesis, which writers such as Ernest Renan and J. A. de Gobineau first presented with a distinction between the Aryan race and the Semitic race (and other races) in the 1850s and 1860s.[322] Richard Wagner's essay "Das Judentum in der Musik" was also influential in the creation of modern antisemitism because of its call for redirection in the negative representation of Jewishness. However, the *Berliner Antisemitismusstreit* represents a new stage of European Jew-hatred since figures such as Heinrich von Treitschke, Adolf Stoecker, and Wilhelm Marr connected antisemitism with national conservative political ideology. For example, Otto Glagau, who was another of the early important founders of modern antisemitism and a union leader for German craftsmen, invented the popular ideological phrase *"Die soziale Frage ist die Judenfrage"* ("The social question is the Jewish question"). Modern antisemitism became a populist ideology which saw modern liberal characteristics such as democracy, capitalism, and the rationalistic science-based mindset as hollow categories that were inadequate to replace the estate and Christian structures of the old world.[323] In the view of the modern antisemites, the modern spirit favored and intensified particular Jewish characteristics.[324] Modern antisemitism thus positioned itself as different from previous traditional antisemitism; as an ideology, it was centered around the idea that it was necessary to initiate a resistance battle against the modern Jewish spirit. The primary enemy was those elements in society which actively supported the continuous acculturation and integration process of Western European Jews. As such, it was not only Jews who the modern antisemites targeted, but also the "philosemitic" liberal parts of the bourgeoisie.[325] Jews and non-Jews "polluted" by the modern Jewish civilization would be equally targeted, though it was the Jewish racial heritage that was viewed as the prime cause of the alleged modern subversion of European national cultures.

In a Danish cultural context, it was mostly the "Jew" Georg Brandes (and his brother Edvard Brandes) who was made responsible for an interpretation of modernity as a time when "everything that was solid melted into air," foreshadowing Marshall Berman's twentieth-century classic. Furthermore, with the figure of the modern Jew in his early writings, Brandes himself had stated that Jews were natural born leaders in the liberal cosmopolitan development of the modern world, and for many decades these early depictions of the modern Jew, particularly the most daring, in "M. Goldschmidt," were remembered and used against him to exhibit his subversive "Jewish" ideas. The effort to silence and ignore Brandes began with the rupture of 1871/1872, when he was effectively stigmatized as a subversive "cosmopolitan Jew" particularly by *Fædrelandet* (*The Mother Country*) and *Dagbladet* (*Daily News*).[326]

Today, with our post-holocaust eyes, it is important to remember that modern antisemitism was not a scandalous set of ideas in Western Europe between 1871 and 1927. It was quite common, including in the Danish civil sphere, to represent Jews and Jewishness in a stereotypical and negative fashion, as the conservative satire magazine *Punch* frequently did, along with the leading bourgeois newspapers of the period. A simple listing of book titles by prominent Danish actors in Brandes' later writings in fact documents how his ideas and writings were constantly identified as subversive and non-Danish "Jewish," and threatening to the order of society.[327] Moreover, it was often former allies and friends who within a few years turned into raging antisemites, blaming Brandes for destroying meaningful, traditional Danish values; many went from being optimistic liberals to national conservative pessimists in this period (like Heinrich von Treitschke). Modern antisemitism became the central cultural code by which the transition from the old world to modern democracy and capitalism was discussed; this is evident all over Western Europe in this period, including in Denmark.

Early on Brandes understood the dangerous potential of modern antisemitism. This can be seen in his journalistic coverage of the Dreyfus Affair from 1896 to 1906. Over the course of 22 articles, Brandes reported on and analyzed this absurd trial. In "Sagens Genoptagelse" ("The Reopening of the Case"), published in *Politiken* in 1903, he creates an overview of the ideological implications of the trial. He characterizes the groundless, antisemitic accusations against Alfred Dreyfus as a sign of a polarized battle of ideas about what the European civilization ought to signify and which direction it should take. He calls the Dreyfus Affair "the fight for and against [...] the modern culture" (*"kampen for og imod [...] den hele moderne kultur"*).[328] Brandes also remarks that, ideologically, antisemitism had become one of the central components in this clash.[329]

However, Brandes does not draw the same conclusion on the basis of the Dreyfus Affair as for example Theodor Herzl did, where the trial is said to be the point at which Herzl lost his last hope that the European Jews would ever be accepted as equal citizens in European societies.[330] Brandes continued to believe that any individual is first and foremost rooted in the *Volksgeist(ern)* into which he is born, and this applied to

European Jews and their European *Volksgeist(ern)*. Accordingly, when Herzl contacted Brandes by letter in 1896 to ask whether Brandes would support his first draft of a Zionist ideology, Brandes replied that he did not believe in Herzl's solution to the so-called Jewish Question.[331] Later, in 1917–18, when the pogroms in Russia and Poland had become more brutal than ever before, it does seem that Brandes changed his view on the Zionist movement. He wrote an article in which he envisioned that one day Israel/Palestine would be a rich and prosperous state, the inhabitants of which would primarily be Eastern European Jews who, understandably, wanted to live in a country in which their equality rights were respected.[332] Brandes also writes that Western European Jews would, on the other hand, continue to be part of the countries they and their families had lived in for generations and in which they had been granted emancipation.[333] Brandes was consequently perceived as a so-called integrationist by supporters of Zionism, including the Danish writer Henri Nathansen.

The fact that Brandes foresaw quite early on the dangerous potential of modern antisemitism (while still believing in the continuous acculturation process of Western European Jews) is the most strategic explanation for why he abandoned his idea of Jewish racial heritage and adopted a general strategy of distancing himself from Jewishness. He most likely feared that, if he continued to represent the modern Jew, and to project such racially based ideas on Jewishness, he would be caught in the claims which Heinrich von Treitschke, for example, had stated in "Unsere Aussichten," that the bourgeois-influenced Western European Jews had a pompous attitude:

And what hollow, insulting hubris! Under constant sneering insults, it is seemingly proven that the nation of Kant was educated and civilized by the Jews, that the language of Lessing and Goethe only became receptive to beauty, spirit and wit thanks to Börne and Heine![334]

In continuing to portray the figure of the modern Jew, Brandes constantly risked being reminded of how he would never amount to anything but a provocative and typical "Jewish intellectual" who considered himself and other modern Jews superior to the rest of society.

Back in the 1860s and 1870s, before the race concept was semantically monopolized by modern antisemitism in the civil sphere, Brandes had in fact found this "clash of races" hypothesis inspirational, particularly in the writings of Ernest Renan.[335] By 1879–81, however, this idea had taken a new, disturbing turn, and the popularity of the new racially based ideology only grew in the following years as it became a central component in many of the nationalistic movements that arose around Europe at this time, particularly in the Eastern European countries.

Shulamit Volkov wrote that the most typical reaction of bourgeois-influenced Western European Jews toward the phenomenon of modern antisemitism was to distance themselves further from Jewishness. This pattern can be observed throughout Brandes' writings, not only in the later ones; he even outlines and recommends this distancing strategy to other European Jews in his first reaction to Treitschke's accusations and the related personal attack from Adolf Stoecker in the German *Reichstag*, in the article "Bevægelsen mod Jøderne i Tyskland" (1881). Having rejected Treitschke's accusations of an overrepresentation of Jews in industries such as journalism and politics, Brandes writes that the most efficient way of bringing modern antisemitism to an end would be for the Western European Jews to continue the process of acculturation that they had begun in the late enlightenment period.[336] Moreover, he urges Western European Jews not to act in a provocatively "Jewish" way in the civil sphere.[337] These two related attitudes towards modern antisemitism do indeed seem to be primary strategies of Brandes in his later writings, as he stops representing the modern Jew and idealizing Jewish racial traits. Furthermore, his de-Judaizing and de-cosmopolitanization of his own work in the context of the publication of his collected writings around the turn of the century also bear witness to how he practised these distancing attitudes.

Brandes' Erasing of Jewish and Cosmopolitan Elements from Samlede Skrifter and Levned

Brandes described his strategy of distancing himself further from Jewishness in an article from 1881 on the construction of modern anti-semitism as an ideology. In this section, I will now examine whether Brandes also had a personal career-oriented motive for this strategy. It is noticeable that the works in which Brandes distances himself the most from Jewishness were written in the same period in which he finally reached his ultimate career goal of becoming a professor at the University of Copenhagen. As is well-known in Jewish Studies, the approval of the Christian-based majority bourgeoisie became a lifelong and failed struggle for many of the gifted and talented scholars of Jewish descent around Western Europe in the nineteenth and early twentieth centuries.[338] Brandes was finally given a professorship at the University of Copenhagen in 1901/1902; he had struggled for 30 years to achieve his goal. In *Professoratet – Videnskabelige Magtkampe i Det Filosofiske Fakultet 1870–1920* (*The Professorship – Scientific Struggles for Power in The Faculty of Philosophy 1870–1920*) (2010), Pelle Oliver Larsen documents how his six previous attempts had failed due to ideological issues and what seem to be cases of structural racism. Larsen lists many examples indicating that it was the link between Brandes' Jewish background and his reputation as simultaneously a liberal cosmopolitan, a freethinker, and an Spinozist materialist/atheist that became the decisive factor, since it was first discussed whether Brandes was worthy of being appointed as a professor in 1871/72.[339] In this context, the leading national liberal and conservative newspapers and their stigmatization of Brandes also played an important role.

Brandes began his characteristic editing process of earlier written texts for his *Samlede Skrifter* shortly after what Pelle Oliver Larsen determines to be his sixth attempt at a professorship in 1896/97. It was once again discussed at the Philosophical Faculty at the University of Copenhagen whether Brandes was now—finally—worthy of the chair.[340]

One of the clearest signs of Brandes' decision to stop articulating the specific Jewish racial heritage is in his editing of his own work for his *Samlede Skrifter*. For example, Brandes includes the essay "M. Gold-schmidt," but in a rather diminished version in which all the passages about the modern Jew and the idealized Jewish race heritage are left out. For instance, the famous part about the particularly innovative free horizon of the modern Jew was removed.[341] Brandes also erases the passage in which he reflects on how a modern Jew, such as M. A. Gold-schmidt, possesses many different cultural "essences," which in combination made Goldschmidt's prose a unique contribution to the Danish cultural tradition.[342] For most of the original readers, this last part of the Goldschmidt essay was the central and most important part. In a letter correspondence in 1902 with Brandes, the later professor in Danish Literature at the University of Copenhagen, Vilhelm Andersen, asks Brandes why he left out these central parts. Brandes replied:

Primarily because I no longer believe at all that north European Jews are Semites, partly because at that time I was influenced by a universal climate of opinion and by racial theories so that I tended to attribute to ancestry what I now believe to be an exaggerated importance.[343]

All the texts that idealized the particular Jewish race heritage and the modern Jew in his early writings underwent a similar editing process for his *Samlede Skrifter*.[344] Jørgen Knudsen has used the term "purism" to describe this process.[345] Its two most significant characteristics are, firstly, the erasure of all passages, sentences, and words that refer to his former thoughts regarding Jewish racial traits, and secondly, as we will see later in this chapter, the replacing of all foreign words and phrases (most often in German or French) with Danish equivalents.[346] On several occasions, Brandes even invents new words because no equivalent exists in Danish.[347] One of the more illustrative examples Knudsen lists is Brandes' substitution of "*optimisme*" with "*gladsyn*." As such, given Knudsen's term "purism," it is not clear how Brandes, ideologically speaking, "purifies" his vocabulary and language of former texts for *Samlede Skrifter*. Yet this editing process shows that he made a strong interrelated effort to de-cosmopolitanize and at the same time de-Judaize his vocabulary in a period when modern antisemitism was on the rise.

Brandes' de-cosmopolitanization strategy can be observed by comparing the vocabulary from two pages in the original version of the essay "M. Goldschmidt," with that of the 1899 version in *Samlede Skrifter*. In this excerpt, I have not used translations of Brandes' words into English. However, non-Danish-speaking readers will most likely be able to recognize the difference between the original so-called foreign words (of which most are common and frequently used Danish words today) and the altered—supposedly more genuine—Danish words:

Reflecteret, p. 404	*Bevidst*, p. 455
Naive, p. 404	*Troskyldige*, p. 455
Charakter, p. 404	*Præg*, p. 455
Coquetteri, p. 404	*Koketteri*, p. 456
Mystisk, p. 404	*Hemmelighedsfuld*, p. 456
Forceret, p. 405	*Anstrengt*, p. 456
Psychologisk, p. 405	*Sjæleligt*, p. 456
Bornerthed (x2), p. 405	*Aandssneverhed* (x2), p. 456
Charakter, p. 405	*Personlighed*, p. 456[348]

Another key example is Brandes' deletion of pages 308–313 in *Benjamin Disraeli* (1878) for the version that appears in his *Samlede Skrifter 9* (1901). These pages are arguably the second most coherent thematization of the modern Jew in his early writings. In the original 1878 work, Brandes discussed whether Disraeli was to be seen as a prime racial example of a modern Jew. Yet, for the version in *Samlede Skrifter 9* (titled "Lord Beaconsfield"), having removed these key pages, Brandes chooses to sum up the political life and writings of Disraeli as truly incarnating English historical events and traits.

Brandes re-worked not just writings with Jewish themes but all his previous writing using these standards. It is also noticeable that his *Samlede Skrifter* was a commercial success, unlike most of his other work.[349]

Another example of how Brandes was eager to self-fashion as a fully assimilated and non-hybridized Dane is the biography of his best friend in his late teenage years, Julius Lange, published in 1898. In this book Brandes presents himself as deeply influenced and even defined by the Danish Romantic period, which he had mainly mocked previously.[350]

Furthermore, in his autobiography *Levned I–III* (1905–08), a de-Judaizing process occurs again. A suitable example of this can be found in one of the most quoted anecdotes from *Levned*—the tale of how, as a boy, he suddenly discovers that he is of Jewish descent when he begins to attend school.[351] It is odd that Jewishness and the Jewish tradition are portrayed as completely absent from his life until he starts school and is mocked for being a Jew (let us remember: two thirds of the people living in the building he grew up in, which was owned by his Danish Jewish grandfather, were also of Jewish descent).

The anecdote appears thus in *Levned I*: When Georg Brandes starts school, and it is a Christian Danish school, he notices that on his way home after lessons some of the other boys shout some sort of abusive word at him and his brother while also throwing rocks at them. Puzzled by this, Brandes asks his mother one day what the swearword means. "Jews!" his mother says, "Jews is a group of people." "Bad people?" asks little Georg—"Yes," his mother answers smilingly, "sometimes rather bad people, but not always." "May I see one of these Jews?" asks little Georg. "You may," the mother replies, and she lifts him up in front of a mirror; he screams in horror.[352]

Clearly, this anecdote is narrated with irony, a tone characteristic of all Brandes' writings. Nevertheless, it functions as a narrative framework by which Brandes constructs his upbringing and his individual "identity" as not particularly Jewish. As has been noted by other researchers, *Levned I–III* is in general very selective in what it focuses on.[353] It leaves out many relevant details.[354] In addition, *Levned I* does not represent a valid historical documentation of how or when Brandes found out he was of Jewish descent. Works by Jørgen Knudsen, Kristian Hvidt, Tine Bach, and Henry J. Gibbons, among others, contradict the de-Judaizing strategy of *Levned*, as Brandes was exposed to much more

Jewish influence in his childhood home than he claims to have been in his autobiography.[355] This is also well documented by friends and acquaintances of the Brandes family such as Edmund Gosse and Peter Nansen, who visited the Brandes' home and described it as "strongly Jewish tinged."[356] Henry J. Gibbons also documents that even as an old man Brandes remained a nominal paying member of the Mosaic Congregation in Copenhagen until 1910.

For works such as *Samlede Skrifter* and *Levned*, a central question must be: What is the historical context of these writings? Why does it become a deliberate strategy of Brandes to write off both Jewishness and strong cosmopolitanism as labels that can be attributed to him?

In this context, it is relevant that, in the late 1890s, Brandes had been striving to become a professor at the University of Copenhagen for almost 30 years. The most important political premise was of course *Systemskiftet* (The Change of Systems) in 1901, by which the conservative bourgeois parties *Højre* (Right) and *De Nationalliberale* (The National Liberal Party), the king, and the aristocracy and landowners accepted for the first time the democratic majority vote for the moderate liberal *Venstre* (Left) party. However, it was still not given that Brandes would be appointed as a professor after *Systemskiftet*. In fact, Brandes himself once again became the prime motor for pursuing the chair.[357] At first, in 1901, the newly appointed *Venstre* minister, J. C. Christensen, who was in fact later responsible for the appointment, actually opposed the idea which Brandes himself had first lobbied for in the newspaper *Politiken*.[358] Still, as Pelle Oliver Larsen has documented, both before and after *Systemskiftet*, the institution of the University of Copenhagen played the most decisive role in appointing new professors. It was a complicated power game; many high-profile people had a say, including the so-called *Konsistorium* (the highest ruling board at the university, counting members of all faculties), *Kultusministeren* (the minister of education) and other members of the parliament who participated in discussions of *Finansloven* (The National Budget), and even the leading Danish theologian and the king demanded that their opinions also be taken into consideration (at least in the 1870s and 1880s). Throughout all seven episodes, it is particularly noticeable how much focus there was on Brandes' Jewish background and the interconnected categorization of him as a liberal freethinker, a cosmopolitan, and a Spinozist materialist/atheist in the notes and official documents circulating between the different actors.[359] Brandes certainly had a career motive for self-fashioning as a fully assimilated Dane who was particularly fond of the Danish Romantic period.

It is also important to clarify that the institution of the University of Copenhagen and particularly the Philosophical Faculty in these years found itself in the midst of an internal struggle. The two factions of what Pelle Oliver Larsen calls the orthodox (feudally orientated conservatives) and modernists (national liberal/conservative secularly orientated actors) were fighting for a majority vote in the faculty, and it would be naïve not to see this political battle as partly a result of Brandes' candidature. Subsequently, throughout the 1890s, the modernists counted more and more tenured faculty members among their ranks.[360] Although this faction gradually won more power and influence, both before and after *Systemskiftet*, the two candidates who were appointed as professors in Aesthetics/Literature, Julius Paludan and Vilhelm Andersen, both focused on national conservative and Romantic topics. Julius Paludan had first made his name known among a wider audience in the civil sphere when in 1877 he had criticized and devaluated Brandes' Modern Breakthrough, claiming that it was without any academic substance, particularly because of its liberal cosmopolitan ideological subtext and its admiration of the French Revolution.[361] Vilhelm Andersen was a follower of the modern secularly orientated national conservativism that became popular, not least in Germany, in the 1880s and the 1890s. As we have seen, Heinrich von Treitschke and works such as Julius Langbehn's *Rembrandt als Erzieiher* (1890) were important factors in the intellectual trend of criticizing modernity and emphasizing the *Volksgeist* and the (homogenic) origins of the national culture instead.[362] Typically, in this romanticization of the *Volksgeist*, certain elements of the old world such as the countryside, the spirit of the people (particularly farmers), and the territory were brought into the foreground.

These elements should prevent the nation from decaying and turning into a Jewish-dominated modernity dystopia. Vilhelm Andersen's favorite book was Langbehn's *Rembrandt als Erzieher*; he definitely also rated the provincial traits of Danish culture as of high importance, as Johnny Kondrup and Per Dahl have shown.[363] Today, Vilhelm Andersen is mostly known for his positive re-evaluation and construction of the Danish Romantic period. The key focus of Andersen's work was subsequently, from the 1890s, to create a narrative of the Danish Romantic period as *Guldalder* (The Golden Age). He portrayed this period as particularly rich in its literature and art production. In comparison, Brandes' Modern Breakthrough and his dictum of "debating problems" was determined to be a failed aesthetical project because of his Jewish background (in the next chapter, we will take a closer look at Andersen's portrayal of Georg Brandes in his work *Tider og Typer Af Dansk Aands Historie. Andel Del: Goethe. Anden Del: Det Nittende Aarhundredes Sidste Halvdel* (*Times and Types in the History of the Danish Spirit. Second Volume: Goethe. Second Volume: The Latter Half of the Nineteenth Century*) (1916), hereafter referred to as *Tider og Typer – Goethe II* (1916)). As mentioned, Brandes had originally mocked the Danish Romantic period, presenting its products in *Emigrantlitteraturen* and *Den Romantiske Skole i Tyskland* as unoriginal reproductions of German Romantic art and literature. Thus, it would not be an overstatement to deduce that candidates who focused on national conservative Romantic subjects, no matter whether these had a neofeudal or a modern and more secularly orientated form, were more likely to be made professors at the University of Copenhagen in the 1890s and 1900s—despite *Systemskiftet* (if the third relevant candidate of this period, Valdemar Vedel, and his academic topics are taken into consideration this fact is only confirmed).[364]

Thus, it was not a coincidence that in the years around the turn of the century, Brandes made a strong effort to self-fashion as a fully assimilated Dane, for whom Jewishness played no important role, and who found the Danish Romantic period particularly rich. Consequently, one could view Brandes' de-Judaizing and de-cosmopolitanizing editing strategies in his *Samlede Skrifter*, as well as the approach in *Julius Lange* and his autobiography, as related to the attitude he had proposed in 1881 in "Bevægelsen mod jøderne i Tyskland." In the following decades, his self-fashioning efforts resulted in some of his greatest publication successes,[365] and he was made a professor at the University of Copenhagen. Although the title he was awarded in reality had little significance—since it entailed no academic responsibilities—there is no doubt that for Brandes it was immensely important. It was a sign of genuine inclusion and proper visible *embourgement*.[366]

Conclusion

In this chapter, we have seen how Brandes continued to distance himself from Jewishness in his later writings. Already after the *Berliner Antisemitismusstreit*, Brandes was reacting to the rise of modern antisemitism and gradually altering his representation of Jewishness. He first abandoned the concepts of race and the racially pre-conditioned modern Jew, who he had otherwise presented as a natural leader of the modern world in his early writings. Later, de-Judaizing and de-cosmopolitanization strategies become central parts of his process when editing texts for his collected works.

These distancing strategies may have helped Brandes achieve his ultimate career goal of becoming a professor at the University of Copenhagen. However, it must also be noted that the title and the chair he finally earned were, in reality, without substance. The title gave him no academic responsibilities and he was not a civil servant. Thus, this final and visible sign of inclusion in the Christian-based Danish bourgeoisie was ambivalent, not least because Brandes was not admitted into the prestigious *Videnskabernes Selskab* (The Royal Danish Academy of Sciences) after he was appointed professor, unlike Vilhelm Andersen.[367]

Still, although Brandes clearly distanced himself even more from Jewishness in his later writings, at the same time, he continued to take part in discussions of the so-called Jewish Question, particularly by emphasizing the Jewish co-construction of Western civilization in many of his later writings. However, like the early writings I examined in the first part of this book, most of these later Jewish-related writings have so far mainly been considered to represent the margins of Brandes' oeuvre. Thus, on the one hand, in writings which were written for commercial success, Brandes clearly self-fashions as a fully assimilated Dane who is worthy of a professorship at the university. On the other, in writings such as *Jobs Bog* and *Kohélet* from the 1890s and through to his last four books, Brandes engaged passionately in specific intellectual discussions on the so-called Jewish Questions by creating counter-narratives to the modern antisemitic interpretation of the historical role of Jews in Europe as parasitical.

Chapter 4

Brandes' Re-Interpretations of the Athens vs. Jerusalem Dichotomy

Introduction

In Chapter 3, we saw that Brandes continued to distance himself from Jewishness in his later writings and that this strategy peaked up to and following his appointment as a professor at the University of Copenhagen. In these works, Brandes made a deliberate effort to self-fashion as a fully assimilated Dane who was no longer a "cosmopolitan Jew."

However, in these same later writings, we find another pattern as regards Brandes' interconnections of Jewishness and cosmopolitanism. This will be pursued in Chapters 4 and 5, in which we will see how Brandes' works on ancient Judaism and early Christianity develop his thoughts on Jews and Jewishness as key in what we today consider to be Western liberal democratic core values. Again, these chapters will mainly focus on texts that have so far been considered unimportant and marginal, including the last four works Brandes wrote before he died in 1927.

In *Smaa Romaner i Det Gamle Testamente* (*Short Novels from the Old Testament*) (1914), Brandes suggests a way of reading the oldest existing books of Judaism and early Christianity. His approach is apparently based on the modern tradition of bible criticism, which Spinoza founded with the *Tractatus Theologico-Politico* and which was further developed in the first half of the nineteenth century, particularly by German philologists (Friedrich Strauss' *Das Leben Jesu* (1835–36) is a classic in the field). Building on this philological bible critical tradition, Brandes often focuses on the fact that these texts were edited and reworked several times. These readings also represent a continuation of his early view of literature, expressed in 1871/72. Thus, in *Smaa Romaner i Det Gamle Testamente*, Brandes firstly states that the books of the Old Testament are all *"tendens-fortællinger"* (stories with a moral lesson/ guidance).[368] In his vocabulary, the term *"tendens-fortælling"* denotes a genre of literature that has the purpose of demonstrating a moral teaching. One could consequently argue that, in his later writings, Brandes links the aesthetical and ethical ideal of the Modern Breakthrough project with this key focus of his later writings. Thus, in *Smaa Romaner i Det Gamle Testamente*, Brandes states that the texts of the Old Testament were written to "debate problems."

At the same time, it is important to emphasize that in the context of Brandes' oeuvre as a whole, the attention he pays to the books of the Old Testament here is not unusual. In some of the earliest written materials of his oeuvre available today, namely the letters he wrote to his parents when he travelled as a teenager, the book he refers to most is the Old Testament. Brandes' many references to the Old Testament in his letters from 1859 to 1871 suggest that he had always used it to provide useful perspectives on his experiences and thoughts.[369] It is pertinent that these letters were written to his parents, and particularly to his mother. While Brandes' childhood home was not influenced much by Jewish religious practice (he did not go to the synagogue, for example), it was Jewish in a cultural sense; these many references to the cornerstone of the Jewish tradition demonstrate that during the upbringing of the Brandes brothers the Old Testament was used as a typical frame of reference. As such, Brandes' later understanding of the stories of the Old Testament as *tendens-fortællinger* correspond to the more culturally oriented use of the Old Testament in these early letters to his mother.

In addressing Brandes' continued elaboration on the Jewish co-construction of Western civilization in his later writings, this chapter will focus on his re-interpretations of the influential cultural code of the Athens vs. Jerusalem dichotomy. Since the Enlightenment, the role of ancient Jewish civilization and Judaism had been downgraded through numerous depictions of the Athens vs. Jerusalem dichotomy by philosophers such as Immanuel Kant, Hegel, Ernest Renan, and Freidrich

Nietzsche; the usual interpretation was that Judaism and the ancient Jewish tradition was a "false start" for European civilization and Christianity. In contrast, Greek and Roman antiquity was typically interpreted as the foundation of Europe.[370] Throughout his later writings, Brandes becomes more and more focused on the past and the historical role of Jews and Jewishness in European history, as the Athens vs. Jerusalem dichotomy merged with the cultural code of modern antisemitism in discussions of the so-called Jewish Question. I propose that Brandes' re-interpretations of the Athens vs. Jerusalem dichotomy were direct reactions to the nationalistic and modern antisemitic fin-de-siècle idea of Jews and Jewishness as subversive strangers in the histories of the different European national traditions.

In the context of the rise of modern antisemitism, the Athens vs. Jerusalem dichotomy was not just an abstract intellectual phenomenon discussed among unworldly philosophers and intellectuals. If we look at the role of the dichotomy in the *Berliner Antisemitismusstreit*, it is significant that a major stir occurred when Heinrich von Treitschke allowed himself to re-interpret the German politician and historian Theodor W. Mommsen's outline of the role of the ancient Jews in shaping Western civilization from his *Römische Geschichte* (1854–85).[371] In the Danish civil sphere, the "Jew" Georg Brandes was continuously mocked for calling himself a Hellene, particularly by the previously mentioned Vilhelm Andersen, the first professor of Danish literature at the University of Copenhagen. Andersen is usually characterized as the most influential actor in the design of Danish language and literature teaching at university and gymnasium level in the twentieth century.[372] However, his racially based national conservative idealizations of the Danish *Volksgeist* are fundamentally connected to modern antisemitism, as can be seen in Brandes' portrayal in *Tider og Typer – Goethe II*.[373]

In the final section of this chapter, we will see how Brandes responds to the modern antisemitic perception of the role of Jews and Jewishness as subversive elements in European history. For Brandes, it was Athens and Jerusalem equally that shaped European civilization; as he writes in "Jobs Bog" (The Book of Job) (1893), "It is Hellas and Israel to which Europe owes its culture."[374] With his juxtaposition of Athens and Jerusalem, he emphasizes the indispensable role of Jewish civilization in the development of European civilization. We will see three examples of this in the analysis section. For the analysis of Brandes' re-interpretations, the following writings are used: *Det unge Tyskland* (1890), *Jobs Bog* (1893), *Kohélet* (1894), *Heinrich Heine* (1897), *Levned I–III* (1905–08), "Jøderne i Finland" (1908), *Smaa Romaner i Det Gamle Testamente, Sagnet om Jesus* (*The Legend of Jesus*) (1925), *Petrus* (1926), and *Urkristendommen* (1927). However, before we reach Brandes' re-interpretations of the dichotomy, we will first examine more substantially how the relation between Athens and Jerusalem became a vital part of the so-called Jewish Question from the Enlightenment onwards. Accordingly, in Brandes' reinterpretations of the Athens vs. Jerusalem dichotomy, his reflections on Jews and Jewishness as a founding and continuously co-constructive part of European civilization, from ancient to modern times, mirrored his own lifelong struggle with gaining proper recognition for his work. In fact, in his early writings, he did not question or seek to reshape the dichotomy. However, as modern antisemitism and the various European nationalistic movements grew from the 1880s on, they turned towards the role of Jews and Jewishness in the history of European civilization, and so did Brandes. He focuses particularly on this Jewish co-construction element in terms of the present-day Western democratic core values of universal justice and free rational thinking. But before we come to his reinterpretations, let us first examine more thoroughly how the Athens vs. Jerusalem dichotomy was developed.

The Athens vs. Jerusalem Dichotomy

The Athens vs. Jerusalem dichotomy is an intellectual historical topos concerning the influence of the ancient Greek and Jewish civilizations and religions on European civilization and Christianity. As Paul Rubow has already made clear in his doctoral thesis *Georg Brandes' Briller* (1932), one of the primary ideals throughout Brandes' oeuvre was indeed Hellenism. Consequently, as we will see in his re-interpretations of the dichotomy, Brandes did not neglect to emphasize the importance of Athens.

The dichotomy was particularly developed during the German Enlightenment, when the idealization of Athens and ancient Greek culture were promoted as part of the modern creation of history as a science. In a German historical context, late eighteenth-century and nineteenth-century "philhellenism" was to a large extent initiated by J. J. Winckelmann's *Geschichte der Kunst des Alterthums* (1755).[375] As Rubow attests, much of Brandes' fascination with Hellenism was arguably derived from J. J. Winckelmann, as well as Hegel's (Winckelmann-inspired) idealization of Athens. In *Geschichte der Kunst des Alterthums*, Winckelmann portrays the ancient Greek human being as a simple but proud, optimistic, strong, and rationally clever individual.[376] In the German Enlightenment, this ideal male Hellene figure came to stand as the authentic predecessor to the Enlightenment's modern human being.

It was an integral part of the Enlightenment movement to create strong narratives, supported by scientific evidence, about the origin of European civilization and Christianity in the Greek/Roman historical context, as Susannah Heschel describes it.[377] The early modern founders of history and historicity were particularly engaged in extricating Christianity from Judaism and making Christianity a fully independent religious tradition. As Heschel writes:

Historicism was not only on the rise in Europe, it was identified as a quintessentially European project, distinguishing the colonizer from the colonized [...] as much as theology gave rise to historicism, it was through the great nineteenth-century historicist project of determining the origins and originality of Christianity that Judaism's "inferiority" was transferred from the theological to the historicist realm.[378]

As Heschel elaborates, it became important to differentiate Christianity from Judaism and furthermore to demonstrate why this particular offspring of Judaism expressed the most truthful image of God and his ethics.[379]

The German Socrates

In the Introduction we saw that the most important eighteenth-century text on the question of the emancipation of the Jews, Dohm's essay *Über der bürgerliche Verbesserung der Juden,* contained deep ambiguities about how the Jews should be treated. These ambiguities came to influence the emancipation and acculturation process of the Western European Jews over the next 150 years. Dohm is convinced that Jews can be transformed into "useful citizens" but he does not argue that they should convert to Christianity and abandon the Jewish religion and its particularities. Yet Dohm also writes that Judaism designates Jews as superstitious and irrational, and he believed that almost all Jews were barbarians. His advice is that Christian teachers guide and instruct Jews on how to become enlightened individuals, leaving behind their "backwards" Jewish characteristics.

The "scandal of Jewish particularity" which Dohm's essay thematizes was also the subtext of many of the Athens vs. Jerusalem discussions of the Enlightenment period. Jewishness and the Jewish religious tradition were rejected as a constructive basis for an enlightened human being. A good example of this is the debate between the German Jewish philosopher Moses Mendelssohn and the Swiss theologian and philosopher Johann Caspar Lavater. Besides having been primarily shaped by an Ashkenazi Jewish *yeshiva* education, Mendelssohn was a self-taught man in the field of the Christian European philosophical tradition. Thus, not only for Lavater but for many Christian enlightenment thinkers, Mendelssohn presented a complex case, challenging the typical view on the *Bildung* Jews were assumed to achieve if they had been primarily formed by the Jewish tradition.

In *Jerusalem* (1783), Mendelssohn challenged the monopoly of Christian enlightenment thinkers over the foundation of Western civilization; he "posits monarchic Jerusalem rather than democratic Athens or republican Rome as his paradigm of the enlightened city."[380] Like Brandes, Mendelssohn also idealized Hellenism, and his *Phaidon* (1767) had earned him the moniker "the German Socrates."[381] *Phaidon* was a philosophical bestseller and Mendelssohn became the first European

Jew since Spinoza to have crossed the line and made a name for himself as a thinker and writer in Christian majority society.[382] In Switzerland, Mendelssohn had also impressed Lavater, who contacted him by letter in 1869. Lavater had become convinced that the author of *Phaidon* had now matured enough that a conversion to Christianity was the next logical step.[383] In other words, Mendelssohn's merits and his philosophical achievements were an unbearable provocation not only for Lavater but for many Christian thinkers, since he was rooted in the Jewish tradition. In his letter, Lavater asked Mendelssohn either to convert to Christianity or to refute Charles Bonnet's idea that Christianity could be proven truthful scientifically.[384] In an open letter answering him, Mendelssohn was able to refute this challenge by argumentation in which he equalized the status of Christianity and Judaism by claiming that both were so-called natural religions. According to Mendelssohn, both Christianity and Judaism were centered around a core of eternal reason that was reflected in their practice.[385] Although Lavater had to accept that Mendelssohn had won this battle in the civil sphere, he would not give up his negative view of Mendelssohn's Jewish background. Later, in his famous *Essay sur la Physiognomie* (1775–78), Lavater presented his theory on physiognomy, by means of which he was convinced that he could detect the underlying character of any individual by reading their facial features.[386] His conclusion after reading Mendelssohn's facial features was that "the antithesis of Mendelssohn's Jewish body and Greek soul was resolved in the synthesis of Christianity."[387] Thus, Lavater continued to label Mendelssohn an individual who transcended his Jewishness. Mendelssohn's talents and abilities reflected typical Christian and ancient European Greek virtues rather than typical Jewish traits, according to Lavater.

Hegel and Heine's Nazarenism

None of the examinations of the origins of the European civilization and Christianity were more controversial than the question of the Jewish identity of Jesus Christ. This is one of the subjects Brandes addresses, arguing in his last books that Jesus (and Christianity as a whole) was mainly based on messianic prophecies of Jewish prophets and fictional myths later constructed particularly by Paul; this was a typical European Jewish claim, which can also be found in many of the Sephardic Jewish writings of the Sephardic Jewish "Golden Age" and the Renaissance from Al-Andalus and the Iberian Peninsula.[388]

However, in the Enlightenment period, the tendency in the Athens vs. Jerusalem arguments was to de-Judaize Jesus and represent his Jewish origins as an aberration. A good example of this is Hegel's essay "Der Geist des Christentums und sein Schicksal" ("The spirit of Christianity and its fate") (1798–99), in which he characterizes the Jews in Jesus' time as a narrow-minded people, entrapped in the dogma of Orthodox Judaism:

In this miserable situation there must have been Jews of a better heart and head who could not renounce or deny their feelings of selfhood or stoop to become lifeless machines, there must have been aroused in them the need for nobler gratification than that of priding themselves on this mechanical slavery, the need for a freer activity than an existence with no self-consciousness, than a life spent in monkish preoccupation with petty mechanical spiritless and trivial usage. Acquaintances with foreign nations introduced some of them to the finer blossomings of the human spirit.[389]

As such, Hegel thought it possible that Jews could experience an "awakening to self-consciousness," indeed the Jews as Jews had "the potential for self-improvement," but this could not occur without the positive influence of an external culture.[390] Thus, Jesus was to Hegel, as for many eighteenth- and nineteenth-century Christian thinkers and writers, a Hellenized Jew: The positive elements of his teachings were derived from Hellenism.

Friedrich Nietzsche

Still, one should be wary of valorizing complex philosophers and their systems according to a cultural code such as that of the Athens vs. Jerusalem discussion; nuancing perspectives are required. If we look closer at how the dichotomy presents itself in the work of another of the afore-mentioned thinkers' work, Friedrich Nietzsche, we also find ambivalent and complex patterns in his interpretations.[391] In this context, it is relevant first to begin with Georg Brandes' unique role in the transformation of Friedrich Nietzsche from (having grown into) a pariah in German academia into a leading European philosopher. When in 1886/87 Friedrich Nietzsche sent his writings to Georg Brandes—who was by then the leading European arbiter of taste—Nietzsche had become desperate to reach his goal of revolutionizing philosophy and the philological tradition. Brandes quickly became fascinated by this eccentric German scholar's peculiar writings, and it was particularly because of the German translation of Brandes' introductory essay on Nietzsche that from 1889–90 Nietzsche's work was circulated among central actors and in-groups of the North European intellectual and artistic circles.[392] At the same time, one should not overestimate Nietzsche's influence on Brandes: It is true that Nietzsche led Brandes to create the ideal of "aristocratic radicalism" in this period,[393] but the idealization of "great men" as a primary force in leading and developing history and nations was already a significant feature in Brandes' doctoral thesis on Hippolyte Taine from 1869.[394] It was the German Romantic tradition of idealizing complex and heterogenic geniuses that first inspired Brandes (and Nietzsche too).[395] Brandes also refers to Ernest Renan and to Thomas Carlyle's *On Heroes – Hero Worship and The Heroic in History* (1841).[396] His early intellectual biographies of Benjamin Disraeli and Ferdinand Lasalle should in this context moreover be viewed as early products of his admiration of great men and their roles in shaping history. Still, Nietzsche doubtlessly revitalized and reinforced Brandes' idealization of great men and radical Romantic individualism in the latter half of the 1880s. In addition, as we will see later in this chapter, although Brandes never mentions Nietzsche in his writings on the Old Testament and early Christianity, his passionate re-positioning of Jerusalem was arguably also influenced by Nietzsche's elaborations on the Athens vs. Jerusalem dichotomy in his philosophical writings.

When enlisting Nietzsche as one of the many German philosophers who continues the dichotomizing tradition of Athens vs. Jerusalem, what has been termed Nietzsche's anti-antisemitism is a relevant nuancing perspective. As part of his representation of Jewishness, Nietzsche scorns the contemporary antisemitic movement in Germany, since antisemites were in his mind true representatives of slave moral. This corresponds to his definition of slave morality as a trait that does not belong only to Jewishness; it is a label for all those who oppose and struggle against the Superman morality. Accordingly, as Reinhard Rürup demonstrated in his classic documentation of the modern antisemitic movement in *Emanzipation und Antisemitismus* (1975), the key actors of this movement unquestionably identified themselves as victims of a Jewish-dominated *haut bourgeoisie* domination. Nietzsche viewed this resentment of the antisemites and their rebellion on the grounds of feelings of defeat and victimization as signs of slave moral.[397]

Nevertheless, it is important also to highlight the centrality of the downgrading of Jerusalem in Nietzsche's philosophy since Judaism clearly is constructed as the hub of the highly negative slave morality trait. Nietzsche does not represent Judaism and Christianity as two somewhat separated religious traditions, with Christianity representing a break from the Jewish religious tradition; rather, for him, Christianity merely reproduces Jewish slave morality.[398] The idea of slave morality is a typical example in eighteenth- and nineteenth-century German philosophy of how Jerusalem was downgraded while Athens was idealized (or at least, in Nietzsche's philosophy, the specific pre-Platonic era of Athens). As Miriam Leonard has argued, it is irrelevant in this context to dismiss Nietzsche's depiction of slave morality as a form of anti-Judaism that is somehow not as dangerous as secular-orientated modern antisemitism, since Nietzsche's depiction of Judaism is riddled with secular-orientated perspectives.[399]

Vilhelm Andersen and Modern Antisemitism

It is also interesting to observe precisely which Danish intellectual discussions of the Athens vs. Jerusalem dichotomy Brandes seems to be reacting to at the time when it became increasingly important for him to re-interpret the Athens vs. Jerusalem dichotomy, in his later writings. As racially based modern antisemitism grew, antisemitic attacks on Brandes also intensified within the Danish civil sphere. These attacks were often sophisticated, and filtered through the cultural code of the Athens vs. Jerusalem dichotomy. This is visible in writings on Brandes such as Konrad Simonsen's *Georg Brandes (Jødisk Aand i Danmark)* (*Georg Brandes (Jewish Spirit in Denmark)*) (1913) and the aforementioned Vilhelm Andersen's *Tider og Typer – Goethe II*.[400] While Konrad Simonsen's antisemitic attacks were not viewed as *salonfähig* in the Danish civil sphere when his book was published, the case of Vilhelm Andersen is different.

From the 1890s, Vilhelm Andersen wanted to create a different view of the Danish Romantic period than Brandes had in his early writings, and it was particularly Brandes' analysis of it as a somewhat unoriginal by-product of the German Romantic period in *Det Unge Tyskland* which provoked Vilhelm Andersen. Thus, today, Andersen is mostly known for his positive re-evaluation and construction of the Danish Romantic period as *Guldalderen* (The Golden Age), a notion that persists today. Through his position as the first professor in Danish literature at the University of Copenhagen, he shaped the way the subject was taught at university level and in the Danish gymnasium school, and he is still celebrated as the founding father of the pedagogy and didactics of literature in a Danish context.[401] However, while these achievements have been much written about,[402] none of the scholarly work on Andersen that I have come across addresses or even mentions the integral role racially based modern antisemitism played in his ideologically based literary method.

In *Tider og Typer – Goethe II*, in the chapter on the work and legacy of Georg Brandes, Andersen examines Brandes' idealization of Hellenism. In the process, he merges a racially based depiction of Brandes with Athens vs. Jerusalem interpretations. In the first pages, Andersen makes it clear that Brandes has never been and can never become a genuine Hellene (unlike Andersen himself), because of his Jewish blood:

No critic would dream of calling Georg Brandes a Greek mind. There is not a drop of Greek blood in him [...] of all the Greek writers, Lucian, an Assyrian, is the only one with whom his style has any similarity.[403]

Brandes' Jewishness means, in Andersen's view, that the only ancient Greek writer he could possibly bear a resemblance to is a Greek-influenced Semite, Lucian. Overall, the purpose of Andersen's *Tider og Typer* was to create a new canon of writers and works that had contributed the most to Danish literary history. He does not aim at isolating the Danish *Volksgeist* or segregating it from other European national traditions. Instead, following the typical patterns of Athens vs. Jerusalem interpretations since the Enlightenment period, he traces key characteristics of the Danish *Volksgeist* back to Athens. By contrast, Jerusalem and Jewishness are categorized as alien, non-European entities; all the European Jewish writers and intellectuals Andersen refers to in *Tider og Typer* are therefore determined as standing outside the European and Danish tradition—according to Andersen, their cultural contributions are useless and often even subversive. According to Andersen, while Danish and German writers such as Julius Lange and Goethe could truly understand the ancient European/Greek culture and fully incarnate the ideal of Hellenism, a non-Danish Jew such as Georg Brandes would never be able to grasp the depths of Athens-based European civilization. In this context, it is certainly interesting that Andersen is one of very few to show that as early as the latter part of the 1860s Brandes was becoming a non-dualistic materialistic Spinozist. According to Andersen, Brandes' cosmopolitan humanism thus fundamentally differs from the Protestant-based, otherwise typical tradition of humanism in Denmark which, according to him, is traceable in the writings of Søren Kierkegaard.[404] However, Andersen then uses his analysis of Brandes as a Spinozist cosmopolitan to reproduce and reinforce some rather stereotypical views. He ends his reflections on Brandes as a follower of Spinoza by referring to the very first reaction Brandes was met with when he participated in a public debate in Denmark. As touched upon already, the leading Norwegian writer Bjørnstjerne Bjørnson made a strong effort to exclude Brandes from *Tro og Viden Debatten* (The Debate on Faith and Science) because, according to Bjørnson, he was un-Danish. In *Tider og Typer – Goethe II*, Andersen refers to this episode and links it to his analysis of Brandes as a Jewish Spinozist: "In a way, Bjørnstjerne, in an article in 'Fædrelandet', was able with some justification to dispute whether he had a 'Danish consciousness'."[405] For Andersen, it is symptomatic that Brandes' understanding of Hellenism was based on a specific Jewish perception of Athens, particularly through the German Jew Heinrich Heine's interpretations of Hellenism.[406] Jørgen Knudsen documents in his biography how Brandes had previously ignored Andersen's characterization of him as an alien Jew who could never become Danish, which Andersen had again and again publicly declared since the 1890s. After *Tider og Typer – Goethe II*, however, Brandes refused to talk to Andersen again.[407]

It is of course relevant to ask whether it is necessary to dwell on racially based modern antisemitism as a fundamental part of what the founding father of Danish literature pedagogy wrote around 1920. This was indeed many years before Hitler gained power in Germany or the Holocaust took place. However, in remembering the legacy of Vilhelm Andersen, it is important to address the unfinished *Tider og Typer* literary history since he himself considered it to be his opus magnum. Furthermore, as mentioned in the Introduction, it is one of the key aims of this book to point out that historical research that focuses merely on the period 1933–45 as the time when racially based modern antisemitism became a dangerously dominant cultural code will only see the culmination of a longer historical course of interconnected events and narratives. Thus, it was not in Hitler's Nazi Germany that the identity characteristics of cosmopolitanism, Jewishness, strangeness, and rootlessness were originally linked and became a dominant cultural code. Still, if we follow the logic of looking only at the 1930s and 1940s and ask whether Andersen continued to connect cultural and political ideological thinking, in 1940 he in fact was among those who signed the declaration of the totalitarian-oriented *Højgaardkreds* (*Højgaard* circle).[408] Consisting of many prominent Danish businessmen alongside intellectuals such as Andersen, *Højgaardkredsen* aimed to overthrow the democratically elected Danish government of the time. It intended to implement a totalitarian right-wing regime in Denmark that, ideologically, resembled the German Nazi regime. In this way, even if we follow this restricted logic, it is about time that the legacy of Vilhelm Andersen is re-considered.

"The Entire Country was Steeped in Judaism"

I will now move on to Brandes' counter-reactions to the dominant pattern of the interpretations of the Athens vs. Jerusalem dichotomy since the Enlightenment period by focusing on three different re-interpretations of the Athens vs. Jerusalem dichotomy in his later writings. As it is the case in the context of most of Brandes' interconnections of cosmopolitanism and Jewishness, all three should be understood as related to contextually bounded discussions of the so-called Jewish Question of the fin-de-siècle period. In this period, as seen through Vilhelm Andersen's *Tider og Typer*, the Athens vs. Jerusalem interpretations merged with racially based modern antisemitism, by which the exclusion and stigmatization of individuals of Jewish descent became *salonfähig*. Brandes' re-interpretations of the dichotomy should also be viewed as developments of his own previous ideas —as well as those of other European Jewish writers—about Jewishness and the role of Jewish civilization in the forming of Western civilization. The first example is Brandes' reaction to a wave of accusations launched against him by the leading Danish bourgeois newspapers when he returned from his exile in Berlin in 1883. His responses to these accusations seem to be closely related to Benjamin Disraeli's idea of the "Semitic Principle," which Brandes had originally argued against in his biography of Disraeli in 1878.[409]

In order to understand why Brandes lived in Berlin from 1877 to 1883, we must go back to 1872. Following the publication of *Emigrantlitteraturen*, Brandes endured attacks from leading Danish newspapers and public figures who argued that his postulated "Jewish" work was a threat to the order of society and an attempt to subvert the national tradition. In the following years, mainly because of the stir that *Emi-grantlitteraturen* had caused, it became difficult for Brandes even to earn a living in Denmark. As a result, he moved to Berlin in 1877. In Berlin, he wrote journalistic articles for German, Austrian, and French newspapers, as well as the few Danish newspapers and magazines that would still publish his work. He returned to Copenhagen in 1883, when a group of men from the bourgeoisie (the majority of whom were also of Jewish descent) offered him a monthly salary to come back and work as a scientist and intellectual.[410] Brandes accepted this offer and moved back to Copenhagen. In his answering letter, he stressed that his reason for accepting was that he would now be able to live as a "Danish scientist."[411] However, the same national conservative/national liberal Danish newspapers that had made a strong effort to stigmatize him as subversive in 1872 reacted by publishing a wave of inflammatory articles, criticizing this offer as well as Brandes as a person. Consequently, in the first example of Brandes' re-interpretations of the Athens vs. Jerusalem dichotomy (taken from his autobiography *Levned I–III* (*Recollections of My Childhood and Youth I–III*), 1905–08), he also recounted this wave of accusations against him in 1883. He sums up the national conservative/national liberal categorization of him as un-Danish. According to Brandes, his opponents framed the conflict as follows: "My standpoint was Jewish, theirs was national" ("Mit standpunkt var jødisk, deres var nationalt").[412] As such, his opponents represented Jewishness as a synonym for being non-Danish, but one could also connect Brandes' use of the word Jewish, *jødisk*, in this sentence with the term "cosmopolitan," since this was/is the most adequate antonym for national.[413] In the following version of his Semitic principle in *Levned*, Brandes sets forth a complex representation of Jewishness while responding to the newspapers' allegations against him.[414] He develops the accusations that he was an un-Danish cosmopolitan Jew into a history lesson in which Jewishness comes to signify the civilizational foundation of Denmark/Europe:

Never in my life had I emphasized or so much as drawn attention to any Jewish view [...]. Without wavering in the slightest [...] I had, from that day when

I made a public appearance, positioned myself, as almost the only person in the country, in clear opposition to Judaism with all of its offshoots, including Lutheranism. The entire country was steeped in Judaism, ancient Jewish culture, ancient Jewish barbarism. All was Jewish, even the peasant names, Hans and Jens [...]. The children were taught Jewish legends before they were taught Danish legends, Jewish history before Danish history, but above all the Jewish religion. A Jewish God was worshipped, as was the son of a Jewish woman as the son of God and God Himself. The festivals of the people were the Jewish festivals, Easter and Whitsun, and Christmas celebrated the son of a Jewish mother seated at the right hand of the Creator. The priests preached to me from the country's pulpits. They stood up for the venerability of Jewish books, nay their [...] infallibility, their eternal value. Their conception of law was Jewish from the year 5000 BC, their notion of grace Jewish from the year 50 AD [...]. To me, however, they talked as though Christianity had sprung from Denmark, as though it was anything but Judaism converted and further developed with added mysticism. [415]

Brandes begins his response to the claim that he has a Jewish mindset by distancing himself from Jewishness: "Never in my life had I emphasized or so much as drawn attention to any Jewish view." However, in the following lines, he also draws attention to the Jewish co-construction of European civilization, identifying the underlying basis for Danish society today (culturally, juridically, and theologically) as originally invented by the ancient Jewish people. For this reason, according to Brandes, it is absurd that his ideas are reduced and stereotyped as negatively "Jewish," since everything in Denmark is based on Jerusalem. In the passage quoted above, there is also an element of denigration of the ancient Jewish/present-day Danish civilization, in the phrase "Jewish barbarism." However, unlike the typical depictions of Jerusalem as backwards—as seen in Lavater's work for example—here the Jewish civilization is not simply a historical entity, and Brandes does not label Christianity as a further developed civilizational stage in comparison to Judaism. By contrast, Christianity is described as "Judaism [...] with added mysticism." Brandes claims that most of present Danish culture and society is still based on a fossilized civilization, meaning nineteenth-century Christianity and Danish society are still caught in pre-modern dogma obstructing a progressive development of the country. Furthermore, he does not count himself as part of this still visible Jewish/Danish stage of civilization: "Never in my life had I emphasized or so much as drawn attention to any Jewish view."

In this context, it could be argued that Brandes drew influence from Nietzsche's distinction between slave and Superman morality. At this time, Brandes indeed believed that he had developed a modern, individualistic mindset, while the majority of the Danish population and the Danish cultural tradition were still caught in a fossilized and backwards pre-modern mindset. In the second version of his reinterpretation of the Athens vs. Jerusalem dichotomy, in "Jøderne i Finland" (The Jews in Finland), he elaborates more on this contrast:

How droll! The one thing I am not, in the deeper sense, is that! [a Jew]. The whole of Denmark [...] is steeped in Judaism, its God is Jewish, its celebrations are Jewish, its religion is Judaism converted and further developed with a few mystical trappings [...]. The Old Testament is [...] written by Jews [...]. There was once a time when I was almost the only person in the country who was not a Jew. And yet one could say that the one thing which is universally known about me in this country and the one thing which is continually communicated about me abroad is that I am that. [...] and although I was the first to return to Athens, they never rest from tracing me back to this Jerusalem, which they cannot let go of.[416]

In both *Levned* and this passage from "Jøderne i Finland", Brandes' argument operates with two civilizational stages (similar to Pontoppidan's "plan" of *Lykke-Per*). The second, more advanced civilization resembles Brandes' idea of modern Jewishness, which Chapters 1 and 2 examined in detail. At this point it seems that Brandes continues to conceive of himself as having achieved this modern mindset, while most Danes have yet to do so. In both versions, Brandes describes two different civilizations struggling with each other in Denmark and across Europe at this time; he clearly perceives most Danes as still caught in a nationally enclosed mindset. According to Brandes, it is as such an historical absurdity to claim that Jews can never be considered Danish since everything in Denmark is built on what were originally Jewish cultural and religious features.

Nazarenism vs. Hellenism

In Brandes' second re-interpretation of the Athens vs. Jerusalem dichotomy, we again observe him reacting against not only typical views on ancient Jewish civilization and Judaism, but also his own former ideas on the dichotomy that he now needed to alter and nuance. The first appearances of the Nazarenism vs. Hellenism version of the dichotomy in his works are in *Det unge Tyskland* (1890) and *Heinrich Heine* (1897) (the portrait of Heinrich Heine in 1897 is mostly a reproduction of that in *Det unge Tyskland* (1890)). In these two books, Brandes characterizes Heine as the climax and leading figure of the literary movement *Das junge Deutschland,* in which both Berthold Auerbach and Karl Gutzkow also participated.[417] Brandes presents the dichotomy while addressing Heine's description of another German Jewish writer, Ludwig Börne, as a "Nazarene":

The reader doubtless remembers the passage in Heine's book on Börne in which he writes on Börne's Nazarenic narrow-mindedness. He tells us that he calls it "Nazarenic" to avoid using the words Jewish or Christian, as to him these words convey the same meaning, and he does not use them to designate a faith but a natural disposition; and he contrasts the word Nazarenic with the word Hellenic, which to him also signifies an innate or acquired disposition and general point of view. In other words, all of humanity is divided into Nazarenes and Hellenes, either people of ascetic, image-hating disposition, inclined to morbid spiritualisation, or people of cheerful, realistic temperament, inclined to self-development. And he designates himself a Hellene.[418]

Although this characterization of Börne is initially Heine's and not Brandes', Brandes appears drawn to the Nazarenism vs. Hellenism dichotomy in *Det unge Tyskland.* Not only does he reuse the exact same passage in his biography of Heine in 1897, he also uses it in the first part of this book on Heine; it frames his further description of Heine as a unique and genius Hellenized German Jewish writer in the biography.[419] Brandes explains that Heine's Nazarenism vs. Hellenism dichotomy paraphrases Hegel's view of Hellenism as the positive foundation and the ancient Jewish religion as a "false start" for European civilization, as we saw earlier in this chapter.[420] Hegel had identified Judaism as the catalyst for Christianity and thus represented Jerusalem (again) as an unconstructive basis for Christianity and European civilization in his (and Heine's) depiction of the dichotomy.[421] It was only due to the Hellenization of Jesus Christ that ancient Jewish characteristics had been made a useful basis for European civilization.

When Brandes first represents Nazarenism vs. Hellenism, imitating Heine (imitating Hegel), it seems that he agrees with Hegel's view on ancient Jewish civilization and Judaism as a "false start" for European civilization. However, in Brandes' two later books, *Sagnet om Jesus* (1925) and *Urkristendommen* (1927), he again calls attention to the term "Nazarenism." In both books, he is oddly engaged in discussing the etymological and historical background of the word; however, according to Brandes, "the Nazarenes" denotes a minor, radical Jewish sect that interpreted Judaism in a radical way compared to the majority of the ancient Jewish people. He explains this new-fangled view of Nazarenism most extensively in *Sagnet om Jesus*:

The second chapter concludes by saying that Joseph came to live in a town called Nazareth so that it should come to pass what the prophets had said. He shall be called a Nazarene. It has been noted in studies that there is no mention anywhere in the Old Testament, in the works of Josephus or in the Talmud of a place called by such name. With the exception of the Gospels, the name is unknown until the fourth century. Recent theologians have certainly wanted to assert the firm belief of first-century Christians that Jesus originated from Nazareth [...]. In all likelihood there was no such place by the name of Nazareth [...]. William B. Smith, upon studying the Epiphanius, proved that a Jewish sect called the Nazarenes existed before the Christian era. In their orthodoxy they recognised no later figure than Joshua, whose name is indeed the same as Jesus, and they seem in some way or another to have merged with the Christians, who merely pronounced their name Nazorean instead of Nazarene. [422]

In *Sagnet om Jesus* and *Urkristendommen*, Brandes does not change his purely negative view of Nazarenism. However, he does alter its scope: It is no longer identical to the whole civilization and the whole religious tradition of the ancient Jewish people. Rather, it was a particular interpretation of Judaism, which originally stemmed from members of a small, extreme sect, who deliberately broke free from the core group's existing perception of Judaism.[423] Later, this small sect developed into and merged with the early Christian movement, according to Brandes.[424]

This view was highly controversial in the 1920s and in his last books on early Christianity Brandes once again—one last time before he died— found himself in the midst of a heated debate when these books were published between 1925 and 1927. In fact, with his re-definition of the term Nazarenism in *Sagnet om Jesus* and *Urkristendommen*, Brandes wrote himself into an old Jewish tradition that later was revitalized as a modern radical Enlightenment tradition; it was particularly present in the Sephardic Jewish Golden Age and later the early eighteenth century. For example, in the Marquis d'Argens' radical Enlightenment text *Lettres Juives* (1738–42), the Sephardic Jewish travelling narrators also label the Christians Nazarenes.[425] According to Adam Sutcliffe, the Marquis d'Argens was as such part of an intellectual trend in which radical European Christian-born thinkers and writers picked up on the Muslim and Jewish tradition of calling Christians Nazarenes in order to subordinate Judaism to Christianity.[426] Sutcliffe also points out that the first of the early radical Enlightenment thinkers to pick up the term "Nazarene" and use it as a synonym for "Christian" was John Toland. Toland's use of the term was not particularly philosemitic—on the contrary, he "draws a sharp distinction between the Nazarene Jews who acknowledges Jesus and those others who did not" by favoring the "Nazarene Jews", the early "Christians" who acknowledged Jesus. It is thus not until later that the use of "Nazarene" by an Enlightenment thinker such as the Marquis d'Argens reflects what could be defined as philosemitism. Thus, "Argens inverts the conventional understanding of the relationship between the two faiths, casting Judaism as the more universal creed, and Christianity as its schismatic offshoot."[427] The radical Enlightenment tradition of calling Christians Nazarenes was a way of challenging the Christian clerical authoritarian power.

To sum up, it is striking that in the last four books Brandes wrote before he died, he was highly preoccupied with re-interpretations of the Athens vs Jerusalem dichotomy. In one of these books, *Petrus* (1926), he even remarks that the antisemitism of the 1920s was originally begun by the early Christians'—in his view—fictional creation of the character of Judas.[428] Moreover, as part of the Athens vs. Jerusalem discussions, in all of these books, he clearly opposes the view that Christianity was a more rational and enlightened religion than Judaism. Instead, he represents Christianity as the product of ascetic, narrow-minded Nazarenism, and as a historically random and irrational "schismatic offshoot" of Judaism.

And Justice For All

The two interpretations of the Athens vs. Jerusalem dichotomy by Brandes presented so far are complex and ambivalent. A less ambivalent version of the juxtaposition of Athens and Jerusalem is to be found in *Jobs Bog* (1893) and *Kohélet* (1894), where Brandes reflects on how the books of the Old Testament reveal the cosmopolitan-oriented values and virtues on which the modern world, in his mind, must be built.

In *Jobs Bog*, the juxtaposition of Athens and Jerusalem is in fact made at the very beginning of the text, as a hint at what the following text aims to demonstrate. Brandes writes that "It is Hellas and Israel to which Europe owes its culture."[429] In both these texts, Brandes then presents a specific Jewish characteristic, traceable back to the ancient Jewish world, as the central virtue which has incarnated the Jewish spirit since ancient times. Accordingly, for Brandes, universal justice is a fundamental Western value that originates in the Jewish tradition.

Brandes' treatment of this virtue as originally Jewish aligned with that of the German Jewish nineteenth-century intellectual, Heinrich Graetz, whom Brandes comments on in *Kohélet*.[430] However, unlike Brandes, Graetz tended to create a reversed dichotomy; he downgraded the contributions of Athens in comparison to those of Jerusalem, whereas Brandes insisted on valuing both of these ancient civilizations.[431] In the following, we see Brandes' reflections on universal justice as a central Jewish trait in his *Jobs Bog*:

The question examined in the Book of Job is the central question of Judaism, namely this: How is it that under the righteous rule of God, evil so often has good fortune on its side, while the righteous are no less often struck by undeserved misfortune? For the Israelite this is the fundamental question. The struggle against this conundrum constitutes the entire inner history of Judaism.[432]

Following this, Brandes philologically determines that the version of the Book of Job which appears in the Old Testament is the work of more than one author. He is mainly interested in the oldest, original part of the text, which he argues was written before Judaism was clerically institutionalized.[433] He then goes on to disqualify the parts which appear to him to have been dictated later by clerical authorities so that the work fitted into a certain religious-clerical system.[434]

As regards *Kohélet*, Brandes determines that it was written by a rational-minded spirit who celebrates free thinking and enjoying life and its pleasures as the most important virtues, besides the question of universal justice.[435] According to Brandes, the text was probably written around the 1st century BC, and he suspects with the primarily ideological purpose of criticizing a specific orthodox interpretation of Judaism which had become popular and influential at the time.[436] He compares this orthodox interpretation of Judaism to the Protestant revival movement of Pietism.[437] Self-abnegation was being preached then, he writes, and the leading authorities of the Jewish state supported the puritan interpretation of Judaism. Still, he believes that the author of *Kohélet* did not intend to criticize Judaism, but to demonstrate that historically a different interpretation of Judaism existed which celebrated the principles of universal justice, free rational thinking, and enjoying life (rather than maintaining a guilt-weighed, dogmatic religious outlook, which Brandes most likely perceived as the opposite of this kind of world view). It is this interpretation of Judaism Brandes wishes to call attention to in his critical reading of *Kohélet*. He shows that this different line of thinking in ancient Jewish civilization and religion continued to exist after the second temple was destroyed, in the Jewish diaspora. For two thousand years the virtue of universal justice continued to be a key element in Jewish thought, according to Brandes, while also contributing to the development of European civilization through the work of different Jewish writers and thinkers:

Not resisting evil is a Christian concept, in which many, from antiquity to Tolstoy in our day, see the essence of Christianity. Never has subjection to injustice been a virtue for the Jew [...]. The man whom the Jew extols is not the holy one; it is the righteous one [...] since Jews have wished to realise the ideal of righteousness here on Earth, they have, in the modern era, had a hand in revolutions. Kabbalistic Jews were instrumental in the establishment of Freemasonry, the Jews in France (again in Paris), few in number, were participants in the revolution, three of them occupied important positions and died on the scaffold, half of the founders of Saint-Simonianism were Jews, men of financial wisdom such as Olinde Rodrigues, Eichtal and Isaa Pereire. Artists such as the composer Felicien David and the poet Heine joined their ranks. At the emergence of liberal thinking, Manin becomes its hero in Italy, Börne its spokesman in Germany, Jellinek its agitator and martyr in Austria, Moritz Hartmann its spokesman in Frankfurt and its champion in Vienna. German socialism is founded by Karl Marx and Lassalle. Russian nihilism has been heavily subscribed to by young Jewish students, many of whom have sacrificed their lives.[438]

Although Nietzsche and the slave morality is not mentioned in any of Brandes' books on the creation of ancient Judaism, Brandes' reflection on justice and his presentation of the will to fight for universal justice as a particular Jewish trait could still be interpreted as a counter-reaction to Nietzsche's idea of slave morality as Jewish virtue which later "poluted" Christianity fundamentally. In the passage quoted above, Brandes constructs a narrative by which the Jewish will to fight for universal justice is emphasized and where sacralized subjugation is a Christian virtue. In *Kohélet*, the Jewish attachment to justice is furthermore linked to the universal virtue of free rational thinking:

He [the author of Kohélet] is the first clear type characterised by liberal, refined Israelite intelligence. After him come Philo and the Alexandrians, after them the Jewish polemicists, who inspired Celsus, who was refuted by Origen; after them follow the group of Talmudists who, in the tenth century, wished to uphold religion through a philosophy emphasising that the authority of reason existed alongside religion [...] they are followed in the eleventh century by Ibn Gabirol, who with his work *The Fountain of Life* strongly influenced Arabic philosophy, and Mainomides, who in his principal work attempted to unite and reconcile Aristotle's philosophy with Judaism [...] from the tenth century to the fifteenth century we see Jewish rationalists and thinkers preoccupied with preparing for that revolution in human history which was the Renaissance. They establish the principles of exegesis, which gradually becomes a liberating force, they criticize the Christian dogmas and symbols, they spread the Arabic philosophy to Europe [...] they were highly active, cherished, even pampered at the court of the great Emperor Frederick II, the centre of religious indifference, of forbearance and of free thinking at the beginning of the thirteenth century. Ibn Gabirol's *Fountain of Life* inspires Giordano Bruno and his adoration of the universe. The thousand-year preoccupation with the Bible by interpreters of Jewish scripture lays the foundation for Luther's translation of the Bible and leads to the principle of free study. In the seventeenth century, this tradition culminates in Spinoza's *Theological-Political Treatise*.[439]

Again, unlike Nietzsche's idea of Judaism as a false start for Christianity and European civilization and also his idea of Plato and Socrates as the first philosophers to focus on rationality as a central virtue, Brandes highlights ancient Judaism as the original source for the European tradition of free rational thinking.

Brandes' focus on the cosmopolitan-oriented virtues of universal justice and free, rational thinking as original Jewish traits are thus key examples of his portrayal of Jerusalem in his later writings. However, in neither *Jobs Bog* nor *Kohélet* does Brandes reverse the dichotomy to denigrate Athens on behalf of Jerusalem. Instead, he maintains that together Athens and Jerusalem are to be seen as the positive underlying basis for European civilization. As he writes in *Jobs Bog*: "It is Hellas and Israel to which Europe owes its culture."[440]

Conclusion

In this chapter, we have seen that although in his later work Brandes abandons the concept of race and ceases to idealize the particular Jewish racial heritage, his interconnections of Jewishness and cosmopolitanism follow the same pattern we witnessed in his early writings. He thus distances himself from Jewishness while simultaneously emphasising the Jewish co-construction of Western civilization. Still, in his later writings, we do find a difference in the pattern of his interconnections. In several writings on ancient Judaism and early Christianity, Brandes develops his thoughts on Jews and Jewishness as playing a key role in the definition of cosmopolitan-oriented Western core values. For example, he presents the Jewish tradition as the hub of the present-day Western liberal democratic virtues of universal justice and free rational thinking.

In Brandes' early writings, the modern Jew and the cosmopolitan ideal of the transnational vision were a vision of the future. He created this vision in support of his own struggles in the civil sphere at the time these writings were published. In this way, the modern Jew and other Jewish-related themes, for example the exile and emigrant/stranger experience in *Emigrantlitteraturen*, became an indispensable part of Brandes' Modern Breakthrough project; they were vital building blocks in putting forward his vision of how to be modern.

In his later writings, Brandes goes back to ancient times, historically speaking. He re-invents the extant interpretations of the past, arguing that Jewishness should be viewed as an ancient foundation of Western civilization. This re-orientation toward the past seems to be part of his reaction to the rise of modern antisemitism. In the "purified" antisemitic versions of the European national histories, migration, mobility, and Jewishness were reduced to threatening external categories in the tracing of the authentic essences of the national traditions. By contrast, Brandes' objective in his re-interpretations of the Athens vs. Jerusalem dichotomy is to demonstrate that the ancient Jewish civilization, together with the ancient Greek culture, is the foundation of European civilization and Christianity and that the most important elements in this Jewish co-construction are cosmopolitan-oriented values. However, his arguments are not limited to the ancient period. He represents Baruch Spinoza, whom he elsewhere calls the father of the modern world, as a key part of this Jewish tradition. It is clear, too, that Brandes' interpretations of the past and ancient Jewish civilization should be viewed as a *Geschehen* bounded to a modern context, and thus as a reaction to growing modern antisemitism in the period when he published them.

In conclusion, at first glance Brandes' self-fashioning in *Levned* and his editing of *Samlede Skrifter* might seem to show him only distancing himself further from Jewishness, and pursuing an identity as a fully assimilated Dane. However, in several writings that so far have mainly been considered marginal and unimportant in his oeuvre, and particularly in his re-interpretations of the Athens vs. Jerusalem dichotomy (and the role Spinoza is given in these re-interpretations, addressed in the following chapter), it is evident that he continues to emphasize the Jewish co-construction of Western civilization. Thus, his new focus on re-inventing the past is better understood as a vital cosmopolitan-oriented reaction to growing nationalism and antisemitism in this period. In short, one could say that Brandes reflects more substantially on Jewishness and the Jewish tradition in his later writings, elaborating on the modern Jewish cosmopolitan ideas about justice as a central virtue found in his early writings.

Chapter 5

Brandes' Spinozist Cosmopolitanism in his Later Writings

Introduction

Georg Brandes' fascination with Baruch Spinoza is visible throughout his adult life. Although his autobiography shows him making a considerable effort to distancing himself from Jewishness, he still describes how as a young man he chose Baruch Spinoza to be his intellectual and spiritual mentor and guide in life. This choice was the culmination of his greatest existential crisis in 1861–1862, catalyzed by his father's bankruptcy and the devastating effect it had on his family. The Brandes family was forced to move from an upper middle-class street in Copenhagen, *Kronprinsensgade* (Crown Prince Street), to a lower class street, *Laksegade* (Salmon Street); in his autobiography, he writes that every night in this neighborhood he could hear the screams of working-class women as they were beaten by their drunk husbands, numb from the consumption of *brændevin* (schnapps).

In this period, Brandes' personal existential crisis had more to do with the fact that he had for some time meditated on two fundamentally different paths in life. Either he should convert to Protestantism, from which quarter the philosophy of Søren Kierkegaard had been his greatest inspiration (as well as the influence and campaigning of friends such as Julius Lange), or he would choose the materialistic and pantheistic world view of Baruch Spinoza. In *Levned*, Brandes explains how this inner conflict escalated during the summer, and describes with great pathos how the crisis peaked as he forced himself to make a choice between these two paths:

Here I stood at the source of the philosophy of Pantheism in the modern era. Here the philosophy was yet more evidently religion, in that it replaced religion [...]. His [Spinoza's] personality fascinated, the human greatness in him, one of the greatest in history. I felt an urge to act as a preacher for the surrounding world, for the thoughtless and hard-hearted [...]. I began to consider it my duty, as soon as I had the skill, to go out into the town and to preach on every street corner, I devised trials with my body to bring it completely under my power, ate as little as possible, slept on the bare floorboards to become accustomed to the hardiness which I sought. I strove to quell the stirring youthful sensuality in me and gradually gained full control over myself so that I could be what I wanted to be, a willing and powerful instrument in the struggle for the triumph of truth. [441]

Thus, Brandes chooses Baruch Spinoza—his pantheism, materialistic philosophy and life example. Yet, in previous research on Brandes, and contrary to Brandes' own choice, there has been a marked focus on Søren Kierkegaard's Protestant-based philosophy influence on him. A number of books and articles have been written about how Kierkegaard directly and indirectly inspired Brandes.[442] However, as can be seen, Brandes himself writes in his autobiography and in several other texts, that it was not Kierkegaard but Baruch Spinoza who was his fundamental intellectual and even spiritual guide in life. It therefore seems more appropriate to focus on this influence.

Baruch Spinoza (1632–1677) is one of the most influential philosophers in modern times. Born in Amsterdam to Portuguese Sephardic immigrants, Spinoza created a non-dualistic materialistic philosophy. With his *Tractatus Theologico-Politicus* (1670), he is also considered the founder of modern Bible criticism. Ideologically speaking, the *Tractatus* is a early modern liberal cosmopolitan manifesto, positing individual freedom, universal justice, and democracy as central ideals humanity must strive to achieve, as a whole and collectively.[443] According to Spinoza, the chief obstacle in his time to liberal universalism was the religious dogmatism of Christianity (and Judaism). The *Tractatus* is first and foremost a critical reading of the Old Testament in its oldest

Hebrew version; Spinoza convincingly demonstrates how some of the most basic Christian interpretations of the Old Testament, in its Greek Vulgate version, can in fact be doubted. By questioning several parts of this canonized Greek translation, he not only secularizes the Old Testament, reading it as a piece of literature influenced by historical context; his ultimate goal was to question and thus dissolve the powerful Christian (and Jewish) dogma and clericalism. According to Spinoza, Christian dogma was the prime force holding European societies in a static, feudal iron grip.

Georg Brandes was a sworn cosmopolitan, and it has already been argued that his cosmopolitanism changed throughout his oeuvre regarding the way he balances his cosmopolitan and particularistic/national outlooks.[444] In his early writings, Brandes was a strong cosmopolitan, and through modern Jewishness and the transnational vision ideal he envisioned a progressive future where a transformed universal humanity had grown out of all religious and cultural particularities. Later, he came to acknowledge that national culture would continue to be a key factor in understanding cultural and political matters, and he was, in particular, engaged in describing growing nationalism and antisemitism around Europe. Nevertheless, so far, there have been no examinations of which tradition Brandes was referring to when he called himself a cosmopolitan; the few times he himself referred to any such tradition, he called Spinoza the father of his cosmopolitanism, both in his early and later writings.[445]

In this chapter, I will shed light on a central element of Brandes' Spinozist cosmopolitanism traceable in his later writings. In *Jobs Bog* (1893), *Kohélet* (1894), and *Smaa Romaner i Det Gamle Testamente* (1914), Brandes portrays Spinoza as part of a Jewish tradition of secular thought, following the cosmopolitan ideals he treasures the most back to this tradition. It is important to note that Brandes investigated Spinozist cosmopolitanism while he was writing his Athens vs. Jerusalem re-interpretations. The two themes are deeply interrelated and frequently the same passages can be said to be both re-interpretations of the Athens vs. Jerusalem dichotomy and examples of Brandes' Spinozist cosmopolitanism.

The aspect of Brandes' Spinozist cosmopolitanism in focus in this chapter is similar to his Athens vs. Jerusalem interpretations in that he again goes against the dominant idea of a solely Christian Western European modernity in which the "backward" and "fossilized" Jewish tradition played no role. As we will see, he argues that the intellectual basis for European modernity was not created primarily by philosophers and writers such as Diderot and Immanuel Kant who were shaped by the Christian Western European tradition. By contrast, he claimed that Baruch Spinoza was the father of European modernity and the culmination of a Jewish tradition of secular thought, which goes back to ancient times. Brandes thus defined a "history of modernity" that was very different from the one typically presented in Europe at the time.

The biased view of the origins of European modernity still exists in today's literature on cosmopolitanism. Most texts see themselves as followers of a tradition in which Immanuel Kant is presented as the founder of Western cosmopolitanism in modern times. As such, Brandes' views represent a valuable alternative cosmopolitan archive, not least because he determines Spinozist cosmopolitanism to be more orientated toward practice and less dreamy than the Christian-influenced Greek/Roman-Kantian cosmopolitan tradition.

This chapter will pursue an understanding of Brandes' reception of Spinoza through one of Brandes' favorite books of the 1860s, Berthold Auerbach's *Bildungsroman Spinoza* (1837/56). Auerbach's novel is part of the vast pool of works of Spinozism containing depictions of the life example of Spinoza combined with different highlighted elements of his philosophy. In this context, it is important to clarify that "works of Spinozism" do not include Spinoza's own work. Rather, Spinozist works are *about* Baruch Spinoza as a life example. In these works, Baruch Spinoza is usually celebrated as a hero, as the first modern man; Auerbach's novel thus depicts Spinoza as a secular Messiah, who actively freed himself from all former particularistic bonds. In his later work Brandes was preoccupied with the study of "great men," geniuses, and

Spinoza was perhaps his favored hero—as Brandes himself attests in *Levned*. The goals of this chapter are therefore: 1) to demonstrate how Spinozist cosmopolitanism differs from the tradition of Kantian cosmopolitanism; 2) to reconstruct Brandes' Spinozist cosmopolitanism and his perception of Spinoza as the culmination of a Jewish tradition of secular thought through a reading of Berthold Auerbach's *Spinoza*; and 3) to demonstrate why Brandes' Spinozist cosmopolitanism is a valuable cosmopolitan archive for today's literature on cosmopolitanism (a topic to which I shall return in the discussion section).

The Philosophical and Literary Background of Brandes' Spinozist Cosmopolitanism

In the blossoming of literature on cosmopolitanism in the last two decades, [446] the research has concentrated on two different but connected areas. The concept of cosmopolitanism has often been used in the analysis of our present sociological condition,[447] as well as in the denouncing of different normative standpoints on the basis of which a particular ethical outlook and practice is emphasized in relation to the increasing mobility, interconnectedness and global exchanges that characterize the modern world.[448] There has been less focus on what Sheldon Pollock, Homi K Bhabha, Carol A. Breckenridge, and Dipesh Chakrabarty have called "cosmopolitan archives," or the "past embodiments" of cosmopolitanisms that are discovered and suggested as useful perspectives for today.[449] Here I will argue that Georg Brandes represents a relevant cosmopolitan archive for today's literature on cosmopolitanism. However, in order to demonstrate this, it is necessary first to point out the difference between the tradition most literature today sees itself as following, namely Kantian cosmopolitanism, and the tradition Brandes referred to when he called himself a cosmopolitan in the Spinozist tradition.

Kant's Cosmopolitanism

When writings on cosmopolitanism today place themselves in an intellectual tradition that sees Immanuel Kant as its founding modern father, the references are predominantly to "Idee zu einer allgemeinen Geschichte in weltbürgerlicher Absicht" (1784) and "Zum ewigen Frieden. Ein philosophischer Entwurf" (1795). Undoubtedly, these two essays by Kant are historically significant texts. The formulation of our modern-day Human Rights, for example, owes a great deal to "Idee zu einer allgemeinen Geschichte in weltbürgerlicher Absicht." Inspired by the Stoics and Diogenes, Kant's overall aim in this text is to present nature as an intelligent and rational system with a particular teleological purpose, since it is determined by divine will. This teleological purpose of nature also determines Kant's view on history as progress. His cosmopolitan vision in "Idee zu einer allgemeinen Geschichte in weltbürgerlicher Absicht" is the ideal completed stage of civilization, where all human beings have reached their potential for reason, and where all enjoy the same equal rights and full individual freedom.

Kant makes it clear that in his time, the human race has not yet completed its teleological purpose ("we are still a long way from the point where we could consider ourselves morally mature"[450]). In this context, Kant refers to an ideal "cosmopolitan existence" that will be realized sometime in the future.[451] The prime obstacle to this in his time was the general lack of *Bildung*, and he consequently calls for all monarchs to contribute actively to the continuing cultivation of all human minds:

But as long as states apply all their resources to their vain and violent schemes of expansion, thus incessantly obstructing the slow and laborious efforts of their citizens to cultivate their minds, and even deprive them of all support in these efforts, no progress in this direction can be expected.[452]

Along these lines, Kant advises the feudal rulers in power to provide and allow education for all individuals within their states. However, he also makes it clear that the political reforms of the Enlightenment period, which have already been accomplished, in general involve the correct historic development:

But this freedom is gradually increasing [...]. Restrictions on personal activities are increasingly relaxed and general freedom of religion is granted. And thus, although folly and caprice creep in at times, enlightenment gradually arises.[453]

In this statement, Kant's perception of equal rights and individual freedom includes all human beings, no matter their religion and cultural background. He supported religious freedom. Yet, in other texts, Kant specifically doubted the civilizational potential of Judaism and thus of Jews in general. His discussion with Moses Mendelssohn in the 1780s on whether Judaism was a natural religion serves as a good example on this matter.[454]

In Kant's view, religion was in essence a moral component.[455] The practice of Christianity, for example, disclosed its positive moral core of reason, and according to Kant, it was therefore a natural religion.[456] In his discussion with Mendelssohn in the 1780s, Kant claimed that Judaism was not a natural religion with a morally eternal inner core like Christianity;[457] it was a historic religion, since the laws, which a faithful Jew had to follow even in the eighteenth century, were the product of a specific historic period—the time in which these laws had been handed down to the Jews by their God. Kant considered Jews to be following a fossilized religious tradition,[458] since they followed laws that had been adequate for a particular society existing thousands of years ago.

One vital consequence of Kant's argumentation in his debate with Mendelssohn is that Jews who continued to be Jews would not be able to contribute constructively to the progress of European civilization in modern times.[459] Kant's ambivalent liberal universalism reveals itself in other places, too; we can also observe it in "Idee zu einer allgemeinen Geschichte in weltbürgerlicher Absicht." This essay states that all human beings must be considered as equals, but even though Kant recommends religious freedom, he also determines the civilizational development of Christian Western Europe to be the only correct path toward the ideal "cosmopolitan existence." He proclaims that in time Europe will teach the rest of the world how to follow its path of civilizational progress:

We shall discover a regular course of improvement in the political constitutions of our continent (which will probably legislate eventually for all other continents).[460]

With Kant's determination that Judaism is not a natural religion, the consequence of this remark would be that European Jews also had to be taught the correct civilizational laws by Christian Europeans (which is similar to what Dohm suggests in his aforementioned essay "Über der bürgerliche Verbesserung der Juden"). Seen through Kant's discussion with Mendelssohn, Jews practising Judaism would not be able to develop and live out their full potential in the modern world since they were not followers of a natural religion.[461]

Kant's Eurocentrism was, historically speaking, the most common world view in Western Europe at the time, and it was also not an uncommon view among nineteenth-century modern Jews like Georg Brandes.[462] In his early writings, Brandes also emphasized how modern Jews (like himself) were more capable of creating innovation within the European tradition than Christian Europeans, due to centuries-old particularistic Jewish racial traits. Some of these racial traits Brandes even dated back to the ancient world.

Moderate and Radical Enlightenment

Georg Brandes studied Immanuel Kant in the 1860s, when he was a dedicated philosophy student of (the Spinozist) Hans Brøchner.[463] It is therefore understandable that Brandes never called himself a Kantian cosmopolitan. However, it was not only that Brandes would never agree with Kant on the question of the Jewish co-construction of European civilization; he would also disagree with many of Kant's so-called moderate enlightenment standpoints in "Idee zu einer allgemeinen Geschichte in weltbürgerlicher Absicht." It was Jonathan Israel who invented this term, "moderate enlightenment." In general, Israel's writings on the Enlightenment (along with, for example, Martin Mulsow's *Enlightenment Underground: Radical Germany 1680–1720* (2015)) consolidate the basic claim of this chapter that more than one historically legitimate tradition of cosmopolitanism exists that are relevant for us today. Israel's works on the topic, for example *Radical Enlightenment*, disclose a variety of liberal-based ideological standpoints throughout the Enlightenment period. These different positions all negotiated and struggled over how radical the transformation of the Christian-based feudal states into modern secular liberal societies should be. This resulted in a diversity of Christian reform movements—some radical, some moderate—particularly in Northern Europe, where the Protestant movement had already succeeded in dissolving the Catholic monopolization of Christianity centuries earlier.

Overall, Israel divides the different pro-modern standpoints into two categories: moderate Enlightenment and radical Enlightenment. Moderate Enlightenment writers and thinkers such as Kant can be said to merge "essential elements of the older structures" with characteristics of universalistic liberal ideology.[464] One example of this is that in his second essay on cosmopolitanism, "Zum ewigen Frieden. Ein philosophischer Entwurf," Kant is hesitant in recommending liberal democracy over autocracy and monarchy.[465]

Israel describes Spinoza as the founder of the Enlightenment tradition, thus normatively favoring the radical Enlightenment. This canonization of Spinoza in many ways resembles Brandes' admiration of Spinoza. Israel and Brandes both venerate Spinoza because he represents a non-dualistic materialistic world view, as well as combining his philosophical ideals with an actual struggle for the realization of these ideals. As early as the Modern Breakthrough lectures of 1871, specifically in the introduction to *Emigrantlitteraturen* (1872), Brandes pointed to the fight against Protestant dogma and clericalism, together with the fight against the remaining authoritarian political structures of the old world, as crucial to Denmark's development into a modern liberal society.[466] With the Modern Breakthrough, Brandes also initiated what would become the key principle of his intellectual career: the non-dualistic combination of publicly announcing which ideals he followed and at the same time practically fighting for them. For example, the most frequent topic of his many later journalistic articles was oppressed European minorities, whose human rights he argued for. The minorities he focused on were diverse, including *Sønderjyder*, Armenians, Sorbs, and Eastern European Jews.

Furthermore, it is important to note that Brandes' idea of Spinozist cosmopolitanism is both multi-faceted and fragmented in his writings. In Chapter 1, I suggested that in his early writings Brandes viewed the modern Jew as exhibiting three characteristics: flexibility, a critical outlook, and considering universal justice a vital virtue. Together they constituted Brandes' cosmopolitan ideal in his early writings, what I call the transnational vision. Brandes, in fact, links all of these characteristics to Spinoza. In *Benjamin Disraeli*, one of his early texts, Brandes discusses the common denominator of some the most important political figures of the nineteenth century—the modern Jews who led the new liberal, anarchistic, and socialistic movements. He determines that universal justice was the most important virtue for these modern Jews, and marks out Spinoza as their forerunner in this in the last pages of the book. In "Shakespeare: 'Kjøbmanden i Venedig'" and "M. Goldschmidt," he identifies Spinoza as embodying the traits of flexibility and a critical outlook. In the following, he directly states that Spinoza is the father of the modern Jew:

But the Jewish spirit is already free at birth, the Roman and anti-Roman culture [...] Catholicism and Protestantism [...] all are equally close and equally distant from him. He is the son of Spinoza. Thus from birth onwards he is against any European narrow-mindedness, he is oppositional, freeborn and emancipated, both as scientific observer and as poetic re-creator. [467]

Here Brandes seems to define a Spinozist cosmopolitanism, drawing on the biography of Spinoza vis-à-vis Spinozism. Thus, one could deduce that Brandes refers to Spinoza's experiences of living in the periphery of Christian Dutch society after his excommunication as facilitating Spinoza's more objective stranger's outlook on the Christian tradition: "Thus from birth onwards he is against any European narrow-mindedness, he is oppositional, freeborn and emancipated." Unlike an individual born into the Christian faith, Spinoza had not been brought up to believe that the seventeenth-century Christian dogma were absolute truths. The image of him as an in-between stranger in the passage quoted above is, however, first and foremost an interpretation of his life example. In general, when Brandes perceives Spinoza as the father of what he calls modern Jewishness in his early writings, this should also be viewed as an example of a contribution to the genre of Spinozism, since Spinoza never wrote anything about modern Jewishness.

In his later writings on the Old Testament, Brandes presents Spinoza as part of a Jewish tradition of secular thought. However, one could interpret this new elaboration on the cosmopolitan tradition, of which Brandes perceives himself a follower, as further developed and matured reflections on modern Jewishness, and specifically on the topic of universal justice as a key Jewish virtue found in *Benjamin Disraeli*. In this way, in his books on the Old Testament, Brandes again seems to have been primarily inspired by the life example of Spinoza, presenting the Dutch Jewish philosopher as part of this secular Jewish tradition. It is suggested in this chapter that Berthold Auerbach's *Bildungsroman Spinoza* (and the branch of Spinozism it represents) laid the foundation for Brandes' idea that Spinoza was influenced by a Jewish tradition of secular thought. The fact that Brandes was particularly drawn by the life example of Spinozism is in keeping with what he himself wrote in *Levned*: "His personality fascinated, the human greatness in him, one of the greatest in history."[468]

The Ex-Jew versus the Eternal Jew Reception of Spinoza

By placing Spinoza in a Jewish tradition of secular thought, interestingly, Brandes differs from Jonathan Israel. One of the basic reasons Israel considers Spinoza's enlightenment project particularly "radical" is that, in his mind, Spinoza completely broke away from the Jewish religious tradition when he created his rationalistic materialistic philosophy.[469]

In fact, Brandes' and Israel's disagreement on the foundation of Spinoza's philosophy reflects probably the most influential sub-discussion in the reception of Spinoza of the last 300 years. There is a long and ongoing discussion of whether his Jewish background plays a role in his philosophical writings. Indeed, masterpieces such as *Tractatus Theologico-Politicus* (1670) and *Ethica [...]* (1677) were written in the period after Spinoza was excommunicated from the Sephardic Jewish religious community in Amsterdam in 1656, so it is clear that he no longer practised Judaism at this stage. But did the Jewish tradition continue to influence his philosophical works? From the time of his death to when the first works on his life and writing were written, a schism arose regarding this question that has resulted in two main factions of scholarly opinion. The two factions have recently been labelled "the ex-Jew" and "the eternal Jew" theories by Daniel B. Schwartz.[470] Israel is at present without a doubt the most prominent spokesperson for the ex-Jew readings. However, this group also counts the first works on Spinoza, for example Colerus' and Lucas' writings.[471] Typically for the "ex-Jew" theorists, in *Radical Enlightenment*, Jonathan Israel views Baruch Spinoza as having entirely separated himself from his Jewish background when he wrote his philosophical masterpieces. In this interpretation, Spinoza thus represents the first fully modern individual, who had actively and entirely freed himself from all former particularistic bonds, whether it be from cultural influences, communities, or institutionalized religion and its social implications. Thus, Israel views the excommunication of Spinoza as a clear break away from all Jewish influence,[472] and he consequently does not highlight any Jewish intellectual influences on Spinoza in *Radical Enlightenment*. Rather, he focuses on figures from Christian-based groups or movements, such as Lodewijk Meyer and Franciscus van den Enden, as shaping Baruch Spinoza in becoming the founder of modernity.

The eternal Jew readings, on the other hand, do not necessarily downplay Meyer and Van den Enden's influence on Spinoza, for example in introducing him to Descartes and thus laying the foundation for Spinoza's philosophical *Bildung*. These readings do however question whether his excommunication really signifies a complete break with his Jewish past. In *Der Spinozismus im Jüdenthumb* (1699), which is considered the first work of the genre,[473] Wachter thus views the Jewish

Kabbalah as one of the main influences on Spinoza in his later philosophical work the *Tractatus*.[474]

A clear risk in the eternal Jew reading of Spinoza shows itself in works that tend to accentuate the Jewish influence too much by, for example, overstating the Kabbalistic influence on his writings without being able to prove this (as Wachter tends to do). This reception of Spinoza gives Jewish history and tradition precedence over all other cultural traditions in the development of modernity, a perspective through which "the essence of modernity" somehow comes to signify particular Jewish elements.[475] The eternal Jew readings do present a convincing case, however, in the way they address questions that representatives of the ex-Jew faction, for example Israel, mostly avoid. These questions include: Was Spinoza's Jewish *Bildung* not an essential inspiration for his later innovative philosophical writings? What about the years Spinoza spent in the *Keter Torah Yeshiva* in Amsterdam, where he learned to write through learning Hebrew, and where he read and discussed the Old Testament alongside great Sephardic Spanish philosophers and bible commentators such as Maimonides and Ibn Ezra? The answers to these questions seem to be self-evident given since Spinoza's bible criticism in the *Tractatus*, for instance, is based on the oldest Hebrew version of the Old Testament. Moreover, Spinoza quotes Maimonides on several occasions in the *Tractatus* and some of his arguments also clearly build on Ibn Ezra's work.[476]

However, as mentioned, one of the clear dangers of reading Spinoza as an eternal Jew is that the Jewish particularistic and religious tradition is often given a continuous precedence in the modern world.[477] There is no indication whatsoever that Spinoza intended such a reading of his works. For this reason, neither the ex-Jew nor the eternal Jew readings seem fully to fit Brandes' reception of Spinoza's Jewish background in his later writings. To take it one step further, I examined works that according to Henning Fenger inspired the young Brandes when he became a Spinozist cosmopolitan in the 1860s. One particular piece of work came to overshadow the others in understanding how Brandes came to view Spinoza as the father of modernity and of what he called modern Jewishness in his early writings: Berthold Auerbach's *Spinoza* (1837/56). According to Fenger's *Georg Brandes' Lærear*, Brandes' reading of Spinoza commenced in the early 1860s and already in 1862 he defines himself as a Spinozian materialist and pantheist.[478] At this time, he also read and became equally fascinated by Auerbach's *Bildungsroman Spinoza* and its depiction of the life example of Spinoza;[479] during the 1860s Brandes returned repeatedly to Spinoza's writings, as well as rereading Auerbach's novel.[480]

One could argue that Berthold Auerbach's *Bildungsroman* seems to have inspired Brandes to appreciate a third way of perceiving how Jewish sources continued to influence Spinoza after his excommunication. Daniel B. Schwartz suggests a related perspective in his description of how Berthold Auerbach depicts the background to Spinoza's writings in his novel:

Auerbach, in line with the idea of *Bildung*, proposed an option between these two extremes – that of perceiving Spinoza's Jewish origins as a shaping influence in the making of the philosopher, while at the same time as only a preliminary stage in a path that ultimately led beyond Judaism.[481]

Auerbach's novel is, as mentioned, part of the literature of Spinozism. In the earliest French and German Enlightenment encyclopedias of the eighteenth century, there are comprehensive entries on both (the philosopher) Spinoza and the genre of Spinozism.[482] The many writings of Spinozism, produced from the latter half of the seventeenth century, were based on only a very small number of documented sources for Baruch Spinoza's life before and after he was excommunicated. However, works of Spinozism mostly celebrate Baruch Spinoza as a hero, and as the first modern man. Influenced by its historical context, Auerbach's novel similarly depicts Spinoza as a romantic genius, who formed himself independently while at the same time his Jewish background continued to influence him even after his excommunication, for example in the shaping of his unique and innovative philosophy.

The primary inspiration for Brandes in representing Spinoza as part of a Jewish tradition of secular thought was, I suggest, not a work by Spinoza himself. It was also not a fully scientific scholarly interpretation of Spinoza's philosophy (if any could be said to exist). Rather, it was a fictional biographical novel depicting the life example of Spinoza, and as such a work of Spinozism. And why would it be any different? Brandes had built his career as a man of the arts. He first became known in the Danish civil sphere as a reviewer of theater and literature in *Illustreret Tidende* in the late 1860s, and he launched his Modern Breakthrough in lectures on nineteenth-century European literary history.

Berthold Auerbach's Spinoza

Interestingly, Brandes came to know Berthold Auerbach personally when the latter was living, as an old man, a secluded life in Berlin; he was a favored target for verbal antisemitic attacks. However, Brandes' first readings of Auerbach's novel appeared before his acquaintance with Auerbach.[483]

For a long time, the vast influence of Berthold Auerbach's two Jewish-related novels *Spinoza* and *Dichter und Kaufmann* (1840) have been neglected. Even a great scholar within Jewish Studies such as David Sorkin disregards these novels in his otherwise rather substantial and influential *The Transformation of the German Jewry, 1781–1840*. Instead, Sorkin highlights what Auerbach has mainly become known for in the more traditional narratives on German literary history: his national-Romantic *Schwarzwalder* stories.[484] The same tendency is observable in research on Brandes. In 1955, Henning Fenger documented that Brandes was extremely fascinated and influenced by Auerbach, and particularly the *Spinoza* novel, in the 1860s.[485] Yet, as mentioned in the Introduction, Fenger dismisses Auerbach's two Jewish-related novels and their influence on Brandes because he judges that they are of poor artistic value. He even calls them "sickly," while claiming that the only reason Brandes could have liked these books was because of his "racial kinship" with their author.[486]

In recent years, the artistic value and historical importance of Berthold Auerbach's two Jewish-related novels has been re-evaluated, particularly by Jonathan Skolnik and Daniel B. Schwartz.[487] Thus, not only for Brandes, but for many nineteenth-century and fin-de-siècle Northern European Jews, it seems that Auerbach's Spinoza in particular became a cornerstone in their *Bildung* and in their determination to become and live as modern Jewish individuals who had perhaps abandoned Orthodox Judaism but not the Jewish tradition and the influences of the millennia-old Jewish civilization per se. In line with this, through his depiction of Spinoza's life example, Auerbach creates a role model for individuals of Jewish descent who felt alienated from and unfamiliar with Orthodox Judaism, while at the same time they had no intentions of converting to Christianity or being fully assimilated into the Christian-based majority societies.

The Story of Auerbach's Spinoza

The original version of Auerbach's *Spinoza* had the subtitle *Bildungsroman.* Following the founding work of the genre, Goethe's *Wilhelm Meister* (1792–98), in its choice of central events and key subordinate characters, the *Bildungsroman* distilled the essential formative characteristics of the individual. Since Auerbach only depicts the time up until Spinoza was excommunicated, the excommunication itself, and a short period after this, the original subtitle of his novel reveals that he considered Spinoza's Jewish background to be formative. However, Auerbach focuses on a particular sub-tradition in his examination of which Jewish traits continued to influence Spinoza after his excommunication, namely one of secular thought and practice in which Spinoza's Sephardic Jewish background is emphasized. At the same time, the novel is the portrayal of an individual who even as a boy instinctively remains at a critical distance from what he is otherwise presented with as absolute truths and scientific facts. We witness how not only the seventeenth-century Orthodox Jewish Sephardic community Spinoza was born into in Amsterdam, but also his new "progressive" radical friends of the Dutch Christian-based society are more interested in subduing him to their principles than listening to his criticism of their traditions. Hence, at the end of the novel, Auerbach portrays Spinoza as the first modern man, who has shaped himself as a product of secular-orientated Jewish sources and rational philosophy, pointing to a third path between the ex-Jew and eternal Jew factions.[488] Yet he also depicts Spinoza as living in lonely solitude, as a result of not subduing himself to any tradition.

Spinoza's Secularly Orientated Interpretations of the Jewish Tradition

As Daniel B. Schwartz and Jonathan Skolnik convincingly point out, Auerbach depicts Spinoza as laying the ground for his later philosophy through his *yeshiva* studies. [489] Yet it is young Baruch's own thoughts on the Jewish canonized texts that are decisive here. An excellent example of this is found in the part where the young Baruch is studying the Five Books of Moses and Ibn Ezra's comments on the books. The eleventh- and twelfth-century Spanish Sephardic Jew Ibn Ezra is primarily known as a highly esteemed bible commentator, who hinted that it was impossible for Moses to have been the author of the Five Books of Moses.[490] In studying Ibn Ezra and the Five Books of Moses, Baruch embarks on a train of thought that would have been utterly denounced by the Orthodox Jewish community of Amsterdam, had he raised such questions in public or put them to his teachers:

It had been made clear to him that the holy scripture, according to its entire contents, was not written by God-blessed men, the glory had disappeared, the whole thing was man's work—how else could later profane hands have daubed into the holy scriptures of God? Who wrote the Bible, who revised it?[491]

It is (indirectly asked) questions such as these that would make Spinoza's later *Tractatus* one of the greatest and most provocative works in the history of philosophy and bible criticism, and would lead authorities all over Europe to ban it and condemn it as the most subversive text ever written. Auerbach emphasizes the importance of Spinoza's scholarly Jewish background in the development of such thoughts, but we are also witnessing the formation of a Romantic genius who independently observes and assembles fragments of secular thought from the Jewish tradition.

The story of how the young Baruch Spinoza identifies a tradition of secular thought in Judaism culminates in the excommunication scene, where the rabbinical court of the Jewish Sephardic community in Amsterdam accuses him of heresy. Standing before the court, Spinoza boldly argues that his way of interpreting the Jewish tradition is no less valid than the Orthodox interpretations represented by the court itself. He even quotes the Five Books of Moses to argue that in the innermost core of the Scriptures, a tradition of interrelated secular thought and practice is endorsed:

The Bible recognizes this sacred right of our reason by acknowledging a godly way of life even in men who lived on Sinai before the revelation, and by speaking of the truth that came forth as a temporal phenomenon in the legislation of Moses, which says: "It is not in heaven that it could be said who will ascend into heaven for us, and fetch it and declare it to us, so that we may act accordingly. For the Word is very near to you: in your mouth and in your heart, that you may act accordingly" (5.B.M. 30:12). In our reason, at the height of pure divine thought, here is Sinai.[492]

Auerbach shows here that Spinoza's final break away from Judaism was not a complete dismissal of the Jewish tradition. Rather, Spinoza's view of Judaism differs too much from the seventeenth-century Orthodox interpretations of the Scripture, which could not acknowledge such secular readings. Still, Auerbach does not suggest that Spinoza continues in some abstract way to be Jewish in a religious sense after he is excommunicated. Instead, he is shown continuing to make use of these secular but Jewish-influenced perspectives within the Dutch Christian civil sphere, once he stops living with his family in the Jewish Sephardic community after his excommunication.

Auerbach also illustrates how a group of Christian Dutch radical Enlightenment men and women introduces early modern rationalistic philosophy (particularly Descartes) and the New Testament to Spinoza.

Almost all of these Dutch Christian subordinate characters are eager for Spinoza to convert to Christianity, although they are also presented as the most progressive individuals at this time. However, in the novel, Spinoza does not want to convert, even when it is the only way for him to marry the daughter of his Latin teacher, Olympia Van den Enden, whom Auerbach depicts as the love of Spinoza's life.

After his excommunication, Spinoza actively chooses to live his life solitarily, on the margins of the Dutch Christian society, where his Jewish background can remain the bedrock of his experience. Auerbach depicts Spinoza as continuing to draw on the knowledge his Jewish background has given him in the conversations he has with Dutch Christian friends and acquaintances.[493] For example, he frequently uses quotations from the Old Testament, the Talmud, and Jewish folklore to provide secularly orientated perspectives on, for instance, the philosophy of Descartes.[494]

Furthermore, Auerbach's fictional depiction of a somewhat phantasmagoric family history also represents Spinoza's identity as entailing traces of all three major world religions: Christianity, Judaism, and Islam. At the end of the novel, it is thus highly symbolic that what has hitherto been a work of historical fiction suddenly morphs into fantasy when the literary and folkloristic trope of the Wandering Jew, Ahasverus, pays Spinoza a visit following his excommunication. Ahasverus, the most widespread Jewish stereotype of the nineteenth century, tells Spinoza that through his existential choices and through all three spheres of experience, he has forged a new path through which not only Jews but all human beings (including Christians and Muslims) have been set free to be themselves.[495] Ahasverus calls Spinoza a secular Messiah, a role model, for all human beings, who has lifted the curse from his shoulders, so that he can finally die in peace.[496]

Subsequently, Auerbach's Spinoza shapes himself as a product of both Jewish (secularly orientated) sources and early Enlightenment philosophy; according to the novel, it is from this remote but near stranger position that he produces his innovative philosophy. One may therefore suggest that the novel represents a synthesis between early modern European modernity and the Jewish tradition, and that it is this synthesis which made Auerbach's depiction of Spinoza's life example a role model for the many cosmopolitan-orientated, bourgeois-influenced modern European Jews. For many of these individuals, including Georg Brandes, the secular bourgeois *Bildung* ideal had indeed replaced the religious Jewish tradition as their primary guide in life.

In *Spinoza*, Auerbach presents elements of the Jewish tradition that Georg Brandes could and would not reject as fossilized relics. As regards Brandes' reception of the book, one of the more important elements is, doubtlessly, that Auerbach shows that secularly orientated Jewish thoughts and practice have always existed alongside the Orthodox tradition and interpretations. In this context, Auerbach sheds light on the culturally pluralistic and secularly orientated Jewish Sephardic historical tradition of the Iberian Peninsula—the Sephardic Jewish golden age—as an important background for Spinoza's *Bildung*, and he points out that already in the eleventh and twelfth centuries Ibn Ezra had hinted at a more secular reading of the Old Testament. Auerbach thus showed his readers that the Jewish religious tradition contains many perspectives that a European Jew of the nineteenth century and the fin-de-siècle period could use to build his modern identity. David Biale's recent book *Not In The Heavens: The Tradition of Jewish Secular Thought* (2011) argues that many different forms of secularization have existed around the world and throughout history, which are just as historically legitimate as the secularization that occurred in the context of the Western Christian tradition.[497] In academia, however, the pervading view has for many years been that there is only one form of secularization: the one that took place in relation to Christianity in Western Europe. Auerbach similarly shows that within the Jewish religious tradition we can find examples of secular thought that are as old as Judaism itself. In the excommunication scene of his novel, Auerbach even suggests that in the holiest books of all, the Five Books of Moses, central passages could be interpreted as mainly orientated toward secular thought and practice.

As mentioned, Georg Brandes himself was a living example of a typical bourgeois-influenced Western European Jew, and he despised the fact that the first thing that was always mentioned about him was that he was a "Jew," as opposed to his ideas or writings. One can only imagine what kind of impact a book such as Auerbach's novel had on Brandes when he read and reread the novel in the 1860s. While Brandes distanced himself many times from the Jewish tradition, many elements of it clearly fascinated him throughout his life, and as we will see next he even developed the idea that a secularly orientated sub-tradition existed within the Jewish tradition. Traceable back to the oldest books in the Old Testament, according to Brandes, this tradition of secular thought emphasized universal justice as the focal point of Judaism.

Brandes' Perception of a Jewish Tradition of Secular Thought and Practice

When in his later writings Brandes presents Spinoza as the culmination of a Jewish tradition of secular thought, we find interesting parallels with Auerbach's depiction of Jewish secular thought and practice influencing Spinoza's *Bildung*. In his books on the Old Testament, Brandes often points to the same examples of secular thought in the Jewish tradition as Auerbach—such as Maimonides' and Ibn Ezra's writings. However, he also expands Auerbach's perception of Jewish secular thought and practice by presenting it as a coherent tradition from ancient times to the modern world. He represents secular thought as a somewhat conscious sub-tradition within the Jewish tradition, which has always existed and which has always opposed Orthodox interpretations of sacred texts.

As seen in Chapter 4, two of the three texts by Brandes in focus here can also be viewed as part of his Athens vs. Jerusalem interpretations (Brandes' essays *Jobs Bog* and *Kohélet*). The fact that Athens vs. Jerusalem appears as a dichotomy demonstrates the dominant interpretation of the relation between the two in the eighteenth and nineteenth centuries. Common to thinkers as diverse as Immanuel Kant, G.W.F. Hegel, Ernst Renan, and Friedrich Nietzsche was the view that the ancient Greek civilization, rather than the ancient Jewish civilization and religion, should be regarded as the most fundamental building block of European civilization.[498] Thus, the Athens vs. Jerusalem dichotomy constitutes an underexposed but historically influential discussion of the Jewish Question in this period, which mainly took place in the sphere of the North European intellectual bourgeoisie.

The Athens vs. Jerusalem dichotomy continues to have a prominent place in academia. For instance, when scholars of cosmopolitanism wish to demonstrate the historical and philosophical background of today's use of the concept, the standard approach is to illustrate how canonical thinkers of Greek and Roman antiquity first laid the foundation for cosmopolitan thought and practice.[499] Typically, Diogenes and/ or the Stoics and Seneca are presented as the fathers of cosmopolitan thought, and Immanuel Kant is submitted as the first modern thinker to have made the concept of cosmopolitanism current again.[500]

Nevertheless, Brandes points to the Book of Job, *Kohélet*, and the books of the prophets in the Old Testament as the first texts which discuss and represent key elements of modern secular thought in a way that is relevant to the development of European civilization, for example the question of universal justice. Furthermore, he considers Baruch Spinoza—and not Immanuel Kant—to be the primary link between the pre-modern and the modern world as regards the revival of secularly orientated ideas about universal justice. As touched upon earlier, one could also argue that Spinoza was himself among the first writers to rebel against the hegemonic Athens vs. Jerusalem dichotomy in modern Western thought; in his *Tractatus*, he argues that the first historical experiment in democracy did not occur in Athens, but in the ancient Jewish cultural and religious community in present-day Israel/Palestine.[501]

Universal Justice

In his books on the Old Testament, Brandes presents the key question of Judaism as one of universal justice, and suggests that in the Jewish tradition of secular thought this question is resolved by focusing on a worldly practice, rather than reliance on divine intervention and/or better conditions in the future.

Brandes had already begun to mark out universal justice—the underlying principle of Western liberal democracy—as a key Jewish topos in his early writings. In *Benjamin Disraeli* (1878), he depicts Spinoza as the father of what he calls modern Jewishness. He goes on to state that he considers Spinoza to be the forerunner of some of the most important political figures of the nineteenth century—the many modern Jews, such as Ferdinand Lassalle and Ludwig Börne, who led or were central figures in the liberal and socialistic movements. Brandes further reflects on how the virtue of justice can be found all around him in the practice of Western European modern Jews like himself:

If the Jews are the most eager to preach to the world that they are by no means God's chosen people [...] might not the source of this be honesty and altruism and self-abnegation rather than base motives? When in 1848 Jews everywhere led the revolt against outdated tradition and entrenched injustice [...] could they not have acted out of a love of liberty, which goes hand in hand with a love of truth? And if Jews – finally rich and wealthy men [...] should have ushered in, if not the Communist, then the Socialist movement in Europe in our age [...] could they not be motivated by a noble and passionate love for mankind, a philanthropy, which [...] applies its vigor to leading democratic ideas forth to victory directly and without further ado?[502]

Brandes does not dwell on this topic in *Benjamin Disraeli*. His later preoccupation with universal justice as the central question of Jewish tradition might nonetheless be seen as a continuation of reflections first expressed in this early work.

The oldest book of the Old Testament with reference to which Brandes addresses Judaism's core question of justice is the Book of Job. Brandes first discusses the overall theme of the text by reflecting on how Jerusalem, no less than Athens, laid the foundation for modern European civilization.[503] Next, he states that what he considers to be the oldest part of the Book of Job does not mention God. As mentioned in Chapter 4, he believes that the version of the Book of Job in the Old Testament comprises different versions of the text written at different times. He speculates that the oldest part, which he considers the most substantial, is much older than for instance the epilogue, in which God is mentioned for the first time and finally answers Job; Brandes suggests that the epilogue was added because clerical authorities demanded it.[504] He also thinks it highly plausible that the original author of the Book of Job was a former exile or a Jewish emigrant. He argues that the oldest part clearly bears the mark of diaspora and migration in the experiences it draws upon, and notes that the exiled author's tale incorporated elements of both Egyptian and Babylonian cultural contexts.[505]

Following this, Brandes' key objective in *Jobs Bog* is to demonstrate that the oldest part of it is essentially a philosophical meditation on the key question of Judaism:

The question examined in the Book of Job is the central question of Judaism, namely this: How is it that under the righteous rule of God, evil so often has good fortune on its side, while the righteous is no less often struck by undeserved misfortune? For the Israelite this is the fundamental question. The struggle against this conundrum constitutes the entire inner history of Judaism.[506]

However, Brandes does not believe that the intention of the Book of Job is to present a solution to the question of justice. What nonetheless makes it a significant discussion of the question, according to him, is that the purpose of its oldest version is to tie the question to a worldly context. Brandes then reflects on the fact that the main question discussed in the Book of Job—a text written millennia ago—is the exact same question that still baffles the finest minds of modern Europe:

For us in the modern age, this question is not resolved – it plagues us daily – but in the face of it, our philosophy has taught us [...] that it is wrongly put and that true wisdom lies in not awaiting any answer. For us, the question has disappeared since we have become accustomed only to seeing, as the world progresses, a subconscious reason gradually growing into greater consciousness and greater potency. We regard righteousness as a duty and an ideal which lies ahead of us in a far-off future.[507]

A younger Brandes, of the 1870s perhaps, would most likely not have distanced himself the way he does here as regards the Enlightenment ideal of progress. In his early writings, he was for the most part a strong cosmopolitan, convinced that Denmark and Europe would eventually progress toward a future in which human civilization would be completed and all human beings would enjoy the same rights and share the same liberal values irrespective of their gender, race, or class background.

In his later writings, however, Brandes changes his view on progress as the ideal of history—or at least, as implied in the above quotation, he begins to doubt it. Nietzsche's influence is likely here. At the heart of Nietzsche's philosophy there is significant opposition to the Enlightenment view of history as progress; inspired particularly by Schopenhauer, he argues it is one of the illusions modern man has come to live by. What Brandes thus rebels against when he begins to question this view is one of the key concepts of the Enlightenment. Kant's cosmopolitan essay "Idee zu einer allgemeinen Geschichte in weltbürgerlicher Absicht" is one of the first texts in which the ideal of history as progress is thoroughly described (though Spinoza also advances it in the *Tractatus*, for example, and this is in fact one of the oldest European versions of it). It is not specifically Kant's essay Brandes argues against in *Jobs Bog* when he suggests that the intellectual quality of the ancient Jews' insights were equal to those of nineteenth-century European thinkers and writers. But he clearly criticizes the widespread perception of a historical teleological purpose of mankind when he compares ancient Jews' level of insight with that of modern-day thinkers.

Brandes goes even further when he states in the above-quoted passage that in some ways the ancient Jews were more advanced in their views, given that they were not constrained by the idea of viewing history as progress. Thus, nineteenth-century modern Europeans "regard universal justice as a duty and an ideal which lies ahead of us in a far-off future".[508]Brandes sees a danger here: Justice might well remain merely an ideal, without ever becoming praxis-orientated, and thus the actualization of justice becomes a futuristic utopia. In contrast, Brandes writes, since ancient times the Jewish tradition has held that discussions and meditations on justice must be followed up by practice.

Brandes' Reading of Kohélet

In Kohélet, Brandes further reflects on how the Jewish historical emphasis on justice is backed up by practice and opposition to worldly injustice:

Not resisting evil is a Christian concept, in which many, from antiquity to Tolstoy in our day, see the essence of Christianity. Never has subjection to injustice been a virtue for the Jew [...]. The man whom the Jew extols is not the holy one; it is the righteous one [...] since Jews have wished to realize the ideal of righteousness here on Earth, they have, in the modern era, had a hand in revolutions. Kabbalistic Jews were instrumental in the establishment of Freemasonry, the Jews in France (again in Paris), few in number, were participants in the revolution, three of them occupied important positions and died on the scaffold, half of the founders of *Saint-Simonianism* were Jews, men of financial wisdom such as Olinde Rodrigues, Eichtal and Isaa Pereire. Artists such as the composer Felicien David and the poet Heine joined their ranks. At the emergence of liberal thinking, Manin becomes its hero in Italy, Börne its spokesman in Germany, Jellinek its agitator and martyr in Austria, Moritz Hartmann its spokesman in Frankfurt and its champion in Vienna. German socialism was founded by Karl Marx and Lassalle. Russian nihilism has been heavily subscribed to by young Jewish students, many of whom have sacrificed their lives. [509]

In *Kohélet* too, Brandes depicts the pattern of idealization of justice without fighting for its actualization as a trait of the Christian tradition, and he states that Christianity has not been influenced by the Jewish tradition in this respect.[510] On the contrary, he discerns a Jewish tradition of secular thought and practice, which in contrast with Christianity's idealization of repression and suffering, emphasizes that injustice must be opposed and fought against. In the passage cited, Brandes also shows that the Jewish tradition of secular thought and practice is a coherent tradition, dating back to ancient times and the writing of the Book of Job up to modern times, Karl Marx, and Ferdinand Lassalle. Indirectly, he also criticizes the Western European ideal of progress—paradoxically perhaps—as limiting the advance of civilization: Europe could already have come further in actualizing universal justice and the full emancipation of mankind if Christian Europeans had not been brought up viewing universal justice as a far-off utopian ideal. In Brandes' opinion, it is primarily thanks to people he called modern Jews, such as Daniele Manin, Georg Jellinek, Ferdinand Lassalle, Karl Marx, and Ludwig Börne, that nineteenth-century European civilization had begun to practise its sophisticated ideals.

In *Kohélet*, Brandes similarly observes that as early as the time of its writing, it was a widespread belief in the Jewish tradition that there was no life after death. Human existence on earth was the only verifiable existence,[511] and he points out that such a secularly oriented view must ultimately lead to a general mistrust in the existence of miracles and supernatural explanations of worldly events. After this, Brandes moves on to describe another central characteristic of the Jewish tradition of secular thought—free, rational thinking:

He [the author of Kohélet] represents [...] Israel's belief that there is no other existence for man than life on Earth. For the Israelite life is a blessing. Life is good fortune. [...] Kohélet is furthermore a reasoning philosopher, a rationalist. He is the type characterized by Jewish reason without hyperbole, with Jewish sophistication of knowledge and criticism, the forefather of the many shrewd ironists, skeptics and polemicists of the people of Israel throughout the millennia. He was by no means a solitary figure in his time.[512]

Besides linking the virtue of justice to the Jewish secular tradition, Brandes also connects it with a coherent tradition of free, rational thinking, which stretches back to the Old Testament and continues as far as until Spinoza in the seventeenth-century, who in this respect is the link between the modern and the pre-modern world:

He [the author of Kohélet] is the first clear type characterized by liberal, re-fined Israelite intelligence. After him come Philo and the Alexandrians, after them the Jewish polemicists, who inspired Celsus, who was refuted by Origen; after them follow the group of Talmudists who, in the tenth century, wished to uphold religion through a philosophy emphasizing that the authority of reason existed alongside religion [...] they are followed in the eleventh century by Ibn Gabirol, who with his work *The Fountain of Life* strongly influenced Arabic philosophy, and Maimonides, who in his principal work attempted to unite and reconcile Aristotle's philosophy with Judaism [...] from the tenth century to the fifteenth century we see Jewish rationalists and thinkers preoccupied with pre-paring for that revolution in human history which was the Renaissance. They establish the principles of exegesis, which gradually becomes a liberating force, they criticize the Christian dogmas and symbols, they spread the Arabic phi-losophy to Europe [...] they were highly active, cherished, even pampered at the court of the great Emperor Frederick II, the center of religious indifference, of forbearance and of free thinking at the beginning of the thirteenth century. Ibn Gabirol's *Fountain of Life* inspires Giordano Bruno and his adoration of the universe. The thousand-year preoccupation with the Bible by interpreters of Je-wish scripture lays the foundation for Luther's translation of the Bible and leads to the principle of free study. It is not until the seventeenth century that their fundamental view culminates in Spinoza's *Theological-Political Treatise*. [513]

Importantly, by projecting this coherent genealogy onto the tradition of rational thinking, Brandes argues that there have always been differ-ent factions in the Jewish tradition—different ways of interpreting the Scripture which existed in parallel with each another (and indeed the newest Bible research backs up Brandes' theory; see for example Paula Fredriksen's *When Christians were Jews: The First Generation* (2019)). He considers it possible that *Kohélet* was in fact written as a rebuttal to and protest against a particular historical regime in ancient Israel, which was de facto ruled by strict Orthodox clerical authorities. This regime attempted to ban Jews from enjoying earthly pleasures, mate-rial effects and hedonism. Their rule was in general based on fear and "pietistic" values, as Brandes writes.[514] Brandes thus describes a similar conflict to the one Berthold Auerbach thematizes in *Spinoza*: Both writers illustrate how in ancient times and in the early modern era, respectively, different views existed within the Jewish tradition—secular thought and practice existed alongside a dominant orthodox clerical interpretation of the Scripture. Yet Brandes expands Auerbach's theme by depicting the Jewish tradition of secular thought as a coherent historic tradition, and by viewing Spinoza's *Tractatus* as its culmination.

Brandes' Spinozist Cosmopolitanism

In his readings of the books of the Old Testament, Brandes does not view the Jewish tradition as backwards and fossilized. On the contrary, he delivers a response to this Christian European Enlightenment notion by observing several examples of secular thought in the Jewish tradition on which a nineteenth-or twentieth-century European Jew could build a modern identity.

Still, it is important to remember that it was not the whole Jewish tradition that Brandes saw as constructive for a nineteenth-century European Jew like himself. In Auerbach's *Bildungsroman*, Spinoza continues to use secularly orientated Jewish modes of thinking after his excommunication while at the same time disposing of what he considered to be unconstructive and irrational elements of the tradition, for example dogmatic interpretations of religious texts. Similarly, in both his early and his later writings, Brandes is critical of the clerical and dogmatic aspects of Judaism, while also highlighting certain secular aspects of it as positive.

In *Smaa Romaner fra Det Gamle Testamente*, Brandes delivers another genealogy on the place of universal justice in the Jewish tradition. He celebrates Spinoza as the culmination of both the virtue of free rational thinking and positioning justice as the central question in the Jewish tradition of secular thought:

They [the Jewish prophets] believed so firmly in universal justice that they succeeded in letting the idea of it take its course throughout the history of Europe. [...]. This spirit has manifested itself throughout time, it has engendered the utmost heresy, it has contributed to the Reformation in Germany, in so far as Luther's translation of the Bible was unthinkable without Raschi's commentaries on the Bible [...]. This spirit has contributed to the Reformation both in France and in England [...], it has given France great Huguenots such as Coligny and d'Aubigné and England great Puritans such as Cromwell, who founded the republic. Furthermore, in a direct line from the prophets Spinoza descends as the founder of intellectual freedom and introduces monism to modern philosophy. [515]

Brandes here argues that the Jewish tradition is to be seen as a key foundation for modern European civilization through its focal point, the discussion of universal justice. The Jewish tradition of secular thought is said to have influenced and catalyzed some of the most innovative ideas in modern Western thinking, such as Luther's Protestant rebellion. And Brandes determines that Spinoza is the link between the pre-modern and modern world; correspondingly, throughout his oeuvre Brandes calls Spinoza the father of modernity.

Regarding the previously presented view that Brandes' books on the Old Testament and early Christianity should be viewed as contributions to discussions of the so-called Jewish Question, it is interesting that he is aware that he argues against the perception—expressed, for example, by Renan—of the Jewish tradition as fossilized. Brandes was clearly influenced by Renan's ideas, but in these later works he calls Renan's perceptions of the Jewish tradition outdated.[516] As a response to such ideas, Brandes' Spinozist cosmopolitanism demonstrates how a Jew or an individual of Jewish descent who refuses to convert can, just as much as a Christian, be viewed as a fully civilized and secularly orientated modern human being. As such, he also asks his readers to put away the many stereotypes that the Athens vs. Jerusalem dichotomy, for instance, has produced.

Yet in present-day literature on cosmopolitanism, it seems that some stereotypes persist still. Within the last two decades, theories of cosmopolitanism have suggested there is just one historically legitimate cosmopolitan tradition, namely the Greek/Roman-Kantian one. In this context, Brandes' Spinozist cosmopolitanism provides a useful piece of advice for other minorities living in a Western context: They should seek out their own path toward an "cosmopolitan existence" in an ever more global world, using sources from the particular tradition in which they have been brought up (I will return to this point in my final conclusion).

Conclusion

As a reader today, it is crucial to be aware of just how important and—for its time—provocative it was that Brandes continued to call himself a cosmopolitan until his death in 1927. As Michael Miller and Scott Ury demonstrate in their article "Cosmopolitanism: The End of Jewishness" (2010), it was one of the essential structures of modern antisemitism to interconnect Jewishness with cosmopolitanism since the first texts by Wilhelm Marr and Heinrich von Treitschke in 1879–81.[517] Richard Wagner's *Das Judentum in der Musik* was another founding text, and right up to the writings of Adolf Hitler the synonymous relation between Jewishness and cosmopolitanism was a focal point of modern antisemitic ideology.

Georg Brandes was originally one of the prime targets for prominent modern antisemites such as Heinrich von Treitscke and Adolf Stoecker, when they determined the alienated, rootless, cosmopolitan modern Jewish spirit as a chief threat to the continued existence of European national cultures. This was not only a German phenomenon: From the 1870s and throughout Brandes' writings, prominent Danish public figures such as Bishop H. L. Martensen, Carl Ploug, Vilhelm Bergsøe, Julius Paludan, Holger Drachmann, Vilhelm Andersen, Jakob Knudsen, and Harald Nielsen (and even the Danish Crown Prince Frederik, as notes from his diary of 1880 suggest)[518] identified Brandes as a subversive, un-Danish "cosmopolitan Jew" who threatened Danish national culture.

Yet from his earliest writings until his death, Brandes continued to call himself a cosmopolitan. The few times he additionally explained which tradition he understood himself to be a descendant of, Brandes appointed Baruch Spinoza the father of his cosmopolitanism. Apart from the texts already analyzed, this can also be observed in an interesting article from 1918, "Das neue Judentum." The overall theme of the article is the Zionist project to create a Jewish homeland in Israel/Palestine, and whether Brandes himself supports it. He did—albeit ambivalently—give his support, after many years of officially opposing Zionism.[519] In this article, however, he first states that, hypothetically, this Jewish homeland in the Middle East region could never become a home to him, since he did not consider himself a Jew. He then makes it his case also to inform readers that he is not an "assimilationist."[520] He explains that he considers himself Danish and a cosmopolitan; elsewhere in the article he furthermore explains that, intellectually, he is first and foremost a product of "Spinoza's Gedanken."[521] There can therefore be no doubt that Brandes considered himself Danish; the listing of different cultural and ideological co-identities/positions that he confirms and denies respectively nonetheless also implies that he is aware that he represents an in-between identity—he is the product of the Danish national cultural tradition, a particular Northern European Jewish interpretation of the *Bildung* ideal (which varied from family to family), and different elements of the pre-modern and modern Jewish tradition.

In his later writings, even though he refused to call himself a Jew, as in this article, Brandes still identifies himself as what in his early writings he called modern Jewish, since he insisted he was a cosmopolitan and a product of "Spinoza's Gedanken." No explanation of this kind would have been needed in 1918, however. By then cosmopolitanism and Jewishness had become part of the same identity anyway, due to the increasingly dominant antisemitic rhetoric. And for the antisemites, nothing was more inflammatory than an individual of Jewish descent who proudly announced himself to be a cosmopolitan. "Das neue Judentum" is a good example of Brandes presenting a culturally pluralistic view, in that he writes that the Western European Christian-based secular "laws" are not the only way to develop a society built on liberal secular universalism. Thus, even while he rejects ever wanting to become a citizen of what would eventually would become Israel (because he considered his home to be Denmark and Europe), in this text, Brandes argues that the state of Israel—which he envisions as mainly consisting of Eastern European Jews—would be fully able to create a modern, secular-based society on the basis of its inhabitants' rich cultural and religious background.[522]

To sum up: this chapter has demonstrated that the cosmopolitan tradition Brandes considered himself a follower of was Spinozist, and as such he mainly draws on sources of Spinozism vis-à-vis the life example of Spinoza, rather than Spinoza's own philosophical work, when he outlines and elaborates on what this type of cosmopolitanism signified. Crucially, it is a cosmopolitanism that highlights the Jewish co-construction of European civilization. In this context, Brandes' Spinozist cosmopolitanism is also to be interpreted as one of his methods of fighting the various European nationalistic and antisemitic movements, which only grew in importance in his later writings. Brandes' Spinozian cosmopolitanism and his perception of Spinoza as the culmination of a Jewish tradition of secular thought opposed antisemitic understandings of the historic role of the Jewish tradition in Europe. Rather than viewing Jews as a negative alien element, as parasites in the histories of the different European national cultures, Brandes emphasized that the Jewish tradition and civilization had always been an indispensable part and even a foundation of European civilization and its intellectual innovations. Nevertheless, his cosmopolitanism endorses cultural pluralism without neglecting the importance of national/local culture; Brandes' key concept for understanding cultural matters thus continued to be *Volksgeist*, and he always insisted on calling himself Danish.

Discussion

Brandes' Representation of Jewishness as a Vital Archive for Today's Cosmopolitanisms

Recapitulation of the Five Chapters

By focusing on the role Baruch Spinoza is given as a life example and as the father of modernity in the writings of Brandes,[523] this book has demonstrated that Brandes considered himself part of a modern Jewish cosmopolitan tradition in both his early and his later writings. His modern Jewish cosmopolitanism highlights virtues such as universal justice, rational thinking, *Bildung*, cultural flexibility in combination with rootedness, and combining idealism with practice. According to Brandes, cosmopolitanism is primarily about the present, and not the future. Indeed, for Brandes, cosmopolitanism was an existential life project in which idealism and practice were always intertwined: At his first entrance to public debates, leading actors tried to stigmatize him as "un-Danish" and a "cosmopolitan Jew." During his career as a public intellectual, the cultural code of racially based modern antisemitism was developed and its popularity grew and grew. In modern antisemitism, the interconnection of Jewishness and cosmopolitanism became almost synonymous; the core belief of modern antisemitism as a populistic ideology is that it is necessary to initiate a resistance battle against the denationalized cosmopolitans and the alienated, rootless Jews who would destroy national traditions from within, through their influential positions in society. Still, Brandes continued to call himself a modern Jewish cosmopolitan until his death in 1927, only a few years prior to Hitler gaining power in Germany.

In this discussion section, regarding the topics of Chapter 1 and 2, I will argue more substantially that the fin-de-siècle idealization of the

Jewish stranger is a useful perspective for the vast pool of literature on cosmopolitanism and ideal strangeness/alienation that has appeared in the last three decades. The idealization of immigrant experience and literature of the exile/diaspora and of strangeness has again become a widespread intellectual trend. However, while the idealization of certain elements of Jewish fin-de-siècle cosmopolitanism reminds us that there are many parallels between the first wave of globalization and the second we now live in, it is also important that we understand the differences. An increased awareness of the historical context of Brandes' modern Jew and Simmel's stranger figure is necessary; we must not reproduce all the elements of the Jewish-related ideal stranger without paying attention to their origins. Brandes' and other fin-de-siècle versions of this ideal stranger will be proposed as useful perspectives for the idealization of a related progressive strangeness, of which writers and thinkers such as Ulrich Beck, Julia Kristeva, Zygmunt Bauman, and Jacques Derrida all represent different but nevertheless related versions. Brandes' and the other fin-de-siècle stranger versions can thus help us to nuance and show the limits of this ideal. At the same time, in the context of today's rising Western right-wing populisms, the modern antisemitic key focus on Jewish strangers also provide valuable perspectives we can learn from today.

The second perspective this discussion will focus on is based on the content of Chapters 3 to 5. As Brandes demonstrates with his Athens vs. Jerusalem re-interpretations and his development of Spinozist cosmopolitanism in his later writings, cultural and religious traditions other than the Christian-based Western European civilization contain valuable examples of universal justice as the focal "secular faith," which we must strive to achieve in our societies in today's period of intensified globalization. Recalling Jeffrey C. Alexander's point that all so-called universalisms bear marks of primordial traits of particularities, it is essential that we acknowledge that other traditions encompass different paths, for example when constructing and further developing a supranational bond of nations such as the EU, and not least in the context of the different nation states we live in today.

The Revitalized Idealization of (Jewish) Strangeness

Michael Miller and Scott Ury have raised awareness of the European Jewish fin-de-siècle tradition of cosmopolitanism as containing many relevant perspectives for writings on cosmopolitanism from the last three decades.[524] They also remark that there have not been many scholarly examinations of this archive to date.[525] In this context, it is important firstly to clarify what I mean by the phrase "writings on cosmopolitanism from the last three decades." Is it possible to refer to all these writings on cosmopolitanism as belonging to one tradition, which can be compared to earlier cosmopolitan traditions? In this section, I will provide a brief overview of some of the key characteristics of writings on cosmopolitanism from the last three decades in order to argue that most of this literature can be interpreted as part of the same tradition. This is necessary to my proposition that Brandes' writings and in more general terms the European Jewish cosmopolitanisms of the nineteenth century and the fin-de-siècle period can provide us with valuable perspectives for today.

In *How Jewish is Jewish History?*, Moshe Rosman focuses on two dominant perspectives of Jewish history in the consideration of whether Jewish history and Jewish experiences contain valuable perspectives for us today. According to Rosman, Jewish history has typically been seen as either a trope or a model. Rosman identifies Homi K. Bhabha as the leading example of making Jews and Jewishness a trope:

One version (popular among non-Jewish theorists as well as some Jews) is to regard Jews, whose identity is always in flux, as an allegory, metaphor, or trope representing all of the people sinned against by modern Western civilization and summarizing all the ways in which they have been harmed. As we learned from Homi Bhabha (...), the Jewish experience is shorthand for the universal experience of all hybridized, colonized, alterior people who have suffered at the hands of modern civilization because they disconcert it. It is studied as an introduction to the need of multiculturalism and for the way in which it problematizes hegemony. It has no intrinsic value, or even significant content, beyond its representative potential and its power to discomfit.[526]

As Rosman argues, this view of Jewish experiences as a trope typically ignores the fact that Jewish history contains particularistic and historically specific traits, which make it difficult merely to reproduce aspects of it without critical reflection on this use. The tendency to use Jewishness as a trope is, besides Rosman's example of Bhabha, also visible in Zygmunt Bauman's famous rendering of the term "sliminess" in *Modernity and the Holocaust*. Bauman consequently proposed "the Jew" (and not: the Jew) as a trope for all individuals and groups who have been stigmatized as in-between strangers, subverting the order of society or threatening national cultural traditions.[527] The idea of the conceptual Jew as a trope for every stranger is also evident in Bauman's *Modernity and Ambivalence*, which is the work I will focus on in this section.

In the other common approach, viewing Jewish history and Jewish experiences as a model—as the Boyarin brothers, for example, have campaigned for—the particularity of Jewish history is respected and acknowledged.[528] When applying Jewish experiences as a model, we can still learn from Jewish history; Jewish experiences still "have something to teach—to contribute."[529] Nevertheless, the Boyarin brothers stress that we must remember to include the historical context of the model and pay attention to its singularistic characteristics, so that we can distinguish between the model and the present use of the model as a *Geschehen*.[530]

European Jewish Fin-De-Siècle Cosmopolitanism as a Model—for What?

Without doubt, Ulrich Beck's *The Cosmopolitan Vision* is the most debated and quoted work among recent writings on cosmopolitanism. Much acknowledgement has rightfully been given to Beck's sociological diagnosis of how all of us today, whether we like it or not, have been cosmopolitanized, so that even our most private spheres are influenced by what Beck calls "cosmopolitanization," particularly through the internet.[531] Beck emphasizes how a sociological description must always be combined with a normative approach.[532] However, while most recent works on cosmopolitanism acknowledge his sociological analysis of our global age, many do not agree with his normative approach. In particular, Beck's ideal of the cosmopolitan outlook has been criticized.[533] An example may be found in the group of scholars who identify themselves as New Cosmopolitans. One of the so-called New Cosmopolitans, Robert Fine, has argued that Beck lacks a realistic understanding of our present time when he envisions that all human beings must transform themselves according to the cosmopolitan outlook and abandon all beliefs and structures that characterize the national outlook.[534] Beck thus clearly understands individuals who continue to view the world through the lens, wholly or partly, of the national outlook as following a somewhat backwards and reactionary mindset.[535] Most of these so-called New Cosmopolitan writers and thinkers acknowledge Beck's argument that everyone everywhere (in Africa, Asia, Europe, etc.) has been cosmopolitanized. However, they do not agree that this necessarily means it is outdated to maintain or at least acknowledge that the national state is still by most people today perceived as being very real (and not merely "imagined") and will probably continue to play an important role for a long time. I have suggested that Gillian Brock and Harry Brighouse's definition of weak vs. strong cosmopolitanism is a useful conceptual frame for understanding how different cosmopolitan theories and writers position themselves.[536] This distinction can also be used to illustrate how the different voices of New Cosmopolitanism view different ideological standpoints. Ulrich Beck, along with Georg Brandes in his early writings, and also Jacques Derrida in *Cosmopolitanism and Forgiveness*, represents a strong cosmopolitanism where both the national state and the individual traits of a national outlook are assumed to have disappeared, or will be on their way to disappearing. Weak cosmopolitanism, on the other hand, holds that national or regional structures and identities, and other such imagined communities, will continue to be important despite increasing globalization processes. However, as regards the ambivalence of our present global age (quoting Karl Marx, it is indeed a time where "everything seems pregnant with its opposite")[537], even the most hardcore right-wing nationalist must acknowledge that some forms of cosmopolitanism exist and are inevitably growing; most likely these hardcore nationalists also practise forms of cosmopolitanism, for example by being part of online (transnational) nationalistic communities. In contrast, most voices of New Cosmopolitanism normatively emphasize that a balance between the cosmopolitan/global and the national/local outlook is necessary.[538]

The Greek/Roman-Kantian Cosmopolitan Tradition

Can we then view the various cosmopolitan writings of Ulrich Beck, Jacques Derrida, and Robert Fine, and the balanced cosmopolitanisms of Brock and Brighouse's anthology of the last three decades, as belonging to the same cosmopolitan tradition? The answer to this is yes—when we look at which tradition all of these writers and thinkers themselves point to as the one they follow. Both Beck and the different scholars of New Cosmopolitanism, as well as Jacques Derrida in *Cosmopolitanism and Forgiveness*, all see themselves as followers of a tradition of Greek/Roman-Kantian cosmopolitanism.[539] Nevertheless, the vast numbers of cosmopolitan writers and thinkers in recent years who view themselves as part of a tradition of Greek/Roman-Kantian cosmopolitanism adapt this tradition in different ways. Particularly, Robert Fine has proposed a useful understanding of the Kantian cosmopolitan tradition today. In *Cosmopolitanism* (2007), he writes (as a representant of New Cosmopolitanism):

The core contention is that the cosmopolitan ideals of the Enlightenment thought are once again pertinent to our own times. The new cosmopolitanism sets itself the task of ironing out inconsistencies in Kant's way of thinking, radicalizing it where its break from the old order of sovereign states was incomplete, freeing it from the old order of metaphysical baggage [...], and applying it to a radically different transformed social context. The basic agenda of cosmopolitan political philosophy is to "think Kant against Kant" in reconstructing the cosmopolitan ideal for our own times.[540]

Fine views himself and the different voices of New Cosmopolitanism as followers of Kantian cosmopolitanism. He acknowledges the great importance of Kant's thinking on cosmopolitanism, while at the same time aiming at "ironing out inconsistencies in Kant's way of thinking." It is not specified what these "inconsistencies" entail. However, as we saw in Chapter 5, Kant's universalism in "Idee zu einer allgemeinen Geschichte in weltbürgerlicher Absicht" is ambivalent. In comparison with Kant's other famous cosmopolitan essay "Zum ewigen Frieden [...]," this is the most quoted work on cosmopolitanism in recent years, and Kant's universalism bears primordial marks of the Christian-based Western European particularistic tradition. For example, he writes that one day Europe will provide the rest of the world with civilizational laws.[541]

There is also a growing awareness that other relevant cosmopolitanisms exist and have existed that we can learn from. With the term "cosmopolitan archive," Sheldon Pollock, Homi K Bhabha, Carol A. Breckenridge, and Dipesh Chakrabarty call attention to other constructive examples from traditions other than the Greek/Roman-Kantian cosmopolitan tradition, which, it seems, also carries with it at least a considerable potential to place ideal and normative approaches over practice.[542] But before we come to Brandes' Spinozist cosmopolitanism as an example of this, let us examine the ways in which cosmopolitan writings of the last three decades, parallel to being part of the Kantian cosmopolitan tradition, also have been influenced by the Jewish cosmopolitanism of the fin-de-siècle period by using it as a trope.

The Jewish-related Ideal Stranger as a Model

In Chapter 2, we have already seen that Georg Simmel's stranger concept influenced contemporary writings on cosmopolitanism. The ideal stranger figure helped to inspire the idealization of alienation by, for example, Julia Kristeva in *Strangers to Ourselves*, Ulrich Beck in *The Cosmopolitan Vision*, Zygmunt Bauman in *Modernity and Ambivalence*, and (as we will see) Jacques Derrida in *Cosmopolitanism and Forgiveness*. It can thus be argued that the idealization of the rootless stranger, a figure with which European Jewish intellectuals were identified and with which many of these individuals also identified themselves positively, has been revitalized in recent years. Central parts of the cosmopolitanisms of European Jewish intellectuals such as Brandes and Simmel resemble key topics of the present-day cosmopolitanisms of Kristeva, Bauman, Beck, and Derrida, particularly the positive representation of migration experience, the exile/diaspora as a topos, rootlessness, liberal free thinking, cosmopolitanism, and strangeness/alienation. Together, these characteristics seem to represent a type of progressive modern identity that meets the challenges of our present global age. Since the 1990s, these different proponents of this line of thought have also been presented as a counter-reaction to the most dominant opposing view of cultural and civilizational encounters of the last three decades, Samuel Huntington's clash of civilization thesis. In this context, it is not unimportant that Huntington wrote his essay on the clash of civilizations as a response to his former student Francis Fukuyama's end of history thesis, which the Introduction elaborated on as a key inspiration for the revitalization of writings on cosmopolitanism in the 1990s. Yet when pointing to specific similarities between cosmopolitanisms of recent years and the fin-de-siècle idealization of Jewish strangeness, we must also outline the fundamental differences.

As demonstrated in Chapter 2, the ideal Jewish strangeness of the fin-de-siècle period was mainly produced as a counter-reaction to modern antisemitism, in that it stressed the Jewish co-construction of Western civilization. Consequently, just as the New Cosmopolitans today are aware that they must resolve the "inconsistencies of Kant's thinking" and reflect on and re-think central elements of Kant's cosmopolitanism, we must also gain a better and more substantial firsthand knowledge of the cosmopolitan archive of ideal strangeness.

In this context, firstly, one notices that the references to the European Jewish cosmopolitan tradition are a lot more subtle than the often rather expressive and substantial references to Kant in works on cosmopolitanism from the last three decades. For example, on the very first page of Beck's *The Cosmopolitan Vision*, we are told that Beck views himself as standing on the shoulders of the cosmopolitanism of Heinrich Heine.[543] Yet Heine's cosmopolitanism is not mentioned again—Kant, however, is quoted and paraphrased on many pages in the book.[544] It is also characteristic that although Simmel's stranger figure appears to form a basis for Beck's "cosmopolitan outlook," there are no direct references to Simmel when Beck defines his cosmopolitan ideal. The reason for this is most likely that, while there has been a renewed substantial focus on the importance of Diogenes', Seneca's, and Kant's cosmopolitanisms, European Jewish cosmopolitanism of the nineteenth century and the fin-de-siècle period has rarely been examined or researched.[545]

The need for greater awareness of this European Jewish cosmopolitanism, and for learning to use it as a model rather than as a trope, can be illustrated in the misleading identification between the strangeness of migrants and refugees and the aforementioned progressive modern stranger identity which Baumann, Kristeva, Beck, and Jacques Derrida all represent as an ideal for present-day Western intellectuals.

It is an inherent part of Brandes' modern Jew and Simmel's ideal stranger that these figures are simultaneously inside and outside the group by which the individual is identified as the stranger. This is the situation and the type of existence which makes the fin-de-siècle ideal stranger equally near and equally remote, to paraphrase Brandes. Historically, the acculturated, bourgeois-influenced Western European Jews occupied such a sociocultural position; they were born into an out-group of society, and were thus identified simply as "Jews" by the Christian-based majority society regardless of their accomplishments or opinions about this identification. In other words, these European Jewish writers and thinkers were both part of an out-group while through their *Bildung*, they were also impressive intellectuals. As intellectuals, they furthermore used the cultural alienation they experienced productively.

However, in many of the writings from the last three decades in which a similar type of strangeness has been idealized, the Jewish-related stranger has in fact been split into two different figures. One is a Western intellectual (or simply a Westerner, as in Beck's book) who incarnates Western values and norms. The other is most often a non-Western/non-Christian migrant and/or refugee. In *Modernity and Ambivalence*, Bauman is clear in perceiving innovative strangeness as a trope and thus, in his analysis, he simply follows the logical consequences of the Jew-as-a-trope view. In the first chapters, he describes the characteristics of this type of strangeness by examining the cultural in-between position of the German Jews in the nineteenth century. Following this, he recommends that "modern intellectuals" should develop a similar intellectually stimulating alienation. [546] In Kristeva's *Strangers to Ourselves*, we also find this identification between Western intellectual creative alienation and the strangeness and alienation of migrants and refugees in her use of exile as a central concept. Up until today, this idealization has continued to be evident. In a recent essay in *Die Welt* on the new literary genre of migrant fiction, German literary critic Richard Kämmerling has similarly expressed that Westerners should particularly focus on the new genre of migrant literature because the stranger experiences of migrants can teach Westerners how to become "strangers to themselves."[547]

In Jacques Derrida's *Cosmopolitanism and Forgiveness*, we also find a related identification between the strangeness of migrants/refugees and the idealized strangeness of present-day Western intellectuals. Derrida proposes that in the Western world "cities of refuge" for incoming strangers should be established. But it is an open question how exactly he identifies who these strangers are in reality.[548] It is not clear whether he is speaking about all refugees and migrants or—as it seems—only about migrating intellectuals, journalists, and scholars fleeing from social injustice and oppression in non-Western countries.[549] Nevertheless, according to Derrida, we should first establish "cities of refuge" for incoming culturally different strangers, and in the course of time these cities will develop into progressive urban centers. Seemingly, "cities of refuge" will also attract certain progressive groups and individuals from the surrounding Western society. These "cities of refuge" will ultimately transform European national states, Western democracy, and the laws by which our shared secular faith in society is defined:

I also imagine the experience of cities of refuge as giving rise to a place (*lieu*) for reflection [...] and for a new order of law and a democracy to come to be put to the test (experimentation). Being on the threshold of these cities, of these new cities which would be something other than "new cities," a certain idea of cosmopolitanism, an other, has not yet arrived, perhaps.

– if it has (indeed) arrived …

… then, one has perhaps not yet recognized it.[550]

Here, it is a new, progressive "we" which comes to transform the Western national state and democracy, a "we" which also seems to dissolve the former separation between the newly arrived non-Western strangers and the Westerners.

With regard to *Cosmopolitanism and Forgiveness*, we must not forget that Derrida wrote it in 2000/2001 and thus before the migrant and refugee situation of the 2010s developed. Within the last six or seven years, migration to Europe has increased and the European debates on this subject have also become a far more dominant part of the civil sphere. Still, even in 2000–2001 there was a discrepancy between the actual groups of migrants and refugees and the demographic Derrida chooses to focus on—fleeing or migrating intellectuals, journalists, and scholars—to illustrate his figure of the stranger.[551] He could be right that this specific sub-group of skilled migrants, along with like-minded groups from Western civil societies, could develop an innovative type of avant-garde strangeness in such visionary "cities of refuge." However, in reality, the influx of migrants and refugees to Europe represents a broad and differentiated group of people, some of whom resemble Derrida's primary examples of specific *haut bourgeoisie* types, while others come from different backgrounds.

As regards the recent decades' revitalization of the less prejudiced and more objective Jewish-related stranger ideal, my point is that there is a difference between the strangeness of non-Western migrants and refugees and the Western intellectual idealized strangeness. The difference is first and foremost that Georg Brandes, Berthold Auerbach, Moritz Lazarus, Heinrich Graetz, Sigmund Freud, Franz Kafka, Georg Simmel, Stefan Zweig, Imre Kertész, Primo Levi, Walter Benjamin, and many others all experienced cultural in-between-ness and were excluded, some in a violent way, because of their Jewish background. They existed in a continuous exile, not fully rooted in the traditional Jewish communities or in any majority groups of society. There was thus a huge degree of personal motivation when these writers reacted to antisemitism's identification of them and other European Jews as negative alien elements, as parasites, through narratives with topoi including exile, cosmopolitanism, alienation/strangeness, diaspora, and rootlessness. However, when today's Western intellectuals label their own alienation as the same as or similar to the struggles of non-Western migrants and refugees, this is a false identification. Undoubtedly, it is important that all Westerners empathize with and can relate to the situation of non-Western refugees and migrants. However, the Western idealized topos of an inner, intellectually stimulating exile striving towards a sophisticated alienated outlook does not correspond to the experiences of non-Western refugees and migrants when they reach Europe. Indeed, Westerners face many difficulties in our global age; turbulent and accelerated global age changes and crises mean that, as Julia Kristeva attests, most Westerners live without roots in any communities, whether it be family, a religious community, or a stable work community. Thus our social world is increasingly turned into a "drama of recognition" as seen through recent years of identity politics.[552] However, when we idealize exile as a topos and use it to explain the form of intensified individualism we experience in the Western world today, we must not forget that the normative systems we constantly reinforce through this denote the exact opposite values of those most non-Western migrants and refugees strive to live by when they come to the Europe. As Homi K. Bhabha writes about Kristeva's ideal strangeness:

Such an emancipatory ideal – so affixed on the flowing, borderless, global world – neglects to confront the fact that migrants, refuges or nomads don't merely circulate. They need to settle, claim asylum or nationality, demand housing and education, assert their economic and cultural rights and seek the status of citizenship.[553]

Indeed, it is necessary to form other views of how cultural encounters should be perceived than Samuel Huntington's clash of civilization thesis, which rather one-sidedly sees cultural encounters as riddled with conflict and ultimately violence, war, and destruction. Still, it is also necessary to show the limits of this ideal stranger type so that the particularistic historical context of the Jewish-related ideal stranger is remembered, acknowledged, and taken into consideration when it is used as a model today. As such, the ideal of the stranger in new cosmopolitan work has been an influential part of debates on migration in recent years (Derrida's essay is the clearest example of this), and related questions of multiculturalism vs. national culture. As in the discussion of the so-called Jewish Question in the fin-de-siècle period, migrants, in-between groups, and new groups of cultural strangers seem once again to have become a widespread cultural code used to discuss, diagnose, and prognosticate the effects of globalization processes and its acceleration of change. But no matter how one views these often unconstructive, polarized discussions on migration and mobility, we must be aware of the normative subtext of this specific stranger type in key works of the new cosmopolitanism.

In the context of the recent rise in right-wing populism, Brandes' and the other European Jewish fin-de-siècle idealizations of the Jewish-related stranger represent a no less important perspective. Thus, today, as in the fin-de-siècle period, we find many examples of various right-wing populisms centering on resistance battles against cultural stranger groups and the so-called rootless and de-nationalized cosmopolitan-oriented "elite" parts of the majority society.

As in our current global age, the vast societal transformation process of the fin-de-siècle period implied new possibilities and advantages for many groups. However, many groups also reacted against globally oriented democratization and capitalism, and did not view the development as "progressive." Some of these groups, including the craftsmanship groups Shulamit Volkov focuses on in her classic study on the origin of modern antisemitism, clearly did not benefit from the new industrial capitalistic forms of production. These craftmanship groups identified themselves and were identified as *Modernisierungsverlie-reren*. Yet it would be too simplistic to blame the lower classes for the development of modern antisemitism as a new populism formulated in catchy slogans such as "Die soziale Frage ist die Judenfrage." The ide-ology of modern antisemitism was all the way through developed by *haut bourgeoisie* figures such as the respected historian Heinrich von Treitschke and pastor Adolf Stoecker. This perspective is useful in the context of the development and spread of right-wing populistic move-ments and ideologies of our global age, for example in taking into ac-count the growing influence of *Génération Identitaire* in Europe or the role that Steve Bannon has played in the establishment of the North American Alt-Right movement. As seen through this book's examina-tions of the Athens vs. Jerusalem dichotomy, modern antisemitic ste-reotypes definitely also thrived in the bourgeoisie, including in the Dan-ish bourgeoisie. Sophisticated and *salonfähig* forms of modern antisem-itism were frequently used by key actors in society to stigmatize and exclude individuals of Jewish descent from firm and secure positions in the bourgeoisie, as we have seen in the case of Vilhelm Andersen. All over Western Europe, the parallel Jewish bourgeoisies continued to exist in the twentieth century. Today, too, we must therefore be aware of intellectual sophistications of racism and the cultural codes by which stranger groups have historically been identified as targets in times of accelerated change.

Hence, most likely, in the coming years of our second global age, more and more people will feel "behind the others" while also being identified by the surrounding society as *Modernisierungsverliereren*. Populists will seek to tap into these feelings of unimportance and not being recognized for one's abilities and potential. In *Homo Deus* (2016), similar to Shulamit Volkov's research on how modern antisemitism be-came a popular cultural code and explanation model, Yuval Harari has described a group of Westerners as having become a "useless class of citizens" as part of recent globalization. Harari also predicts that this group will continue to grow. Thus, if we want to continue to work and to understand the world and be relevant to what is happening, in general, we will all have to reinvent, adapt, and transform ourselves again and again, faster and faster, if we want to keep up with these accelerated processes of change and the type of work market that comes with this development (particularly as regards the constant flow of new "revolutionizing" technology that we must adapt to, for example in the context of the job market). Already now, the increasing amount of digitalized information we are expected to consume is experienced by many—and not just groups of so-called "losers of modernity"—as a difficult and somewhat futile challenge. Rightfully, Ulrich Beck and other significant voices of the new cosmopolitanisms have been criticized for not paying enough attention to the unintended consequences of the globalization process, which Jeffrey C. Alexander has called *The Dark Side of Modernity* (2012). Accordingly, just as we must be aware of reckless liberal cosmopolitanism, not least in the context of unregulated global "free market" capitalism, we must also be aware of what seems to be a fundamental human tendency to point out and blame stranger groups for the unintended consequences and dark sides of major social, political, and economical changes. Drawing on Koselleck's analysis of how and when the gap between *Erfahrungsraum* and *Erwartungshorizont* increases, one can even argue that it is somewhat logical that stranger groups have yet again become our favorite objects in the increased utopian and not least dystopian human imagination of the future in this globalized period of accelerated change. The European Jews of the fin-de-siècle period are moreover far from the only relevant case when it comes to stranger groups being identified as media for vast social change and transitions in other historical periods. In a specific Danish context, besides the common European topos of the Muslim stranger, migrating wolves and wild pigs have even played an important role in discussions on migration and mobility in recent years. Furthermore, the mainstream media and the leading politicians who passionately take part in the often intense discussions on Muslim strangers or the effects of migrating wolves and wild pigs do not seem to be conscious of the point when these discussions develop into chimerically based cultural codes by which it seems to be more general discussions on migration and mobility that is being debated. In this context, the most important lesson of Brandes' interconnections of cosmopolitanism and Jewishness and the antisemitic reactions to these interconnections is that we must try to discuss the accelerated processes of change themselves. Particularly, we must try more directly to discuss the Western intellectual and capitalist economical understanding of growth and civilizational progress that drives these accelerated processes of change—instead of discussing them through indirect cultural codes such as the ones targeted at the Muslim stranger or migrating wild pigs. Instead of blindly following this ideal of hasty and accelerated change through a particular understanding of how our society must progress according to certain economical ideological based growth perceptions, we should again let ethics and the question of universal justice be our primary guideline.

In the context of the recent increase in right-wing populism, the archive of Georg Brandes' oeuvre can teach us another important lesson: It took more than five decades from when modern antisemitism was first developed as a new ideology and populism in the *Berliner Antisemitismusstreit* until Hitler and the Nazi party won a majority of the votes in the German democratic election of 1933. Many forms of modern antisemitism existed in the in-between period, and Hitler's final version should be seen as having been built on many different drafts of modern antisemitic ideologies. One of the most significant attempts to create a powerful and cohesive modern antisemitism can be found in Otto Weininger's *Geschlecht und Character* of 1903. Hitler was later influenced by Weininger's book. However, there are also ideas in *Geschlecht und Character* that the Nazi ideology later wiped out. For example, Weininger developed Treitschke's and the early modern antisemitic idea of a necessary resistance battle against the Jewish domination of society into the idea that only two types of mindsets existed at the turn of the century in Germany: The Arian and the Jewish mindset, or the meaningful, nationally rooted *Gemeinschaft* versus the rootless, alienated, cosmopolitan *Gesellschaft*. As such, each individual faced an ultimate life-or-death choice as to which side of this polarized battle they supported. Thus, Weininger did not view Jewishness as a biological, racially determined category, as the Nazis later would. He believed that individuals who had a so-called Jewish mindset could rescue themselves and develop an Arian mindset. As such, the road to 1933 and the Holocaust of World War II was long and, as a populism offering understandable ways of interpreting the world and its different forms of hasty *Geschehen*, modern antisemitism developed in various but interrelated forms before the Nazis took power. Now and in the future, different rightwing populisms will also compete with each other over establishing ultimate life-or-death crisis narratives that will make it possible for them to win a majority of votes in democratic elections; their creators will learn from earlier failures and seek to develop ever more popular crisis narratives, for example by synthesizing with other crisis narratives on migration and mobility, pandemics, climate change, financial crisis, Western democracy crisis, and so on. Hopefully, we will be able to avoid that similar regimes as those that came about in Europe in the 1930s will develop in the 2020s or 2030s although even today some countries indeed seem to stand in the middle of life-or-death choices regarding whether they will remain democracies.

I will now elaborate more on one of Brandes' counter-reactions to modern antisemitism, since it is now more than ever necessary that we, as Westerners, acknowledge that other traditions contain different paths that can ultimately lead to the same mutually shared democratic universal justice values.

Different Paths to the Same Civil Sphere

The second vital aspect of Brandes' representations of Jewishness as a valuable cosmopolitan archive for recent work on cosmopolitanism is the Spinozist cosmopolitanism of his later writings, and his idea of a Jewish tradition of secular thought. In his analyses of the Old Testament, Brandes thematizes a Jewish tradition of secular thought positioning Baruch Spinoza as the father of Western modernity. We have however also seen that Brandes' interest in the ancient Jewish tradition should not be limited to the last decades of his life. In the letters Brandes wrote to his parents when he was travelling as a teenager, the book

Brandes refers to the most is the Old Testament. While his childhood home was not particularly influenced by Jewish religious practice, these many references to the cornerstone of the Jewish tradition demonstrate that Brandes was much culturally influenced by the Jewish tradition. He was what in Danish would be called *kulturjødisk* (culturally influenced by Judaism), a parallel to the frequently used term *kulturkristen* (culturally influenced by Christianity). Regarding the lack of previous research on the Jewish cultural influence on Brandes, a parallel can be drawn to Inger Hammar's perspective of how historical and cultural studies have all too long been "religion blind," in the same way that feminist research termed earlier work "gender blind."[554] The impact of religious practices and ideas on secular cultural phenomena that are not bound into ecclesiastical contexts is under-researched, generally and also specifically in relation to Brandes.

In terms of the cosmopolitan-orientated Western European Jews that have been the particular focus of this book, in *Not in the Heavens: The Tradition of Secular Jewish Thought* (2011), David Biale writes that it was not only Brandes who, in the nineteenth and early twentieth centuries, found sources of relevant secular thought in the books of the Old Testament. It is not difficult to understand why:

In many of the works that can be dated to the Persian or Hellenistic periods, such as Esther, Job and Ecclesiastes, God is transcendent or even completely absent. He no longer walks among humans, as he did in the literature of the First Temple period and his communication with them has become indirect if not mute [...]. [In the book of the Ecclesiastes] the writer finds no meaning in the world, starting and concluding that "all is futile." Although the coda to the book recommends revering God and obeying his commandments, one has the sense that this pious ending was tacked on to make the less-than-Orthodox text more palatable. Exactly what the philosophical position of the author actually was remains hotly contested, and he may or may not have been the follower of a Greek school of philosophy like that of Lucretius or Epicurus. But the book was certainly ripe for the picking by a modern secularist.[555]

For example, the German Jewish historian Heinrich Graetz and the communist founder Karl Marx were preoccupied in their letter correspondence, like Brandes, with the secularizing visions of *Kohélet/Ecclesiastes*.[556]

In the nineteenth and early twentieth century, Brandes was moreover far from the only European Jewish intellectual who considered Baruch Spinoza and not Immanuel Kant the father of modernity. In this book, Berthold Auerbach and Moritz Lazarus have been proposed as other significant nineteenth-century and fin-de-siècle European Jewish intellectuals who also advanced Baruch Spinoza as a central reference for how to be modern, and in fact Georg Simmel was also a Spinoza follower. My conjecture is that these European Jewish intellectuals would not represent themselves as followers of Kantian cosmopolitanism because they were aware of Kant's ambivalent universalism. Besides stating that non-European nations will someday learn from "our" civilizational laws, at one point in the essay, Kant also writes that a "wise creator" has designed nature with a particular teleological purpose.[557] It is thus not surprising that European Jewish intellectuals such as Georg Brandes and Berthold Auerbach, who refused to convert to Christianity, would insist that other traditions existed which considered universal justice the most central virtue of human civilization. They were aware of the "inconsistencies" within Kant's cosmopolitanism and they most likely viewed Kantian cosmopolitanism as Christian-based. With reference to Spinoza, they communicated that they wanted to be recognized as equals to Christian-born men without having to convert and subdue themselves. Subsequently, they each constructed their own forms of Spinozism, which also reflected their own particular ideas of what it meant to be a modern secular-orientated European/Danish/German Jew, since these so-called integrationists also considered themselves part of the national European traditions and Western civilization into which they were born.

Still, for some readers, Brandes' evaluation of the Jewish tradition of secular thought probably appears to be an overestimation of the Jewish co-construction of European civilization. In the last part of Chapter 5, we saw how Brandes interprets the Jewish tradition of secular thought as having catalyzed some of the most innovative ideas in modern Western thinking, including Luther's Protestant rebellion and Cromwell's reforms in Great Britain. A necessary question subsequently emerges: Does Brandes in fact create yet another cultural chauvinistic idea of the foundations of European modernity and secularization with his Spinozist cosmopolitanism? He does argue, for example, that the Jewish tradition of secular thought is more advanced than the Christian equivalent since it demands that ideals are followed by practice. Like Kant's Christian-based universalism in "Idee zu einer allgemeinen Geschichte in weltbürgerlicher Absicht," one could ask whether Brandes simply proposed a Jewish-related *Bildung*, which non-Jews must experience before they can become truly modern secularized individuals? Here, it is important to observe that Brandes formulated his Spinozist cosmopolitanism at the same time as his Athens vs. Jerusalem interpretations. The two themes are deeply related and often they appear side by side in the same books. In Chapter 4, I read Brandes' interpretations of the Athens vs. Jerusalem dichotomy as a counter-narrative to the hegemonic idea that the ancient Jewish civilization was a degenerative "false start" for European civilization. With his juxtaposition of Athens and Jerusalem, Brandes emphasized the contribution of ancient Jewish civilization to Europe. Similarly, with his cosmopolitanism, he is concerned with finding Jewish cosmopolitan archives that oppose the typical Enlightenment narrative regarding the ancient Jewish religious tradition. In his books on the Old Testament, he does not repeat Kant's or Renan's ideas that the ancient Jewish tradition can be synthesized as superstitious, dogmatic, and irrational. Thus, when antisemitism began to grow, it became crucial for Brandes to demonstrate that different interpretations of the Old Testament existed in the course of Jewish history, beyond the clerical orthodox ones. His claim that Spinoza was the culmination of a tradition of secular thought points to one of these different Jewish "histories." Brandes' agenda is not, however, to demand that all non-Jews experience a Jewish *Bildung* before they can become truly "modern." In *Jobs Bog* and *Kohélet*, he does not neglect to inform us that the ancient Greek culture is also full of constructive examples of ideal secular virtues and let us remember that, at the beginning of *Jobs Bog*, Brandes writes "It is Hellas and Israel to which Europe owes its culture."[558] Thus, by insisting that Jewish examples of secular thought must be considered equivalent to, for instance, Athens' innovative ideas, he demonstrates that in the modern world parallel particular "histories" can exist, demonstrating that certain ideals, such as universal justice, are fundamental humanistic values. Here, I level with David Biale, who in *Not in the Heavens* points out that the pervading view in academia has for many years been that there is only one form of secularization—the one that took place in relation to Christianity in Western Europe. As Biale suggests, it would be productive also to consider the secularization that took place and indeed takes place in relation to Judaism, Hinduism, Islam, and so on. Brandes' Spinozist cosmopolitanism represents a vital cosmopolitan archive for literature on cosmopolitanism today since he legitimately points out examples of another tradition of secular thought, one that is different from the dominant Western narrative in which Diogenes and Kant stand as the founding fathers of secularism. In the context of Jeffrey C. Alexander's definition of the modern civil sphere, Brandes' perception of these previous Jewish cosmopolitan archives is therefore useful for us today. Hence, most present-day debates and struggles of our different Western civil spheres focus primarily on the same topic that Brandes proposes as the focal point in the ancient Jewish as well as modern Jewish tradition, the question of universal justice. In this way, non-Christians, who are not familiar with Seneca, Kant, or Grundtvig's *Nordens Mytologi* (*Mythology of the North*) (1832), can still participate equally and valuably in these fundamental contextually bound discussions of our mutual "secular faith." Implicitly, Brandes argues that other cultural and religious traditions similarly contain examples of traditions of secular thought and this is indeed a valuable perspective for our current, second intensified globalization period, where cultural pluralism and cosmopolitanized national identity is an everyday experience for most people. If we can agree that democratic universal justice is an ideal we strive to live by when we meet each other in the civil sphere, it is less important which cultural and religious paths brought us to this meeting point.

Brandes' Spinozist cosmopolitanism can thus teach us that we must also revitalize other past embodiments of relevant cosmopolitan archives. On the basis of the Greek/Roman-Kantian cosmopolitan tradition, it might seem as though cosmopolitan thought is only about the future—particularly as seen through the texts of Kant, Ulrich Beck and Jacques Derrida, in which all humanity at some unclear point in the future is envisioned as living together in harmony in a new, progressed form of Western order. However, Brandes' Spinozist cosmopolitanism and in general the nineteenth-century and fin-de-siècle European Jewish cosmopolitan tradition shows us that cosmopolitanism is more than anything about the present, and the challenges and struggles of the future for which we need to prepare and act out on now. Yet, Cosmopolitanism is also about the past; cosmopolitan existences have already been lived (in this context, I am not thinking about Kant's secluded existence in Königsberg). Therefore, we must also begin to understand cosmopolitanisms as histories that can influence and alter how we perceive the present and build the future through their potential to become new forms of *Geschehen* having impact on how we meet and solve the crises and challenges of our present-day global age.

Conclusion

This book has focused on the interconnections between representations of Jewishness and cosmopolitanism in Georg Brandes' (1842–1927) writings. I have argued that Georg Brandes—one of the most influential European intellectuals in the fin-de-siècle period—and his Jewish-related and cosmopolitan themes together constitute a crucial archive for studies on this significant interconnection, which became a dominant cultural code in the period covered by the book. Brandes was also a favored target for influential early modern antisemites such as Adolf Stoecker, who, based on a Dano-Norwegian pamphlet written against Brandes, argued he was a key example of subversive Jewishness in the German *Reichstag*.

While Brandes has typically been viewed as a liberal cosmopolitan, the existing research on his ideas and practice addresses his representation of Jewishness only to a limited degree, despite the fact that Brandes, even in his first published works, presented himself as a modern Jewish cosmopolitan. In fact, previous research typically does not move beyond the presentation of Brandes as a so-called "assimilated Jew" who distanced himself from Jewishness.

In his early writings (1867–1883(/1897)), Brandes is mainly concerned with interconnecting Jewishness and cosmopolitanism in terms of creating a cosmopolitan vision of the future. He dreams of a transformed mankind in which everyone shares the same universal rights and values and in which the figure of the modern Jew is the primary role model for this transformation. In his later writings, his interconnections primarily reflect the more general tendencies in Europe after 1879–81. Through racially based modern antisemitism, Jews and Jewishness were increasingly identified as negative alien elements within the histories of different European national cultures. Brandes' interconnections consequently came to emphasize Jews and Jewishness as a founding and continuous part of the history of Western civilization.

Chapter 1 shed light on the representations of Jewishness in Brandes' early writings. The main focus was on Brandes' cosmopolitan ideal of the transnational vision through the figures of the modern Jew, the emigrant, and the critic, and through the topos of exile. Brandes claims that, as a result of the Jewish racial *Volksgeist* heritage, the modern Jew has precedence in the development of the transnational vision. In this period, he in fact proposes that the modern Jew is the most innovative individual in the development of the cosmopolitan-orientated modern world. Consequently, this chapter argued that Brandes' modern Jew must be seen as an essential but somewhat disguised and thus far overlooked subtext to his Modern Breakthrough project.

Chapter 2 elaborated further on Brandes' figure of the modern Jew and sought to demonstrate how, through the ideal stranger figure, Brandes was part of an interesting intellectual pattern at this time in which different Jewish-related ideal stranger figures were put forward as a counter-reaction to a specific stereotypical depiction of Western European Jews as rootless. Chapter 2 proposed that Georg Simmel's *Exkurs über der Fremde* (1908) should be considered not as the founding text for the concept of the stranger in academia, but the culmination of an ideal that had gestated for a longer period.

The last three chapters focused on the interconnection of Jewishness and cosmopolitanism in Brandes' later writings and the effects of increasing modern antisemitism, which led him to develop his Jewish-related cosmopolitanism more substantially while at the same time seeking to avoid being stigmatized as a "cosmopolitan Jew." Chapter 3 showed that Brandes distances himself from Jewishness and cosmopolitanism even more in his later work, particularly through the two significant strategies of "de-Judaizing" and "de-cosmopolitanization," which are most evident in his editing process for his *Samlede Skrifter* (1899–1910) and in his autobiography *Levned* (1905–08). These distancing strategies were also read as related to Brandes' goal of becoming a professor at the University of Copenhagen. In his earlier attempts, Brandes had again and again experienced that his Jewish background and cosmopolitan ideas had prevented his appointment.

Chapters 4 and 5 demonstrated how Brandes developed his Jewish-related cosmopolitanism by stressing the Jewish co-construction of Western civilization in his later writings. Thus, while he distanced himself even more from Jewishness in works which he intended for commercial success, another significant pattern is observable. In several writings on the Old Testament and early Christianity, Brandes is occupied with illustrating how Jews and Jewishness were an indispensable and founding element of Western civilization. In Chapter 4, the key focus was on Brandes' original re-interpretations of the influential nineteenth-century dichotomy of Athens vs. Jerusalem, which had been central to the Jewish Question since the Enlightenment in the course of works by Immanuel Kant, G. W. F. Hegel, and Friedrich Nietzsche, for example. In writings such as *Jobs Bog*, *Kohélet* and *Urkristendommen*, Brandes re-constructs this historically influential discussion of the Jewish Question so that Athens vs. Jerusalem becomes Athens *and* Jerusalem.

Chapter 5 elaborated further on Brandes' writings on the Old Testament and early Christianity with an analysis of the role accorded to Baruch Spinoza. This chapter demonstrated how, in his later works, Brandes formulates a unique Spinozist cosmopolitanism. Influenced in particular by Berthold Auerbach's *Bildungsroman Spinoza*, Brandes defines a coherent tradition of Jewish secular thought that runs from the Old Testament to modern times and which was a crucial factor in the shaping of European modernity and modern secular thought. His Spinozist cosmopolitanism should thus also be seen as a reaction to the various right-wing nationalistic and antisemitic movements and actors of this period, since he again emphasizes that Jews and Jewishness were a founding and continuous part of Western civilization from ancient to modern times.

Based on Chapters 1 to 5, the Discussion then presents two perspectives that make Brandes' work a valuable cosmopolitan archive for today's literature on cosmopolitanism. Brandes' and other fin-de-siècle versions of the Jewish-related ideal stranger can help clarify the idealization of a related progressive strangeness in the cosmopolitan literature of our present global age. Moreover, in the context of the current increase in Western right-wing populisms, we can learn from the modern antisemitic focus on Jewish strangers, since many global age populisms are again eager to use stranger figures as explanation models in the context of the unintended consequences of globalization processes today. The second perspective offered a solution to the problems of our transitive age: It is essential that we acknowledge that traditions other than Western Christianity have paths that can lead to the same mutually shared secular faith of the civil sphere, for example, in the context of understanding how we can create constructive and dynamic social cohesions in national states of the global age.

Appendix

Quotations from Brandes in their Original Danish Form

Chapter 1

Page 52: Hvis den jødiske Natur er den mest haardnakkede af alle, saa er den til Gjengæld en af de smidigste: i Oldtiden Bærer af det mest eksklusive Nationalitetsprincip og derigennem Monotheismens Verdenstanke, i den nyere Tid opløsende sig i de forskellige moderne Folkestammer og gjørende sig til Et med dem uden at tabe eller tilsætte sit Præg, snart romansk, snart germansk, i den nyeste Tid Deltager i og ofte i Spidsen for nationale og liberale Bevægelser, indenfor en og samme Stamme, f. Ex. den tydske, snart kosmopolitisk som Heine, snart som hos Auerbach saa fuldstændigt nationaliseret, at han, en Jøde, bliver den der giver Tydskland de Bondenoveller og Landsbyhistorier, som næsten alle andre Lande efterligne [...]. Hvilke modsætninger inden for den lille stamme![559]

Page 53: Ligeoverfor en Natur og en Virken som Goldschmidts har en uvillig Betragter ordet "rodløs" paa rede Haand; men Ordet passser ikke. Vil man sammenligne denne Forfatter med et Træ, da ligner han ikke et rodløst Træ, men et flyttet og podet, hvis Grene spreder sig stærkt i det Brede, hvis Stamme ikke groer højt i Veiret, og hvis glatte Frugter har en fin og blandet Smag.[560]

Page 54: Naar jøder ere de ivrigste til at forkynde Verden den Lære, at jøderne ingenlunde ere Guds udvalgte folk [...] skulde da ikke snarere dette have sin Kilde i sanddru Uegennyttighed og Uselviskhed end i lave Bevæggrunde? [...] Naar jøder i 1848 overalt stode i Spidsen for Oprøret mod forældet Tradition og hævdsikker uret [...] kan det da ikke have beroet på den Kærlighed til Frihed som er Sandhedskærlighedens Tvillingesøster? Og naar Jøder endelig, velhavende formuende mænd [...] have indvarslet om ikke den communistiske så dog den socialistiske Bevægelse i vore Dages Europa [...] kan dette da ikke til sin Aarsag have en ædel og brændende Kærlighed til Menneskene, en Filanthropi, der langt fra at ville hævde den Handlendes egen Race Rangen som "det naturlige Aristokrati," er gennemtrængt af den ægte menneskelige Uvilje mod Fødselsaristokratiet og derfor anvender sin Kraft paa direkte og uden Omsvøb at føre de demokratiske Ideer frem til Sejr.[561]

Page 56: Det var en Virksomhedsdrift, der søgte Modstand og kun levede og aandede i Opposition [...], altså en Handlekraft, der opsøgte Hindringer og overvandt Hindringer.[562]

Page 57: Men den jødiske Aand staar ved Fødselen allerede frit, den romanske og anti-romanske Cultur, [...] Katholicisme og Protestantisme, classisk og romantisk Civilisation, Alt er ham lige nær og lige fjernt. Han er Søn af Spinoza. Derfor er han fra Fødselen af polemisk stillet mod enhver europæisk Bornerthed, oppositionel, fribaaren og frifødt baade som videnskabelig Betragter og som poetisk Gjenfremstiller.[563]

Page 58: Seet i dette Lys viser den jødiske Races Genius et forskelligt Fysiognomi, et straalende og aabent; det er en kritisk og forskende, ingen dogmatisk Aand.[564]

Page 58-59: Det er klart, at den moderne Jøde [...] har den uvurderlige Fordel, at han [...] staar paa et archimedisk Punkt udenfor begge de ariske Stammers medfødte Begrændsning, ligesom

paa et højt sted med fri horisont. Der er heri noget Lykke-
ligt. Paa den anden Side er det klart, at den moderne Jøde,
der saasnart som hans Natur begynder at tale føler sig som
det sorte Faar i flokken, uden samme Religion, uden samme
Temperament, som det folk midt i hvilket han boer, uden
Fællesskab med det i de Anskuelser, som følge af Tempera-
mentet, og uden at fornemme samme Forfædres Aand røre
sig i sig, maa føle sig mere aandelig hjemløs end nogen Anden. Der er heri noget virkelig Tragisk.[565]

Page 62:   Hvo der ikke har kjæmpet den møisomme Kamp for at forstå
en helt fremmed Races Synsmaade, veed ei hvor vanskeligt
det er i dette Punkt at løsrive sig fra de medfødte Stamme-
fordomme. Det er dertil nødvendigt at indaande den samme
Luft, at leve en Tid lang i de samme Naturomgivelser som
den fremmede Race. Uden de Reiser, hvortil Mme de Stäel
ved sin Landsforvisning blev tvungen vilde det have været
hende umuligt saaledes at udvide sin Intelligents. Jeg tror i
al Beskedenhed at kunne tale med derom af Erfaring. Jeg tør
sige at det først under ensomme Spadserture i i Omegnen
af Sorrent lykkedes det mig at få Shakespeare paa en saadan
Afstand at jeg kunne overskue ham og virkeligt forstå ham
og derigjennem hans Modsætning [...]. Det begyndte at blive
mørkt, Venus lyste stærkt og Bjergenes kraftige Sider og
Kløfter begyndte at antage den phantastiske Charakter, som
det hører Mørket til at give. Men Charakteren blev ikke hvad
vi Nordboere kalde romantisk. [...] Jeg forstod, hvor naturligt
det er at et Land som dette ikke har frembragt en Shakespeare eller trængt til en Shakespeare, fordi Naturen selv her
har paataget sig det Hverv, som Digterne maa udfylde i Norden.[566]

Page 63:   Men grundigst paavirket af de fremmede Omgivelser blev
dog den Klasse af Mennesker, der ved alle hine store Be-

givenheder så sig tvunget til et fast og langvarigt Ophold udenfor Fædrelandet […]. Den franske Emigrant nødtes til at lære
det fremmede Sprog på en mere end overfladisk Maade, om ei
af anden Aarsag så for i det fremmede land at kunne give Un-
dervisning i sit eget Sprog. Fra intelligente franske Emigranter
udbredte da en ny Aand over Frankrig og heri ligger det at det
nye Aarhundredes Litteratur i dette Land begynder som "Emi-
grantlitteratur.[567]

Page 64: Der gives en eneste stor Idee som er den farligste af alle for
den despotiske Magt som hvert enkelt Samfunds fastslaaede
Anskuelser og Vedtægter udøve. Det er ikke Ideen om det
Logiske […]. Nei! mere end noget Andet vækker og forbauser
det Mængden, ifald man er i stand til at gøre det relivt for
den […] at det Ideal som den antager anerkjendt af Alle, kun
betragtes som Ideal af saa og saa mange sammenarbejdede
Gemytter medens andre Folkeslag […] have et helt forskelligt
Begreb om det Tilhørlige og Skønne […]. Skulde jeg derfor
charakterisere Mme de Stäels Fortjeneste af det franske Samfund, dets Cultur og Litteratur, […] da vilde jeg udtrykke mig
saaledes: Hun gjorde især i sine to Hovedværker "Corinne"
og "Om Tyskland", Frankrigs, Englands, Tysklands og Italiens
humane og litterære Anskuelser og Synsmåder relative for Be-
boerne af de forskellige lande.[568]

Page 65-66: Dels er der endeligt et Element, som den Fremmede lettere
opdager end den Indfødte, det er Racemærket, det i den tydske
Forfatter, der betegner ham som Tysker. For den indfødte Betragter bliver det at være tydsk og det at være Menneske alt
for let Et og det samme, da han er vant til overalt, hvor han
behandler behandler et Menneske, at have med en Tydsker at
gøre. Den Fremmede forekommer Meget paafaldende, hvis
Ejendommelighed den Indfødte overser, fordi han er vant til at
see det, og især fordi han selv har det eller er det.[569]

Page 66: Han [Kritikeren] maa til sin nationale og naturlige Aand føje fem til sex konstige og erhvervede Aander, idet hans bøielige Sympathi indfører ham i udslukte eller fremmede Følelser. Den bedste Frugt af hans Gjerning er maaske den, at den river ham løs fra sig selv, nøder ham til at beregne Indflydelsen af de Omgivelser, i hvilke han er nedsænket, lærer ham at udskille Gjenstandende af den forbigaaende Farvetone, Hvori hans Charakter og vort Aarhundrede aldrig undlade at indhylde dem. [...] Vi opdage, at Farven ikke er i Gjenstandende men i os selv, vi tilgive vore Naboer at se anderledes end os selv, vi erkjende, at de maa se blaat, hvad der forekommer os gult. [...] Man seer, hvorledes Kritikeren, der er saa sikker pa de andre Aanders medfødte Begrændsning, er forvisset om at kunne overskride sin Egen. Han ser alle de Andre tøirede og mener at kunne udvide sit Tøir.[570]

Page 67: Den Reaction som det 19de Aarhundrede i sine første Aartier førte mod det 18des Litteratur og dennes Reactions Overvindelse. Denne historiske Begivenhed er efter sit Væsen europæisk og kan kun forstaas ved en sammenlignende Litteraturbetragtning. [...] Den sammenlignende Litteraturbetragtning har den dobbelte Charakter at nærme det Fremmede til os saaledes at vi kunne tilegne os det og at fjerne vort Eget fra os saaledes, at vi kunne overskue det [...]. Det gjælder om at bruge den saaledes, at vi med den corrigere det naturlige Syns Illusioner.[571]

Page 68: Han [Heinrich Heine] gjengiver, som lidt senere Disraeli i England, Lassalle i Tyskland, Gambetta i Frankrig, den brydning, hvorunder hans Races Egenskaber gnistrede, da den moderne Kultur brød ind over den og ramte den som Staalet Flinten.[572]

Chapter 4

Page 147-48: Aldrig i mit Liv havde jeg betonet eller blot fremdraget noget
jødisk standpunkt […] Uden ringeste Usikkerhed […] havde
jeg fra den Dag da jeg offentlig traadte op så godt som ene i
Landet stillet mig i afgjort Opposition til det Jødiske med alle
dets Aflæggere, Lutheranismen iblandt. Det hele Land var
gennemtrængt af Jødedom, al ældgammel jødisk Kultur, æld-
gammelt jødisk Barbari. Alt her var jødisk, indtil Bøndernes
Navne, Hans og Jens […] Man lærte Børnene jødiske Sagn før
man lærte dem danske, jødisk Historie før dansk men først
og fremmest jødisk Religion. Man tilbad en jødernes Gud
og tilbad en jødisk Kvindes Søn som Guds Søn og Gud selv.
Folkets Fester var de jødiske, Påske og Pintse, og man fejrede
i Julen den Søn af en jødisk Moder hvem man gav Plads ved
"Skaberens højre Hånd." Præsterne prækede mod mig fra
Landets Prædikestole. De forsvarede mig mod jødiske Bøgers
Ærværdighed, mere: deres […] Ufejlbarhed, deres evige
Værdi. Deres Begreb om Loven var jødisk fra år 5000 før vor
Tidsregning, deres begreb om Naaden var jødisk fra Aar 50
efter den […] Men overfor mig udtrykte de sig som om Kris-
tendommen var udgaaet fra Danmark og var hvadsomhelst
andet end omdannet og mystisk udviklet Jødedom.[573]

Page 149: Hvor er det pudsigt! Er der noget jeg i dybere forstand ikke er,
så er det dette (en jøde) Hele Danmark […] er gennemtrængt
af Jødedom, dets Gud er jødisk, dets Fester er jødiske, dets
Religion er omdannet, videre udviklet Jødedom med nogle
mytiske tilføjelser. Det gamle Testamente er […] skrevet af
Jøder […] Der var en Tid, hvor jeg noget nær var det eneste
menneske i Landet, som ikke var Jøde. Og ikke desmindre er
snart sagt det eneste, alle Mennesker i Landet ved om mig, og
det eneste, de stadigt meddeler Udlandet om mig, det at jeg
er det.[574]

Page 150: Man mindes vistnok fra Heines Skrift om Börne det sted, hvor han taler om Börnes nazarenske Indskrænkethed. Han siger "nazarenisk" forklarer han, for hverken at bruge udtrykket jødisk eller kristelig, da begge disse Udtryk for ham er synonyme og af ham anvendes ikke til at betegne en Tro men et Naturel; og han stiller ordet nazarenisk i modsætning til hellenisk, der ligeledes for ham betegner en saavel medfødt som tilegnet Aandsretning og synsmaade. Med andre ord: alle Mennesker er for ham enten Nazarener eller Hellenere, enten Mennesker med asketisk, billedfjendtligt, sygeligt spiritualiserende Hang eller Mennesker med livsklart, udviklingsstolt og virkelighedskært Væsen. Og han betegner så sig selv som Hellener.[575]

Page 151-52: I andet Kapitels Slutning hedder det om Josef at han kom og boede i en Stad, som kaldes Nazareth for at det skulle fuldbyrdes hvad der var sagt ved Profeterne: Han skal kaldes Nazaræer. Forskningen har lagt Mærke til at hverken det Gamle Testamente eller Josephus eller Talmud nogensinde nævner en By der hedder saadan. Fraset Evangelierne er navnet ubekendt indtil det fjerde Aarhundrede. Vel har nyere Teologer villet hævde en fast tro hos det første Aarhundredes Kristne paa at Jesus havde hjemme i Nazareth [...]. Sandsynligvis har det ikke existeret nogen Landsby ved navn Nazareth. [...] William B. Smith har ved Studiet af Epiphanus bevist, at der før vor Tidsregning gaves en jødisk Sekt Nazaræerne. I deres Rettroenhed anerkendte de ingen senere Personlighed end Josva, hvis Navn jo er det samme som Jesus, og de synes paa en eller anden Maade at have smeltet sammen med de Kristne, der kun har udtalt deres Navn Nazoræer i stedet for Nazaræer.[576]

Page 153: Det er Hellas og Israel som Evropa skylder sin kultur.[577]

Page 154:   Det Spørgsmål der behandles i Jobs Bog er det, som er
Kærnespørgsmålet i Jødedommen. Og spørgsmålet er
dette: Hvorledes gaar det til at under den retfærdige Guds
Herredømme den onde hyppigt har Lykken med sig, medens
den retfærdige ikke mindre hyppigt rammes af uforskyldte
Ulykker? Det er Grundspørgsmålet for Israeliten. Kampen
imod denne Vanskelighed er Judaismens hele indre Historie.[578]

Page 155:   Det ikke at gøre Modstand mod det onde er en kristelig Ide
[...] i hvilken mange fra Oldtidens Dage af til vore dages
Tolstoj har set Kristendommens inderste Væsen. Aldrig har
Underkastelse under Uretten for Jøden været en Dyd. [...]
Den mand, Jøden lovpriser, er ikke den Hellige; det er den
Retfærdige. [...] Fordi Jøden har villet virkeliggøre Retfær-
dighedsidealet paa Jorden, er han i den moderne Tid bleven
medvirkende ved Revolutioner. Kabbalistiske Jøder var
virksomme ved Frimurerordenens Indstiftelse, Frankrigs faa
Jøder (i alt atten i Paris) var deltagere i Revolutionen, tre af
dem indtog vigtige Stillinger og døde på Skafottet. Halvdelen
af Saint-Simonismens Grundlæggere var Jøder, økonomisk
indsigtsfulde Mænd som Olinde Rodrigues, Eichtal og Isaa
Pereire. Kunstnere som Komponisten Felicien David og Dig-
teren Heine sluttede sig til dem. Da Liberalismen opstaar,
bliver Manin dens Helt i Italien, Börne dens Ordfører i Tyskland, Jellinek dens Agitator og Martyr i Østerrig, Moritz
Hartmann dens Talsmand i Frankfurt og dens Stridsmand
i Wien. Den tyske Socialisme grundlægges af Karl Marx og
Lassalle. Den russiske Nihilisme er blevet stærkt rekrutteret
af unge studerende Jøder og Jødinder af hvilke mange har
ofret deres liv.[579]

Page 156:   Han [forfatteren til Kohélet] den første tydelige Type paa
fri, forfinet, israelitisk Intelligens. Efter ham kommer Philon
og Alexandrinerne; efter dem de jødiske Polemikere, der

inspirerede hin Celsus mod hvem Origenes skrev; efter dem følger den Gruppe af Talmudister, der i det 10. Aarhundrede ville opretholde Religionen ved Filosofi, betonede, at der gaves en Fornuftens Autoritet ved Siden af Skriften [...]. Paa dem følger i det 11te Aarhundrede Ibn Babirol, der ved sit værk "Livets Kilde" stærkt paavirkede den arabiske Filosofi og Mainomides, der i sit Hovedværk [...] stræbte at forene og forsone Aristoteles' Filosofi med Judaismen [...]. Lige fra det 10de Aarhundrede af indtil det 15de Aarhundrede ser vi jødiske Rationalister og Tænkere sysselsatte ved at forberede den Omvæltning i Menneskeaandens Historie, som Renæssancen betegner. De grundlægger Bibelfortolkningen, der lidt efter lidt bliver en frigørende Magt, de kritiserer de kristne dogmer og sindbilleder, de forplanter den arabiske filosofi til Europa [...]. De var højest virksomme, yndede, ja forkælede ved den store kejser Frederik den andens Hof, Midtpunktet for den religiøse Ligegyldighed for Taalsomheden og Fritænkeriet i begyndelsen af det 13de Aarhundrede. Ibn Gabirols Livets Kilde faar Indflydelse paa Giordana Bruno og hans forguden af Verdensaltet. De jødiske Skriftfortolkeres tusindaarige Syslen med Biblen muliggør Luthers Oversættelse af den og fører til den fri Forsknings Princip. Deres grundanskuelse udmunder først i det 17de Aarhundrede i Spinozas Teologisk-politiske Traktat.[580]

Chapter 5

Page 160: Her stod jeg ved den panteistiske Filosofis Ophav i nyere tid.
Her var Filosofien endnu tydeligere Religion idet den erstat-
tede Religionen. [...] Hans personlighed drog [Spinoza], det
store Menneske i ham, et af Historiens største. [...] Jeg følte
en Drift til at optræde som Forkynder for Omverdenen,
for de Tankeløse og Haardhjertede. [...] Jeg begyndte at
betragte det som min Pligt, saasnart jeg dertil havde Evne,
at gaa ud i Byen og præke på hvert Gadehjørne [...]. Jeg an-
stillede Prøver med mit Legem for at få det helt i min Magt,
spiste saa lidt som muligt, sov saa lidt som muligt, lagde mig
mangen Nat udenfor min Seng paa det blotte trægulv for at
vænne mig til den Haardførhed hvorfor jeg havde brug. Jeg
stræbte at døde den vågnede ungdommelige Sanselighed i
mig, og fik efterhånden fuldt Herredømme over mig, saa jeg
kunne være, hvad jeg vilde være, et villigt og kraftigt Redskab
i Kampen for Sandhedens Sejr.[581]

Page 182: For os moderne er spørgsmålet ikke løst – det er vor daglige
kval – men vor filosofi har lært os overfor dette [...] at det er
urigtigt stillet og at den sande visdom bestaar i ikke at vente
svar derpaa. For os er det bortfaldet, siden vi har vænnet os
til i Verdens Gang kun at se en ubevidst fornuft bevægende
sig langsomt frem imod større bevidsthed og mere omfat-
tende magt. Vi betragter retfærdigheden som en opgave og
et ideal, der ligger foran os i en fjern fremtid.[582]

Page 185: Han [Kohélets forfatter] repræsenterer [...] Israels Tro paa
at der ikke gives nogen anden Eksistens for Mennesket end
Livet paa Jorden: For Israeliten er Livet et Gode. Liv, det er
Lykke. [...] Kohélet er dernæst ræsonnerende Filosof, en ra-
tionalistisk Filosof. Han er typen paa jødisk Forstand uden
Sværmeri, paa jødisk Finhed i Vid og Kritik, Stamfaderen for

alle skarpsindige Ironikere, Tvivlere, Polemikere af Israels Folk Aartusinder igennem. Han stod ingenlunde ene i sin tid.[583]

Page 187-88: De [de jødiske profeter] troede saa fast paa Retfærdigheden at de fik dens Ide til at gaa sin Gang gennem Europas Historie. [...] Denne Aand har virket gennem Tiderne, skabt Middelalderens ypperste Kætteri, den har medvirket til reformationen i Tyskland, forsaavidt Luthers Bibeloversættelse var utænkelig uden Raschi's Bibelfortolkning [...]. Denne Aand har medvirket til Reformationen baade i Frankrig og i England [...] skænkede Frankrig store Huguenotter som Coligny og d'Aubigné, England store Puritanere som Cromwell der grundede Republikken. I lige Linje fra Profeterne nedstammer dernæst Spinoza som Grundlægger af Aandsfriheden og indfører Enhedslæren i den moderne Filosofi.[584]

German Quotations in Original Language
(translated by SBH)

Page 102: Jedes Volksthum, welches eine hohe Stufe der Entwicklung erreichen soll, muss mit einer grossen Mannigfaltigkeit der Bedingungen sowohl, wie der Bestrebungen ausgestattet seyn. Den Unterschieden von Küsten- und Binnenland, von erzhaltigen Bergen und Fruchtbaren Thälern und Ebenen, müssen auch eine Vielheit geistiger Gaben entsprechen.[585]

Page 102-03: Die Juden haben nicht eine eigene Nationalität mehr; es gibt schlechterdings keinen Juden mehr, der nur noch einen jüdischen Geist hat. Darum schöpfen sie nothwendig aus allen Volksgeistern deren Theile sie geworden sind und wirken auf dieselben zurück; auch in ihrem ursprünglichen und Eigensten, in ihrer Religion selbst, sind sie wesentlich zugleich nach den Nationen, in denen sie leben individualisiert, und können darum [...] energischer ihre receptive Theilnahme an der Cultur auch in eine productive verwandeln. Philo hat griechisch, Maimonides arabisch, Spinoza lateinisch, Mendelssohn deutsch geschrieben.[586]

Page 103: Diese Aneignungs- und Angleichungskraft, diese Nahrfähigkeit und das Nahrungsbedürfniss des eigenen Geistes durch den fremden ist gewiss ein hervorragender Zug.[587]

Page 104: Erkennt das Judenthum in Ubereinstimmung mit den Prinzipen der neuen Gesellschaft und des rechtsstaates [...] In Übereinstimmung mit dem Prinzip der Einheit des Menschengeschlechtes, der Gleichheit aller vor dem Gesetze, der Gleichheit aller in Pflichten und Rechten dem Vaterland und den Staate gegenüber, sowie der völligen Freiheit des Individuums in seiner religiösen Übersetzung und dem Bekenntniss derselben.[588]

Page 105:   Dass [...] wir deutschen Juden [...] bereits Theil nehmen
            durften ist für uns ein stolzes Bewusstsein, eine unvergleich-
            bare befreidigung. Um felde haben wir mitgekämpft, in den
            Parlamenten mitberaten, vermeil auch auf den communalen
            Rathstuhlen, gesessen, in den Laboratorien mitgearbeitet,
            in den Krankenhåausern mitgeheilt og mitgepflegt, auf den
            Kathedern mitgelehrt.[589]

Page 121:   Und welche hohle, beleidigende Selbstüberschätzung! Da
            wird unter beständigen hämischen Schimpfreden bewiesen
            dass die Nation Kants eigentlich erst durch die Juden zur
            Humanität erzogen, dass die Sprache Lessings und Goethes
            erst durch Börne und Heine für schönheit, Geist und Witz
            empfänglich geworden ist![590]

Page 175:   Es war ihm klar dargetan, dass die heilige Schrift nicht nach
            ihrem ganzen Inhalte von gottbeseelten Männers geschrie-
            ben war, die Glorie war verschwunden, das Ganze war Men-
            schenwerk – wie konnten sonst spätere profane Hände in
            die heiligen Schriftzüge Gottes hineinklecksen? Wer hat die
            Bibel verfasst, wer sie überarbeitet?[591]

Page 176:   Die Bibel erkennt diese heilige Recht unserer Vernunft an,
            indem sie einen gottseligen Lebenswandel auch in Männern,
            die vor der Offenbarung auf Sinai gelebt, anerkennt, und
            indem es sogar von der Wahrheit, die in der Gesetzgebung
            Mosis als zeitliche Erscheinung heraustrat, heisst: "Sie ist
            nicht im Himmel, dass man sagen könnte, wer will für uns in
            den Himmel steigen, sie holen und uns verkünden, auf dass
            wir danach handeln. Den das Wort liegt dir sehr nahe: in
            deinem Munde und in deinem Herzen, auf dass du danach
            handelst" (5. B. M. 30, 12). In unserer Vernunft, auf der Höhe
            des reinen göttlichen Gedankens, hier ist Sinai.[592]

Bibliography

Albertsen, Leif Ludwig. *Engelen Mi: En bog om den danske jødefejde*. Independently published, 1984.

Alexander, Jeffrey C. *The Civil Sphere*. New York: Oxford University Press, 2006.

Alexander, Jeffrey C. *The Dark Side of Modernity*. Boston: Polity Press, 2013.

Allen, Julie. *Icons of Danish Modernity, Georg Brandes and Asta Nielsen*. Seattle: University of Washington Press/Museum Tusculanum Press, 2012.

Andersen, H.C. *Mit Livs Eventyr*. Copenhagen: C.A. Reitzels Forlag, 1877.

Andersen, Vilhelm. *Tider og Typer af Dansk Aands Historie. Anden Del: Goethe. Anden Bog: Det Nittende Aarhundredes Sidste Halvdel*. Copenhagen: Gyldendal, 1916.

Appiah, Kwame Anthony. "Cosmopolitan Patriots," *Critical Inquiry* 23, no. 3 (Spring, 1997): 617–639.

Arendt, Hannah. *The Origins of Totalitarianism*. New York: Harvest, 1968.

Auerbach, Berthold. *Spinoza. Romanbiografie*. Berlin: Europäischer Literaturverlag, 2014.

Bach, Tine. *Exodus – Om den hjemløse erfaring i jødisk litteratur*. Copenhagen: Forlaget Spring, 2004.

Bak, Sofie Lene. "Den røde Synd. Brevvekslingen mellem Olga Eggers og Georg Brandes," *Fund og Forskning* 43 (2004): 267–302.

Bak, Sofie Lene. *Ikke noget at tale om – Danske jøders krigsoplevelser 1943-45*. Copenhagen: Det jødiske Museum, 2010.

Baumann, Zygmunt. *Modernity and the Holocaust*. Cambridge: Polity Press, 1989.

Baumann, Zygmunt. *Modernity and Ambivalence*. New York and Ithaca: Cornell University Press, 1991.

Bauman, Zygmunt. "Allosemitism: Premodern, Modern and Postmodern." In *Modernity, Culture and "the Jew"*, edited by Bryan Cheyette and Laura Marcus, 143–157. Stanford: Stanford University Press, 1998.

Bay, Carl Erik. "Mellem Kultur og politik, mellem magt og ret. Georg Brandes og forfatningskampen i 80´erne." In *Den politiske Georg Brandes*, edited by Sven Møller Kristensen and Hans Hertel, 99–114. Copenhagen: Hans Reitzels Forlag, 1973.

Bay, Carl Erik. "Georg Brandes som 'jøde." In *Kulturradikale Kapitler*, 37–56. Copenhagen: C.A, Reitzels Forlag, 2003.

Bech, Henning. *Kvinder og Mænd*. Copenhagen: Hans Reitzels Forlag, 2006.

Beck, Ulrich. *The Cosmopolitan Vision*. Cambridge: Polity Press, 2004.

Bergmann, Werner. *Geschichte des Antisemitismus*. Munich: C.H. Beck Verlag, 2002.

Berthelsen, Sune and Ditte Maria Egebjerg. "Europa i Danmark, Danmark i Europa." In *Det stadig moderne Gennembrud – Georg Brandes og hans tid set fra det 21. århundrede*, edited by Hans Hertel, 99–123. Copenhagen: Gyldendal, 2004.

Bhabha, Homi K. "Our Neighbours, Ourselves: Contemporary Reflections on Survival." In *Hegel Lectures*, edited by Joachim Küpper et al., 1–19. Berlin: De Gruyter, 2011.

Biale, David. *Not in the Heavens*. Princeton: Princeton University Press, 2011.

Birnbaum, Pierre and Ira Katznelson. *Paths of Emancipation: Jews, States and Citizenship*. Princeton: Princeton University Press, 1995.

Birnbaum, Pierre. *Geography of Hope*. Stanford: Stanford University Press, 2008.

Borup, Morten (ed.). *Georg og Edvard Brandes. Brevveksling med Nordiske Forfattere og Videnskabsmænd*, Volume 2. Copenhagen: Gyldendal, 1940.

Boyarin, Daniel and Jonathan Boyarin. "Diaspora: Generation and the Ground of Jewish Identity," *Critical Inquiry* 19 (1993): 693–725.

Brandes, Georg. *Den Franske Æsthetik i Vore Dage, en Afhandling om H. Taine*. Copenhagen: Gyldendal, 1870.

Brandes, Georg. "M. Goldschmidt." In *Kritiker og Portraiter*, 387–409. Copenhagen: Gyldendal, 1870.

Brandes, Georg. *Kritiker og Portraiter*, 2nd edition. Copenhagen: Gyldendal, 1885.

Brandes, Georg. "M. Goldschmidt." In *Samlede Skrifter* 2, 447–461. Copenhagen: Gyldendal, 1899.

Brandes, Georg: "Shakespeare: 'Kjøbmanden i Venedig'." In *Kritiker og Portraiter*, 113–127. Copenhagen: Gyldendal, 1870.

Brandes, Georg. "Shakespeare: 'Kjøbmanden i Venedig'." In *Kritiker og Portraiter*, 25–41. Copenhagen: Gyldendal, 1885.

Brandes, Georg. *Emigrantlitteraturen* (1872). Copenhagen: Gyldendal, 1971.

Brandes, Georg. *Forklaring og Forsvar*. Copenhagen: Gyldendal, 1872.

Brandes, Georg. *Den romantiske Skole i Tydskland*. Copenhagen: Gyldendal, 1873.

Brandes, Georg. "Ferdinand Lassalle (Første Afsnit)." In *Det nittende Aarhundrede – Maanedsskrift for Literatur og Kritik*, edited by Edvard Brandes and Georg Brandes. October–December 1874.

Brandes, Georg. "Ferdinand Lassalle (Sidste Afsnit)" In *Det nittende Aarhundrede – Maanedsskrift for Literatur og Kritik*, edited by Edvard Brandes and Georg Brandes. January–March 1875.

Brandes, Georg. *Benjamin Disraeli*. Copenhagen: Gyldendal, 1878.

Brandes, Georg. *Ferdinand Lassalle*. Copenhagen: Gyldendal, 1881.

Brandes, Georg. *Det moderne Gjennembruds Mænd*. Copenhagen: Gyldendal, 1883.

Brandes, Georg. "Bevægelsen mod jøderne i Tyskland" (1881). In *Berlin Som Tysk Rigshovedstad*, 372–380. Copenhagen: P.G. Phillipsens Forlag, 1885.

Brandes, Georg. *Indtryk fra Polen*. Copenhagen: Gyldendal, 1888.

Brandes, Georg. *Indtryk fra Rusland*. Copenhagen: Gyldendal, 1888.

Brandes, Georg (and Harald Høffding). *Fr. Nietzsche, tre essays*. Aarhus: Akademisk Boghandel, 1972.

Brandes, Georg. *Det Unge Tyskland*. Copenhagen: Gyldendal, 1890.

Brandes, Georg. "Jobs Bog," *Tilskueren* 10 (1893): 653-671, 737-754.

Brandes, Georg. "Kohélet," *Tilskueren* 11 (1894): 817-838.

Brandes, Georg. *Heinrich Heine*. Copenhagen: Gyldendal, 1897.

Brandes, Georg. *Julius Lange*. Copenhagen: Det Nordiske Forlag, 1898.

Brandes, Georg. "Lord Beaconsfield" (2nd edition of *Benjamin Disraeli* (1878)). In *Samlede Skrifter* 9, 273–527. Copenhagen: Gyldendal, 1901.

Brandes, Georg. "Jødiske og kristne rumænere" (1901). In *Samlede Skrifter 11*, 456–477. Copenhagen: Gyldendal, 1902.

Brandes, Georg. "Rumænsk Indfødsret" (1901). In *Samlede Skrifter 11*, 477–482. Copenhagen: Gyldendal, 1902.

Brandes, Georg. "Sionismen" (1901). In *Samlede Skrifter 11*, 482–486. Copenhagen: Gyldendal, 1902.

Brandes, Georg. "Om Nationalfølelse" (1894). In *Samlede Skrifter 12*, 187–204. Copenhagen: Gyldendal, 1902.

Brandes, Georg. "Danskheden i Sønderjylland" (1899). In *Samlede Skrifter 12*, 220–234. Copenhagen: Gyldendal, 1902.

Brandes, Georg. "Sagens Genoptagelse" (1903). In *Samlede Skrifter 16*, 188–192. Copenhagen: Gyldendal, 1906.

Brandes, Georg. "Zionismen" (1905). In *Samlede Skrifter 18*, 407–412. Copenhagen: Gyldendal, 1910.

Brandes, Georg. "Jøderne i Finland" (1908). In *Samlede Skrifter 18*, 437–446. Copenhagen: Gyldendal, 1910.

Brandes, Georg. *Levned I*. Copenhagen: Gyldendal, 1905.

Brandes, Georg. *Levned II*. Copenhagen: Gyldendal, 1907.

Brandes, Georg. *Levned III*. Copenhagen: Gyldendal, 1908.

Brandes, Georg. "Raceteorier." In *Fugleperspektiv*, 167–173. Copenhagen: Gyldendal, 1913.

Brandes, Georg. *Smaa Romaner fra det Gamle Testamtente*. Copenhagen: Gyldendal, 1914.

Brandes, Georg. *Verdenskrigen*. Copenhagen: Gyldendal, 1916–1917.

Brandes, Georg. *Cajus Julius Cæsar*. 2 volumes. Copenhagen: Gyldendal, 1918.

Brandes, Georg. *Tragediens anden del. Fredsslutningen*. Copenhagen: Gyldendal, 1919.

Brandes, Georg. *Heinrich Heine*, 2nd edition. Copenhagen: Gyldendal, 1922.

Brandes, Georg. *Sagnet om Jesus*. Copenhagen: Gyldendal, 1925.

Brandes, Georg. *Hellas*. Copenhagen, Gyldendal 1925.

Brandes, Georg: *Petrus*. Copenhagen: Gyldendal, 1926.

Brandes, Georg. *Urkistendommen*. Copenhagen: Gyldendal, 1927.

Brandes, Georg. "Das neue Judentum" (1918). In *Georg Brandes – Et Portræt*, edited by Nathansen Henri, 257–266. Copenhagen: Nyt Nordisk Forlag, 1929.

Brandes, Georg. *Breve til Forældrene 1859–71*, 2 volumes. Copenhagen: Det Danske Sprog- og Litteraturselskab, 1978.

Brandes, Georg and Arthur Schnitzler. *Ein Briefwechslung*, (ed.) Kurt Begel, Bern: Francke Verlag Bern, 1956.

Bredsdorff, Elias. *Henrik Pontoppidan og Georg Brandes*. Copenhagen: Gyldendal, 1964.

Bredsdorff, Elias. *Henrik Pontoppidan og Georg Brandes, en redegørelse for brevvekslingen*. Copenhagen: Gyldendal, 1964.

Brennan, Timothy. *Cosmopolitanism Now*. Cambridge (Mass.): Harvard University Press, 1997.

Brock, Gillian and Harry Brighouse. *The Political Philosophy of Cosmopolitanism*. Cambridge: Cambridge University Press, 2002.

Bruer, Albert. "Aufklärung im Spannungsfeld von Philosemitismus und Antisemitismus." In *Geliebter Feind – Gehasster Freund: Antisemitismus und Philosemitismus in Gechichte und Gegenwart*, edited by Irene A. Diekmann and Elke-Vera Kotowski, 259–280. Berlin: Verlag für Berlin-Brandenburg, 2009.

Busk-Jensen, Lise. *Romantikkens Forfatterinder I–III*. Copenhagen: Gyldendal, 2009.

Cheyette, Bryan. *Constructions of "The Jew" in English Literature and Society*. Cambridge: Cambridge University Press, 1993.

Christensen, Hilda R. *Mellem Backfische og Pæne Piger*. Copenhagen: Museum Tusculanum, 1995.

Christensen, Erik M. "Georg Brandes, virkelig?" In *Danske Studier* 86, edited by Iver Kjær et al., 76–94. (Copenhagen: C.A. Reitzels Forlag, 1991).

Clausen, Jørgen Stender. *Det nytter ikke at sende hære mod idéer: Georg Brandes' kulturkritik i årene omkring 1. Verdenskrig*. Copenhagen: C.A. Reitzels Forlag, 1984.

Clausen, Jørgen Stender. *Georg Brandes og Dreyfussaffæren*. Copenhagen: C. A. Reitzels Forlag, 1994.

Cohen, Richard I. "'Jewish Contribution to Civilization' and its Implication for Notions of 'Jewish Superiority'." In *The Jewish Contribution to Civilization: Reasssessing an Idea*, edited by Richard I. Cohen and Jeremy Cohen, 11–23. Portland: The Littman Library of Jewish Civilization, 2008.

Dahl, Per. *Om at skrive den danske ånds historie*. Copenhagen: Gyldendal, 1985.

Danstrup, John and Hal Koch (ed.). *Danmarks Historie*, Volume 12, *De Nye Klasser 1870–1913*. Copenhagen: Politikens Forlag, 1965.

Derrida, Jacques. *Cosmopolitanism and Forgiveness*. London: Routledge, 2001

Derrida, Jacques. *Disseminations*. London: Continuum, 2004.

Dohm, Christian Wilhelm von. *Ueber die bürgerliche Verbesserung der Juden. Mit Königl. Preußischem Privilegio* (1781). Duisburg: Duisburger Institut für Sprach- und Sozialforschung und vom Salomon Ludwig Steinheim-Institut für deutsch-jüdische Geschichte, 2009.

Dohm, Christian Wilhelm von. *Ueber die bürgerliche Verbesserung der Juden. Zweyter Theil. Mit Königl. Preußischem Privilegio* (1783). Duisburg: Duisburger Institut für Sprach- und Sozialforschung und vom Salomon Ludwig Steinheim-Institut für deutsch-jüdische Geschichte, 2010.

Drachmann, Holger. "Ostende-Brügge." In *Poetiske Skrifter*, Volume 6, 241–312. Copenhagen: Gyldendal, 1911–12.

Elf, Nikolaj. *Undersøgelse af danskfagets didaktik*. Odense: Forlaget Dansksiden.dk/ Syddansk Universitet, 2017.

Elon, Amos. *The Pity of It All: A Portray of the German-Jewish Epoch 1743–1933*. New York: Penguin Books, 2002.

Eriksen, Thomas Hylland. *Overheating: An Anthropology of Accelerated Change*. London: Pluto Press, 2016.

Feldt, Jakob Egholm. "Forskellige i Fællesskab. Moses Mendelssohn og Frigørelsen." In *Jøderne som frie borgere*, edited by Bent Blüdnikow, 24–35. Copenhagen: Det Jødiske Samfund, 2014.

Feldt, Jakob Egholm. *Transnationalism and The Jews*. London: Rowman & Littlefield, 2016.

Fenger, Henning. *Georg Brandes' Læreår*. Copenhagen: Gyldendal, 1955.

Fukuyama Francis. *The End of History or The Last Man Standing*. New York: The Free Press, 1992.

Geller, Jay. *The Other Jewish Question – Identifying The Jew And Making Sense Of Modernity*. New York: Fordham University Press, 2011

Gibbons, Henry J.. "The Reluctant Jew." In *The Activist Critic*, edited by Hans Hertel and Sven Møller Kristensen, 55–89. Copenhagen: Munksgaard, 1980.

Gilman, Sander L. *Smart Jews: The Construction of the Image of Jewish Superior Intelligence*. Lincoln: University of Nebraska Press, 1996.

Gilman, Sander L. *Jewish Self-hatred*. Baltimore: Johns Hopkins University Press, 1986.

Goetschel, Willi. *Spinoza's Modernity: Mendelssohn, Lessing, and Heine*. Madison: University of Wisconsin Press, 2004.

Goldschmidt, M. A. *En Jøde, Fortælling*. Copenhagen: Andr. Fr. Høst, 1852.

Gordon, Milton. *Assimilation in American Life: The Role of Race, Religion and National Origins*. New York: Oxford University Press, 1964.

Greenblatt, Stephen. *Renaissance Self-fashioning*. Chicago: University of Chicago Press, 1980.

Gutzkow, Karl. *Uriel Acosta. Trauerspiel in Fünf Aufzügen*. North Charleston: CreateSpace Independent Publishing Platform, 2013.

Hansen, David T. "Dewey and Cosmopolitanism." *E&C/ Education & Culture* 25, no. 2 (2009): 126–140.

Hansen, Thomas Illum. *Kognitiv Litteraturdidaktik*. Copenhagen: Dansklærerforeningens Forlag, 2011.

Hammar, Inger: "From Fredrika Bremer to Ellen Key: Calling, Gender and the Emancipation Debate in Sweden, c. 1830-1900" in *Gender and Vocation: Women, Religion, and Social Change in the Nordic Countries, 1830-1940*, ed. by Pirjo Markkola, Helsinki: Finnish Literary Society, 2000.

Hammerschlag, Sarah. *The Figural Jew: Politics and Identity in Postwar French Thought*. Chicago: The University of Chicago Press, 2010.

Heinrichs, Wolfgang E. "Juden als ideelle Hoffnungs- und Heilsträger im Protestantismus des 18. und 19. Jahrhunderts." In *Geliebter Feind, Gehasster Freund. Atnisemitismus und Philosemitismus in Geschichte und Gegenwart*, edited by Irene A. Diekmann and Elke-Vera Kotowski, 213–232. Berlin: Verlag für Berlin-Brandenburg, 2009.

Hertel, Hans and Sven Møller Kristensen (ed.). *Den politiske Georg Brandes*. Copenhagen: Hans Reitzels Forlag, 1973.

Heschel, Susannah. "Judaism, Islam, and Hellenism: the conflict in Germany over the origins of Kultur." In *The Jewish Contributions to Civilization: Reassessing an Idea*, edited by Jeremy Cohen and Richard I. Cohen, 98–124. Portland: The Littman Library of Jewish Civilization, 2008.

Heuch, J. C. *Dr. G. Brandes' Polemik mod Kristendommen*. Copenhagen: Gyldendal, 1877.

Hvidt, Kristian. "Edvard og Georg Brandes opfattelse af deres jødiske herkomst." In *Judisk liv i Norden*, edited by Gunnar Broberg et al., 209–222. Uppsala: Svanberg og Tydén, 1988.

Hvidt, Kristian. *Edvard Brandes – Portræt af en Radikal Blæksprutte*. Copenhagen: Gyldendal, 1987.

Hvidt, Kristian. "Det folkelige gennembrud (1850–1900)" In *Den Store Danske, Danmarkshistorien*, 2nd edition, edited by Olaf Olsen. Copenhagen: Gyldendal, 2002–2005. http://denstoredanske.dk/Danmarkshistorien/Det_folkelige_gennembrud

Israel, Jonathan. *Radical Enlightenment*. Oxford: Oxford University Press, 2001.

Jeppesen, Bent Haugaard. *Henrik Pontoppidans Samfundskritik*. Copenhagen: Vinten, 1977.

Jordheim, Helge. "Against Periodization: Koselleck's Theory of Multiple Temporalities." *History and Theory* 51 (2012): 151–171.

Juncker, Beth. "Debatten omkring *Emigrantlitteraturen*." In *Den politiske Georg Brandes*, edited by Sven Møller Kristensen and Hans Hertel, 88–114. Copenhagen: Hans Reitzels Forlag, 1973.

Kant, Immanuel. "Idea for a Universal History with a Cosmopolitan Purpose." In *Political Writings*, edited by Hans Reis, 41–53. Cambridge: Cambridge University Press, 1970.

Kant, Immanuel. "Perpetual Peace." In *Political Writings*, edited by Hans Reiss, 93–130. Cambridge: Cambridge University Press, 1970.

Kämmerling, Richard. "Man sollte uns zwingen den Flüchtlingen zuzuhören." *Die Zeit*, February 8, 2016. https://www.welt.de/kultur/literarischewelt/article151957006/Man-sollte-uns-zwingen-den-Fluechtlingen-zuzuhoeren.html.

Karp, Jonathan and Adam Sutcliffe (ed.). *Philosemitism in History*. New York: Cambridge University Press, 2011.

Katz, Jakob. "German Culture and the Jews." In *The Jewish Response to German Culture*, edited by Jehuda Reinharz and Walter Schatzberg, 85–99. Hanover, University of New England, 1965.

Kinzig, Wolfram. "Philosemitismus – was ist das? Eine kritische Begriffsanalyse."In *Geliebter Feind, Gehasster Freund. Antisemitismus Und Philosemitismus In*

Geschichte Und Gegenwart, edited by Irene A. Diekmann And Elke-Vera Kotowski, 25–60. Berlin: Verlag Für Berlin-Brandenburg, 2009.

Klautke, Egbert. *The Mind of the Nation: Völkerpsychologie in Germany, 1851–1955.* Oxford: Berghahn Books, 2013.

Knudsen, Jørgen. *Georg Brandes. Frigørelsens Vej 1842–1877.* Copenhagen: Gyldendal, 1985.

Knudsen, Jørgen. *Georg Brandes. I Modsigelsernes Tegn 1877–1883.* Copenhagen: Gyldendal, 1988.

Knudsen, Jørgen. *Georg Brandes. Symbolet og Manden,* 2 volumes. Copenhagen: Gyldendal, 1994.

Knudsen, Jørgen. *Georg Brandes. Magt og Afmagt,* 2 volumes. Copenhagen: Gyldendal, 1998.

Knudsen, Jørgen. *Georg Brandes. Uovervindelig Taber 1914–27,* 2 volumes. Copenhagen: Gyldendal, 2004.

Knudsen, Jørgen. "Georg Brandes og det jødiske." *Rambam* 7 (1998): 6–17.

Kondrup, Johnny. *Levned og Tolkninger.* Odense: Odense Universitetsforlag, 1982.

Kondrup, Johnny. *Livsværker. Studier i dansk litterær biografi.* Copenhagen: Amadeus, 1986.

Koselleck, Reinhart. *Begreber, tid, erfaring. En tekstsamling,* edited by Jeppe Nevers and Niklas Olsen. Copenhagen: Hans Reitzels Forlag, 2007.

Kramer, Michael P. "The Art of Assimilation: Ironies, Ambiguities, Aesthetics." In *Modern Jewish Literature: Intersections and Boundaries,* edited by Sheila E. Jelen, Michael Kramer, and L. Scott Lerner, 303–326. Philadelphia: University of Pennsylvania Press, 2011.

Kramer, Michael P. "Race, Literary History and the 'Jewish' Question." *Prooftexts* 21, no. 3 (Fall 2001): 287–321.

Kristensen, Sven Møller "Georg Brandes, liberalist and activist." In *The Activist Critic,* edited by Hans Hertel and Sven Møller Kristensen, 9–20. Copenhagen: Munksgaard, 1980.

Kristeva, Julia. *Strangers to Ourselves.* New York: Columbia University Press, 1991.

Larsen, Pelle Oliver. "Professoratet – Videnskabelige Magtkampe i Det Filosofiske Fakultet 1870–1920." PhD Diss., University of Aarhus, 2010.

Lausten, Martin Schwarz. *Jøder og Kristne i Danmark, fra middelalderen til nyere tid.* Frederiksberg: Anis, 2012.

Lazarus, Moritz. *Was heisst national?* Berlin: Ferd. Dümmlers
Buchhandlungsverlag, 1880.

Leonard, Miriam. *Socrates and the Jews: Hellenism and Hebraism from Moses
Mendelssohn to Sigmund Freud*. Chicago: University of Chicago Press, 2012.

Lessing, G. E. *Nathan den Vise. Et dramatisk digt i fem akter*, translated by Villy
Sørensen. Copenhagen: Vandkunsten, 2010.

Levenson, Alan T. "From recognition to consensus: the nature of philosemitism in
Germany, 1871–1932." In *Geliebter Feind, Gehasster Freund. Antisemitismus
und Philosemitismus in Gechichte und Gegenwart*, edited by Irene A.
Diekmann and Elke-Vera Kotowski, 295–310. Berlin: Verlag für Berlin-
Brandenburg, 2009.

Liska, Vivian. *German-Jewish Thought and its Afterlife*. Bloomington: Indiana
University Press, 2017.

Lützen, Karin. *Hvad hjertet begærer. Kvinders kærlighed til kvinder*. Copenhagen:
Tiderne Skifter, 1986.

Mack, Michael: *German Idealism and the Jew: The Inner Anti-Semitism of
Philosophy and German Jewish Responses*. Chicago: University of Chicago
Press, 2003.

Maier, Charles S.: *Once Within Borders – Territories of Power, Wealth and
Belonging since 1500*. Cambridge: Harvard University Press, 2016.

Malitz, Jürgen: "'Auch ein Wort über unser Judenthum' Theodor Mommsen und
der Berliner Antisemitismusstreit." In *Theodor Mommsen: Gelehrter, Politiker
und Literat*, edited by J. Wiesehöher and H. Börm, 137–164. Stuttgart: Franz
Steiner Verlag, 2005.

Mannow, Phillip. *Die Politische Ökonomie des Populismus*. Berlin: Suhrkamp, 2018.

Martensen, H. L.: *Den christelige Ethik I–III*. Copenhagen: Gyldendal, 1871–78.

Marx, Karl: "Speech at Anniversary of People's Paper" in Karl Marx & Friedrich
Engels, *Selected Works*, Vol. 1, Moscow: Progress Publishers, 1969, p. 500

McMurran, Mary Helen. "The New Cosmopolitanism and the Eighteenth Century."
Eighteenth-Century Studies 47, no. 1 (2013): 19–38.

Miller, Michael and Scott Ury. "Cosmopolitanism: The End of Jewishness?"
European Review of History 17, no. 3 (2010): 337–359.

Morris-Reich, Amos. "Three Paradigms of 'the Negative Jew': Identity from Simmel
to Zizek." *Jewish Social Studies* 10, no. 2 (2004): 179–217.

Morris-Reich, Amos. *The Quest for Jewish Assimilation in Modern Social Science.* New York: Routledge, 2008.

Mortensen, Klaus P. *Ironi og Utopi.* Copenhagen: Gyldendal, 1982.

Mosse, George L. *Toward the Final Solution.* Madison: The University of Wisconsin Press, 1978.

Mosse, George L. "Jewish Emancipation – between Bildung and Respectability." In *The Jewish Response to German Culture – From Enlightenment to the Second World War,* edited by Jehuda Reinharz and Walter Schatzberg, 1–16. Hanover: University Press of New England 1985.

Nadler, Stephen. *Spinoza. A Life.* Princeton: Princeton University Press, 1999.

Nadler, Stephen. *A Book Forged in Hell: Spinoza's Scandal Treatise and the Birth of the Secular Age.* Princeton: Princeton University Press, 2011.

Nathansen, Henri. *Af Hugo Davids Liv I–IV.* Copenhagen: V. Pios Boghandel, 1917.

Nathansen, Henri. *Georg Brandes – Et Portræt.* Copenhagen: Nyt Nordisk Forlag, 1929.

Nielsen, Harald. *Usurpatoren.* Copenhagen: Achehoug, 1922.

Pollock, Sheldon, Homi K Bhabha, Carol A. Breckenridge, and Dipesh Chakrabarty. "Cosmopolitanisms." *Public Culture* 12, no. 3 (2000): 577–589.

Pontoppidan, Henrik. *Lykke-Per.* Copenhagen: Gyldendal, 2006.

Pontoppidan, Henrik. *Lucky Per,* translated by Naomi Lebowitz. New York: Peter Lang Publishing, 2010.

Rahden, Till van. *Jews and Other Germans: Civil Society, Religious Diversity and Urban Politics in Breslau, 1860–1925.* Madison: University of Wisconsin Press, 2008.

Reitter, Paul. *The Origins of Jewish Self-hatred.* Princeton: Princeton University Press, 2012.

Rosa, Hartmut. *Social Acceleration: A New Theory of Modernity.* New York: Columbia University Press, 2013.

Rose, Paul Lawrence. "Renan versus Gobineau: Semitism and Antisemitism, Ancient Races and Modern Liberal Nations." *History of European Ideas* 39, no. 4 (2013): 528–540.

Rosman, Moshe. *How Jewish is Jewish History?* Portland: Littman Library of Jewish Civilization, 2008.

Rosman, Moshe. "From Counterculture to Subculture to Multiculture: The 'Jewish

Contribution' Then and Now." In *The Jewish Contribution to Civilization*, edited by Richard I. Cohen and Jeremy Cohen. Portland: Littman Library of Jewish Civilization, 2008.

Roudometof, Victor. "Transnationalism, Cosmopolitanism, and Glocalization." *Current Sociology* 53, no. 1 (January 2005): 113–135.

Rubow, Paul. "Georg Brandes' forhold til Taine og Sainte-Beuve." In *Litterære Studier*, 38–101. Copenhagen: Levin og Munksgaards Forlag, 1928.

Rubow, Paul. *Georg Brandes' Briller*. Copenhagen: Levin og Munksgaard, 1932.

Rubow, Paul. *Georg Brandes og hans lærere*. Copenhagen: Pio, 1927.

Rürup, Reinhardt. "Die 'Judenfrage' der bürgerlichen gesellschaft und die Entstehung des modernes Antisemitismus." In *Emanzipation und Antisemitismus: Studien zur "Judenfrage" der bürgerlichen Gesellschaft*, 74–94. Göttingen: Fischer Verlag, 1975.

Rürup, Reinhardt and Thomas Nipperdey. "Antisemitismus – Entstehung, Funktion und Geschichte eines Begriffs." In *Emanzipation und Antisemitismus: Studien zur 'Judenfrage' der bürgerlichen Gesellschaft*, 95–114. Göttingen: Fischer Verlag, 1975.

Samuels, Maurice. *The Betrayal of the Duchess: The Scandal that Unmade the Bourbon Monarchy and Made France Modern*. New York: Basic Books, 2020.

Schlör, Joachim. *Das Ich in der Stadt. Debatten über Judentum und Urbanität, 1822–1938*. Göttingen: Vandenhoeck & Ruprecht, 2005.

Schnurbein, Stefanie von. "Darstellung von Juden in der dänischen Erzählliteratur des poetischen Realismus." *Nordisk Judaistik* 25, no. 1 (2004): 57–78.

Schnurbein, Stefanie von. "Literarischer Antisemitismus bei Knut Hamsun und Henrik Pontoppidan: zwei Varianten mit unterschiedlicher Tendenz." *European Journal of Scandinavian Studies* 44, no. 1 (2014): 90–102.

Schorske, Carl E. *Fin de Siècle Vienna – Politics and Culture*. New York: Random House, 1981.

Schwartz, Daniel B. *The First Modern Jew: Spinoza and the History of an Image*. Princeton: Princeton University Press, 2012.

Silverstein, Michael. "Shifters, Linguistic Categories, and Cultural Description." In *Meaning in Anthropology*, edited by Keith H. Basso and Henry A. Selby, 11–55. Albuquerque: University of New Mexico Press, 1976.

Simmel, Georg. "Ekskurs om den fremmede." In *Hvordan er samfundet muligt*, 95–103. Copenhagen: Gyldendal, 1998.

Simmel, Georg. "The Stranger." In *Social Theory: The Multicultural and Classic Readings*, edited by Charles Lemert, 3rd edition, 181–184. Boulder: Wesleyan University, 2004.

Simonsen, Konrad. *Jødisk Aand i Danmark (Georg Brandes)*. Copenhagen: Nationale Forfatters Forlag, 1913.

Skolnik, Jonathan. "Writing Jewish History between Gutzkow and Goethe: Auerbach's Spinoza and the Birth of Modern Jewish Historical Fiction." *Prooftexts* 19, no. 2 (May 1999): 101–125.

Skolnik, Jonathan. *Jewish Cultural Memory and the German Historical Novel*. Stanford: Stanford University Press, 2014.

Sorkin, David. *The Transformation of German Jewry, 1780–1840*. New York: Oxford University Press, 1987.

Skriver, Svend. "Europæere i 1800-tallets danske litteratur. Om Jens Baggesen, P.L. Møller og Georg Brandes." PhD Diss., University of Copenhagen, 2007.

Spinoza, Baruch. *Theologisch-politisch Abhandlung*. Berlin: Contumax, 2010.

Spinoza, Baruch. *Teologisk-politisk Afhandling*, translated by Niels Henningsen. Copenhagen: Forlaget Anis, 2009.

Stanislawski, Michael. *Zionism and Fin de Siécle*. Los Angeles: University of California Press, 2001.

Stanislawski, Michael. *Autobiographical Jews: Essays in Jewish Self-Fashioning*. Seattle: University of Washington Press, 2004.

Stoeltzer, Marcel. "Cultural difference in the national state: from trouser-selling Jews to unbridled multiculturalism." *Patterns of Prejudice* 42, no. 3 (2008): 245–279.

Sutcliffe, Adam. *Judaism and Enlightenment*. Cambridge: Cambridge University Press, 2003

Thing, Morten. *Den historiske Jøde*. Copenhagen: Forum, 2001.

Tjørnehøj, Henrik. *Rigets Bedste Mænd*. Copenhagen: Gyldendal, 1990.

Tudvad, Peter. *Stadier på antisemitismens vej, Søren Kirkegaard og jøderne*. Copenhagen: Rosinante, 2010.

Valdez, Damian. *German Philhellenism – The Pathos of Historical Imagination from Winckelmann to Goethe*. New York: Palgrave Macmillan, 2014.

Volkov, Shulamit. *Jüdisches Leben und Antisemitismus im 19. Und 20. Jahrhundert*. Munich: C. H. Beck, 1990.

Wagner, Thorsten. "Fællesskabets nationalisering og jødespørgsmålet i en liberal kultur. Jøderne i Danmark mellem inklusion og eksklusion" In *Folk og fællesskab. Træk af fællesskabstænkningen in mellemkrigstiden*, edited by Uffe Østergaard and Cecilie Banke, 47–61. Aarhus: Werks, 2001.

Wagner, Thorsten. "Jøderens ligestilling – et europæisk perspektiv." In *Jøderne som frie borgere*, edited by Bent Blüdnikow, 10–23. Copenhagen: Det Jødiske Samfund, 2014.

Yovel, Yirmiyahu. *Spinoza and Other Heretics*, Volume 1, *The Marrano of Reason*. Princeton: Princeton University Press, 1989.

Yovel, Yirmiyahu. "Sublimity and Ressentiment: Hegel, Nietzsche, and the Jews." *Jewish Social Studies* 3, no. 3 (1997): 1–25.

Yovel, Yirmiyahu. *The Other Within: The Marranos – Split Identity and Emerging Modernity*. Princeton: Princeton University Press, 2014.

Zemon Davies, Nathalie. "The Sacred and the Body Social in Sixteenth-Century Lyon." *Past and Present* 90, no. 1 (February 1981): 40–70.

Zweig, Stefan. *Verden af i går*. Copenhagen: Gyldendal, 2014.

Notes

1   Francis Fukuyama, *The End of History or The Last Man Standing* (New York: the Free Press, 1992), p. xi, xvi.

2   Fukuyama, *The End of History*, p. xvii–xvii.

3   "Although this political body exists in the present only in its roughest of outlines, it nonetheless seems as if a feeling is beginning to stir [...]. And this encourages the hope that, after many revolutions with all their transforming effects, the highest purpose of nature, a universal cosmopolitan existence, will at last be realized as the matrix within which all the original capacities of the human race may develop." See Immanuel Kant, "Idea for a Universal History with a Cosmopolitan Purpose" in *Political Writings*, ed. Hans Reiss (Cambridge: Cambridge University Press, 1970), 51.

4   See Ulrich Beck, *The Cosmopolitan Vision* (Cambridge: Polity Press, 2006), 1–14.

5   Beck defines the cosmopolitan outlook like this: "Global sense, a sense of boundarylessness. An everyday historically alert, reflexive awareness of ambivalence in a milieu of blurring differentiations and cultural contradictions. It reveals not just the 'anguish' but also the possibility of shaping one´s life and social relations under conditions of cultural mixture." Beck, *The Cosmopolitan Vision*, 3.

6   Beck, *The Cosmopolitan Vision*, 70.

7   See Phillip Manow, *Politische Ökonomie des Populismus* (Berlin: Suhrkamp, 2018), 7–25.

8   Ibid.

9   Reinhart Koselleck, *Begreber, tid, erfaring. En Tekstsamling*, ed. Jeppe Nevers and Niklas Olsen (Copenhagen: Hans Reitzels Forlag, 2007).

10 Hartmut Rosa, *Social Acceleration: A New Theory of Modernity* (New York: Columbia University Press, 2013); Thomas Hylland Eriksen, *Overheating: An Anthropology of Accelerated Change* (London: Pluto Press, 2016).

11   See Charles S. Maier, *Once Within Borders: Territories of Power, Wealth and Belonging since 1500* (Harvard University Press: Cambridge, 2016), 1–13, 277–296.

12   Charles S. Maier, *Once Within Borders*, 185–232.

13   Michael Miller and Scott Ury, "Cosmopolitanism: The End of Jewishness?" *European Review of History* 17, no. 3 (2010). 337–359.

14   In this book, I divide Brandes' work into what I call his early writings, from 1867–1883(/1897), and his later writings, from 1883(/1897)–1927. This division is based on his changed view on the concept of race in the 1880s and 1890s as a reaction to modern antisemitism. This abandonment of the race concept changed the way Brandes represented Jewishness. I elaborate on this matter later in the Introduction and in Chapter 1.

15   See e.g. Georg Brandes, *Benjamin Disraeli* (Copenhagen: Gyldendal, 1878), 308–313.

16   The books and articles which have specifically thematized Georg Brandes' relation to and representation of Jewishness are: Henri Nathansen, *Georg Brandes – et portræt* (Copenhagen: Nyt Nordisk Forlag, 1929); Henry J. Gibbons, "The reluctant Jew," in *The Activist Critic* (Copenhagen: Munksgaard, 1980); Carl Erik Bay, "Georg Brandes som 'jøde'," in *Kulturradikale Kapitler* (Copenhagen: C.A. Reitzels Forlag, 2003), 37–56; Kristian Hvidt, "Edvard og Georg Brandes' opfattelse af deres jødiske herkomst," in *Judisk liv i Norden* (Uppsala: Svanberg og Tydén, 1988), 209–222; and Tine Bach, *Exodus* (Copenhagen: Spring, 2004). See also Jørgen Knudsen, *Frigørelsens Vej 1842–1877* (Copenhagen: Gyldendal, 1985) and Volume 1 of *Magt og Afmagt* (Copenhagen: Gyldendal, 1998). Most Brandes researchers whose main focus lies elsewhere still comment on Brandes' relationship to his Jewish background, though they usually downplay it. Most significantly, Henning Fengers does this in his otherwise solid *Georg Brandes' Læreår* (Copenhagen: Gyldendal, 1955). However, the lack of focus on Brandes' relationship to and representation of Jewishness is also seen in, for example, the otherwise politically and ideologically focused anthology edited by Hans Hertel and Sven Møller Kristensen, *Den politiske Brandes* (Copenhagen: Hans Hertels Forlag, 1973).

17   See for example Michael Mogensen, "October 1943. The Rescue of the Danish Jews," in Mette Bastholm Jensen and Steven B. Jensen (eds.): *Denmark and the*

Holocaust. Copenhagen: Institute for International Studies, Department for Holocaust and Genocide Studies, (2003), 35–50.

18 Sofie Lene Bak, *Ikke noget at tale om – Danske Jøders Krigsoplevelser 1943–45* (Copenhagen: Dansk Jødisk Museum, 2010).

19 Mogens R. Nissen, *Til fælles bedste – Det danske landbrug under besættelsen* (Copenhagen: Lindhardt og Ringhoff, 2005).

20 Henri Nathansen, *Georg Brandes – et portræt* (Copenhagen: Nyt Nordisk Forlag, 1929); Henry J. Gibbons, "The reluctant Jew," in *The Activist Critic* (Copenhagen: Munksgaard, 1980); Carl Erik Bay, "Georg Brandes som 'jøde'," in *Kulturradikale Kapitler* (Copenhagen: C.A. Reitzels Forlag, 2003), 37–56; Kristian Hvidt, "Edvard og Georg Brandes' opfattelse af deres jødiske herkomst," in *Judisk liv i Norden* (Uppsala: Svanberg og Tydén, 1988), 209–222; and Tine Bach, *Exodus* (Copenhagen: Spring, 2004). See also See also Jørgen Knudsen, *Frigørelsens Vej 1842–1877* (Copenhagen: Gyldendal, 1985) and Volume 1 of *Magt og Afmagt* (Copenhagen: Gyldendal, 1998).

21 See Jørgen Knudsen, "Georg Brandes og det jødiske," *Rambam* 7 (1998): 6–17.

22 See Erik M. Christensen, "Georg Brandes, virkelig?" in *Danske Studier 86*, ed. Iver Kjær et al, (Copenhagen: C. A. Reitzels Forlag, 1991), 81.

23 Bach, *Exodus*, 212–213; Gibbons, "The reluctant Jew," 75.

24 See, for example, Paul Rubow, *Georg Brandes' Briller* (Copenhagen: Levin og Munksgaard, 1932); Henning Fenger, *Georg Brandes' Læreår* (Copenhagen: Gyldendal, 1955); Jørgen Knudsen, *Frigørelsens Vej 1842–1877*, 55–67; Svend Skriver "Europæere i 1800-tallets danske litteratur. Om Jens Baggesen, P.L. Møller og Georg Brandes" (PhD diss., University of Copenhagen, 2007), 210–212, pointed out that Paul Rubow tends to emphasize Kierkegaard's influence on Brandes in *Georg Brandes' Briller*.

25 Fenger, *Georg Brandes' Læreår*, 80, 120–121, 131–143.

26 "It is difficult to say anything pleasant about Auerbach except that he was probably a good human being. [...] His work can in no way be compared to the masculine art of Gottfried Keller. In his Jewish *pseudo–historical* novels, there is a sickly humanism and tolerance, with which even the most passionate admirer of Lessing and Lessing's Nathan will have difficulties. [...] Brandes' admiration should be understood on the basis of the historical context – and the racial kinship." (Translated from the Danish: "Det er svært at sige andet

pænt om Auerbach, end at han sikkert var et godt menneske. [...] Hans værker tåler slet ikke sammenligning med Gottfrieds Kellers mandige kunst. I hans jødiske pseudohistoriske romaner er der en vammel humanitet og tolerance som dels den varmeste beundrer af Lessing og hans Nathan kan have svært ved at kapere. [...] Brandes' beundring må skrives på tidens regning – og på raceslægtskabets.") See Fenger, *Georg Brandes' Læreår*, 120–121.

27 Ibid.

28 See Thorsten Wagner: "Fællesskabets nationalisering og jødespørgsmålet i en liberal kultur. Jøderne i Danmark mellem inklusion og eksklusion," in *Folk og fællesskab. Træk af fællesskabstænkningen in mellemkrigstiden*, ed. Uffe Østergaard and Cecilie Banke (Aarhus: Werks, 2001), 47–61.

29 See Jørgen Knudsen, *Magt og Afmagt*, Vol. 2 (Copenhagen: Gyldendal, 1998), 488.

30 See Reinhard Rürup and Thomas Nipperdey, "Antisemitismus – Entstehung, Funktion und Geschichte eines Begriffs," in *Emanzipation und Antisemitismus: Studien zur 'Judenfrage' der bürgerlichen Gesellschaft* (Göttingen: Fischer Verlag, 1975).

31 See Jørgen Knudsen, *I modsigelsernes tegn* (Copenhagen: Gyldendal, 1988), 85–86.

32 See Wolfgang E. Heinrichs, "Juden als ideelle Hoffnungs- und Heilsträger im Protestantismus des 18. und 19. Jahrhunderts," in *Geliebter Feind, Gehasster Freund. Atnisemitismus und Philosemitismus in Geschichte und Gegenwart*, ed. Irene A. Diekmann and Elke–Vera Kotowski (Berlin: Verlag für Berlin–Brandenburg, 2009), 223.

33 See Jeffrey C. Alexander, *The Dark Side of Modernity* (Cambridge: Polity Press, 2013), 1–4.

34 Michael Stanislawski, *Zionism and the Fin de Siècle: Cosmopolitanism and Nationalism from Nordau to Jabotinsky* (Los Angeles: University of California Press, 2001), 9.

35 Jay Geller, *The Other Jewish Question – Identifying The Jew And Making Sense Of Modernity* (New York: Fordham University Press, 2011), 2.

36 See Georg Brandes, "M. Goldschmidt," in *Kritikerog Portraiter* (Copenhagen: Gyldendal, 1870), 401; Brandes, *Levned III* (Copenhagen: Gyldendal, 1908), 308.

37 "With the rise of the national state, 'cosmopolitan' increasingly became a word of opprobrium. In 1879, for example, the German historian Heinrich von Treitschke (1834–96) observed that 'a specific Jewish civilization will always flourish, as befits a historically cosmopolitan power.' Treitschke did not intend to conjure up the moral and ethical cosmopolitanism of Kant and other Enlightenment thinkers, but rather the moral and ethical incompatibility of Jews (qua cosmopolitans) with the German national project. Indeed, Treitschke – who in the same essay coined the slogan, 'the Jews are our misfortune' – viewed the Jews' inherent cosmopolitanism as a threat to the young German national state, one which was still trying to strike roots and find its place among the European nations. Anti–cosmopolitanism, which was central to Treitschke's writings on 'the Jews', was also a dominant motif in the other anti–Semitic writings that came into vogue at the time. Wilhelm Marr (1819–1904), who coined the term 'anti–Semitism' in 1879, rejected the 'bored cosmopolitanism' that ruled Germany in the 1870s and 1880s, disparaging the Jews as its carriers and spokespeople. Reflecting on the liberal spirit of the 1830s and 1840s, Marr observed that 'we all became supporters of the cosmopolitan spirit, so much so that we related to Israel [i.e. the Jews] as the representative of cosmopolitanism, and it was considered fashionable to be a philo-Semite.' Marr, who considered it fashionable to be an anti-Semite, helped establish the inextricable link between anti-Semitism and anticosmopolitanism, two terms that would become almost interchangeable in the reactionary, anti-modern imagination. As Adolf Hitler put it in Mein Kampf, 'I had ceased to be a weak-kneed cosmopolitan and become an anti-Semite.'" See Michael Miller and Scott Ury, "Cosmopolitanism: The end of Jewishness?" *European Review of History* 17, no. 3 (2010), 347.

38 Sheldon Pollock, Homi K Bhabha, Carol A. Breckenridge, and Dipesh Chakrabarty, "Cosmopolitanisms," *Public Culture* 12, no. 3 (2000), 578.

39 Sheldon Pollock, Homi K Bhbaha, Carol A. Breckenridge, and Dipesh Chakrabarty, "Cosmopolitanisms," 585–586.

40 See Derrida, *Cosmopolitanism and Forgiveness*, 18–23; Beck, *Cosmopolitan Vision*, 9, 20, 46–47; Robert Fine, *Cosmopolitanism* (London: Routledge, 2007), ix–xvii, 4, 22–38; Mary Helen McMurran, "The New Cosmopolitanism and the Eighteenth Century," *Eighteenth–Century Studies* 47, no. 1 (2013): 19–38.

41   Miller and Ury, "Cosmopolitanism: The End of Jewishness?"

42   Ibid.

43   Julie K. Allen, *Icons of Danish Modernity: Georg Brandes and Asta Nielsen* (Seattle: University of Washington Press, 2012), 68.

44   Rürup, *Emanzipation und Antisemitismus*, 74–78.

45   Ibid.

46   See Jakob Egholm Feldt, "Forskellige i Fællesskab. Moses Mendelssohn og Frigørelsen," in *Jøderne som frie borgere*, ed. Bent Blüdnikow (Copenhagen: Det Jødiske Samfund, 2014); Thorsten Wagner, "Jødernes ligestilling – et europæisk perspektiv," in *Jøderne som frie borgere*, ed. Bent Blüdnikow (Copenhagen: Det Jødiske Samfund, 2014).

47   See C. W. von Dohm, *Ueber die bürgerliche Verbesserung der Juden. Mit Königl. Preußischem Privilegio* (1781) (Duisburg: Duisburger Institut für Sprach- und Sozialforschung und vom Salomon Ludwig Steinheim-Institut für deutsch-jüdische Geschichte, 2009), 40–41.

48   See Dohm, *Über der Bürgerliche Verbesserung der Juden*, 14.

49   See Dohm, *Über der Bürgerliche Verbesserung der Juden*, 46.

50   See Feldt, "Forskellige i Fællesskab," 25–26.

51   See Wagner, "Jødernes ligestilling – et europæisk perspektiv," 15–20.

52   Translated by Nancy Aaen (NA) from the Danish: "ei allene haandhæve jøderne I deres borgerlige rettigheder men endog bane vei for dem til at amalgamere sig med landets ældre borgere." See Wagner, "Fællesskabets nationalisering og jødespørgsmålet i en liberal kultur," 53.

53   Ibid.

54   See, for example, M. A. Goldschmidt, *En Jøde, Fortælling* (Copenhagen: Andr. Fr. Høst, 1852); Henri Nathansen, *Af Hugo Davids Liv I–IV* (Copenhagen: V. Pios Boghandel, 1917).

55   See Knudsen, *Frigørelsens Vej 1842–1877*, 12–13.

56   Paul Reitter, *The Origins of Jewish Self-hatred* (Princeton: Princeton University Press, 2012), 5–45.

57   Cf. Jørgen Knudsen, "Georg Brandes og det jødiske", 6–17; Tine Bach, *Exodus*, 207.

58   See Nathansen, *Georg Brandes*, 100–104.

59 Sander L. Gilman, *Jewish Self-hatred* (Baltimore: The Johns Hopkins University Press, 1986), 2.

60 Gilman, *Jewish Self-hatred*, 106–7, 334.

61 Reitter, *The Origins of Jewish Self-hatred*, 6.

62 Bach, *Exodus*, 207.

63 For a short overview of some of the minorities Brandes defended most passionately, see, for example, Jørgen Knudsen, *Magt of Afmagt*, Vol. 2, 360–377. Jørgen Stender Clausen's two anthologies contain some of Brandes' most significant articles on the rights of both Eastern European Jews and Western European Jews (as seen in the Dreyfus Affair). See Jørgen Stender Clausen, *Det nytter ikke at sende hære mod idéer: Georg Brandes' kulturkritik i årene omkring 1. Verdenskrig* (Copenhagen: C.A. Reitzels Forlag, 1984); Jørgen Stender Clausen, *Georg Brandes og Dreyfussaffæren* (Copenhagen: C.A. Reitzels Forlag, 1994).

64 See Jeffrey C. Alexander, *The Civil Sphere* (New York: Oxford University Press, 2006), 3–22.

65 See Alexander, *The Civil Sphere*, 4.

66 Alexander, *The Civil Sphere*, 16

67 Alexander, *The Civil Sphere*, 8.

68 Alexander, *The Civil Sphere*, 428.

69 See, for example, David Sorkin, *The Transformation of German Jewry, 1780–1840* (New York: Oxford University Press, 1987), 107–123; Amos Morris–Reich, *The Quest for Jewish Assimilation in Modern Social Science* (New York: Routledge, 2008), 1–12.

70 Alexander, *The Civil Sphere*, 427.

71 See Alexander, *The Civil Sphere*, 48.

72 Natalie Zemon Davies, "The Sacred and the Body Social in Sixteenth-Century Lyon," in *Past and Present* 90, no. 1 (1 February 1881), 40–70.

73 Alexander, *The Civil Sphere*, 462–463.

74 Sutcliffe, *Judaism and Enlightenment*, 7.

75 See Reinhard Rürup and Thomas Nipperdey, "Antisemitismus – Entstehung, Funktion und Geschichte eines Begriffs," in *Emanzipation und Antisemitismus: Studien zur 'Judenfrage' der bürgerlichen Gesellschaft* (Göttingen: Fischer Verlag, 1975), 95–114.

76 Paul Rubow also observed Brandes' changed view on and use of the race con-
    cept; he also suggested that Brandes' abandonment of the race concept was a
    consequence of the rise of modern antisemitism. See Rubow, "Georg Brandes'
    forhold til Taine og Sainte-Beuve," in Paul Rubow, *Litterære Studier* (Copenha-
    gen: Levin og Munksgaard, 1928), 87–88.

77 Helge Jordheim, "Against Periodization: Koselleck's Theory of Multiple Tem-
    poralities," *History and Theory* 51 (May 2012): 151–171.

78 Jordheim, "Against Periodization," 151.

79 Jordheim, "Against Periodization," 159.

80 Jordheim, "Against Periodization," 157.

81 In this book, I use the term "the Old Testament" rather than e.g. "the Tanakh"
    or "the Hebrew Bible" because Georg Brandes himself consistently used this
    term.

82 See Hans Hertel, "Nødigt men dog gerne – da Danmark blev moderne. Det
    nye samfund, det nye livssyn, det nye kulturliv 1870–1900," in *Det Stadig Mod-
    erne Gennembrud*, ed. Hans Hertel (Copenhagen: Gyldendal, 2004), 40–41.

83 In particular, Brandes' Spinozist cosmopolitanism will be elaborated on in
    Chapter 5. Brandes declares himself a liberal cosmopolitan in the tradition of
    Baruch Spinoza in texts such as "M. Goldschmidt," 401; *Benjamin Disraeli*,
    309–313; *Levned I*, 114–118.

84 Georg Brandes, *Emigrantlitteraturen* (Copenhagen: Gyldendal, 1971 (1872)).

85 See Allen, *Icons of Danish Modernity*, 60.

86 See, for example, Hans Hertel and Sven Møller Kristensen, eds., *Den politiske
    Brandes* (1973); Jørgen Knudsen, *Frigørelsens Vej 1842–77* (Copenhagen: Gyl-
    dendal, 1985); Hans Hertel (ed.), *Det stadig Moderne Gennembrud* (Copenha-
    gen: Gyldendal, 2004).

87 "Through emancipation and acculturation [...], in the course of the transition
    from counterculture to subculture Jews adopted more and more of the values
    of majority society, but they also used various forms of covert aggression to
    combat continuing manifestations of majority hostility and the desire to keep
    them marginalized. In the customs of minority groups, one important form of
    this covert aggression was expressive hostility; verbally denigrating and other-
    wise casting aspersions on the majority group. One type of expressive hostility
    is ethnocentric interpretation of both history and current events. Minorities

often create myths asserting – appearances to the contrary notwithstanding – that they stand at the center of events, wield unseen power over the majority and in some significant measure determine society's fate [...]. It is an expression of the minority's internalization of majority values as well as an assertion of the minority's right to internalize them. It means minority members believe they should belong. In addition, this ethnocentrism is a counter reaction to the majority's continued exclusionary practices; its apparent preference that the minority remains a counterculture rather than a subculture." Moshe Rosman, *How Jewish is Jewish History* (Portland: Littman Library of Jewish Civilization, 2008), 115–116.

88   Knudsen, *Frigørelsens Vej 1842–77*, 125.

89   In one of the most significant attacks on Brandes and his ideas at this time, a journalist at the newspaper *Fædrelandet*, Rudolf Schmidt, wrote these words claiming that because of his Jewish descent, Brandes was unable to deliver a genuine constructive contribution to the Danish cultural tradition. Typically and like the discourse in Wagner's essay, Schmidt acknowledges that Brandes has mastered the technical aspect of the Danish language as "an inheritance which everywhere follows the Semitic tribe," but he is unable to produce any legitimately original ideas because of his Jewish decent. See Knudsen, *Frigørelsens Vej 1842–77*, 262.

90   See Knudsen, *Frigørelsens Vej 1842–77*, 125.

91   See Knudsen, *Frigørelsens Vej 1842–77*, 262–268.

92   See Gilman, *Jewish Self-hatred*, 209–210.

93   Cf. Bauman, *Modernity and the Holocaust*, 34–46. Here, Bauman defines the trope of the destabilizing "slimy Jew" that fundamentally threatens the order of society.

94   Translated by NA from the original version in Thing, *Den historiske jøde*, 16.

95   Gilman, *Jewish Self-hatred*, 209–210. Other researchers have also emphasized the importance of Wagner's essay as a proto-text for the later construction of modern antisemitism; see, for example, Shulamit Volkov, *Jüdisches Leben und Antisemitismus im 19. und 20. Jahrhundert* (Munich: C. H. Beck, 1990), 61; Michael Mack, *German Idealism and The Jew: The Inner Anti-Semitism of Philosophy and German Jewish Responses* (Chicago: University of Chicago Press, 2003), 70–72.

96   See Gilman, *Jewish Self-hatred*, 209–210; Sander L. Gilman, *Smart Jews – The Construction of the Image of Jewish Superior Intelligence* (Lincoln: Nebraska University Press, 1996), 44–45.

97   Ibid.

98   Ibid.

99   See Stephen Greenblatt, *Renaissance Self-fashioning* (Chicago: University of Chicago Press, 1980), 1–3; Michael Stanislawski, *Autobiographical Jews – Essays in Jewish Self-fashioning* (Seattle: University of Washington Press, 2004), 1–18.

100 See Morten Borup (ed.), *Georg og Edvard Brandes. Brevveksling med Nordiske Forfattere og Videnskabsmænd*, Vol. 2 (Copenhagen: Gyldendal, 1940), 321.

101 Knudsen, *Frigørelsens Vej 1842–77*, 261–262

102 See Pelle Oliver Larsen,"Professoratet – Videnskabelige Magtkampe i Det Filosofiske Fakultet 1870–1920," PhD Diss., University of Aarhus, 2010, 62–77.

103 Ibid.

104 See Paul Rubow, *Georg Brandes og hans lærere* (Copenhagen: Studier fra sprog- og oldtidsforskning udgivne af det filologisk-historiske samfund, No. 144, 1927), 7–10.

105 See Rubow, *Georg Brandes og hans lærere*, 7; Knudsen, *Frigørelsens Vej 1842–77*, 68–71

106 See Knudsen, *Frigørelsens Vej 1842–77*, 68–71.

107 Larsen, *Professoratet*, 62.

108 See Larsen, *Professoratet*, 64–65.

109 Georg Brandes, *Den Franske Æsthetik i Vore Dage – En Afhandling om H. Taine* (Copenhagen: Gyldendal, 1870), 154–194.

110 However, it seems that Brandes agrees more with Ernest Renan than with Hippolyte Taine on some aspects of the concept of race. In an 1869 letter to his mother from Paris, Brandes writes that he agrees more with Renan when it comes to the strength of racial ties, stating that Taine's view of racial ties is too deterministic and that he agrees with Renan that racial traits can loosen their grip on the individual due to the influence of the national *Volksgeist* into which the individual is born. See Georg Brandes, *Breve til Forældrene 1859–71, Vol. I: 1859–71* (Copenhagen: Det Danske Sprog- og Litteraturselskab og C. A. Reitzels Boghandel, 1978), 260.

111 Berthelsen and Egebjerg, "Europa i Danmark, Danmark i Europa," 102–105.

112 Brandes, "M. Goldschmidt," 122–124.

113 Ibid.

114 *Illustreret Tidende* April 11, 1869.

115 See e.g. Knudsen, *Frigørelsens Vej 1842–77*, 132–134.

116 Note, for example: "Clear waters are often shallow," translated by NA from Brandes, "M. Goldschmidt," in *Kritiker og Portraiter* (Copenhagen: Gyldendal, 1870), 394.

117 See Brandes, *Levned I* (Copenhagen: Levin og Munksgaard, 1905), 245–251.

118 Part of a letter from Brandes to Henri Nathansen (18 Aug. 1912), translated by NA, in Georg Brandes, *Samlede Skrifter 2* (Copenhagen: Gyldendal, 1899), 464.

119 Brandes' autobiographical descriptions in *Levned I* on p. 20 and p. 38. In comparison, see Brandes, "M. Goldschmidt," 398–399.

120 Brandes, "M. Goldschmidt," 399.

121 See Kondrup, *Levned og Tolkninger*, 12–13. In particular, the structure of Goethe's novel *Wilhelm Meisters Lehrjahre* (1795–96) functioned as a role model for Danish autobiographies and biographies in the nineteenth century.

122 Ibid.

123 Georg Brandes, "Ferdinand Lassalle (Første Afsnit)," in *Det nittende Aarhundrede – Maanedsskrift for Literatur og Kritik*, ed. Edvard Brandes and Georg Brandes (October–December 1874 to January–March 1875), 257.

124 Brandes, "Ferdinand Lassalle (Sidste Afsnit)," in *Det nittende Aarhundrede – Maanedsskrift for Literatur og Kritik*, ed. Edvard Brandes and Georg Brandes (October–December 1874 to January–March 1875), 326–389.

125 Georg Brandes, *Ferdinand Lassalle* (Copenhagen: Gyldendal, 1881), 4.

126 Georg Brandes, "Ferdinand Lassalle (Første Afsnit)," in *Det nittende Aarhundrede – Maanedsskrift for Literatur og Kritik*, ed. Edvard Brandes and Georg Brandes (October–December 1874 to January–March 1875), 253–255.

127 See Jørgen Knudsen, *I Modsigelsernes Tegn 1877–83* (Copenhagen: Gyldendal, 1988), 72–73.

128 Ibid.

129 See Georg Brandes, "Bevægelsen mod jøderne i Tyskland," in *Berlin Som Tysk Rigshovedstad – Erindringer fra et femaarigt ophold* (Copenhagen: Gyldendal, 1885), 372–380.

130 Knudsen, *I Modsigelsernes Tegn 1877–83*, 85–86.

131 Brandes, "Bevægelsen mod Jøderne i Tyskland," 379–380.

132 See e.g. Brandes, *Benjamin Disraeli*, 183.

133 Translated by NA from Brandes, "M. Goldschmidt," 119.

134 Translated by NA from Brandes, "Shakespeare: 'Kjøbmanden i Venedig,'" in *Kritiker og Portraiter* (Copenhagen: Gyldendal, 1870), 119–120.

135 Brandes, "M. Goldschmidt," 120.

136 See Gilman, *Jewish Self-hatred*, 209–210; Gilman, *Smart Jews*, 44–45.

137 Translated by NA from Brandes, "M. Goldschmidt," 409.

138 Translated by NA from Brandes, "M. Goldschmidt," 402.

139 See Georg Brandes, "Raceteorier," in *Fugleperspektiv* (Copenhagen: Gyldendal, 1913), 167–173.

140 Translated by NA from Brandes, *Benjamin Disraeli*, 311–312.

141 Translated by NA from Brandes, *Benjamin Disraeli*, 308–311.

142 See pp. 308–313 in Brandes, *Benjamin Disraeli*, where Brandes elaborates on this term "the Semitic principle."

143 "As a politician, Goldschmidt, by virtue of his familiarity with repression in the Middle Ages, with which he had become acquainted from birth as a member of a pariah caste, and with his race's hatred of slavery, has taken the side of liberty." Translated by NA from Brandes, "M. Goldschmidt," 408.

144 Translated by NA from Brandes, "Ferdinand Lassalle (Første Afsnit)," 251–252.

145 Brandes, "Ferdinand Lassalle (Første Afsnit)," 248–255.

146 Ibid.

147 Ibid.

148 "Here we come to the racial characteristic of his disposition, the basic shape of his temperament [...], the Jewish word *Chutspe* [...], which can be easily understood as the extreme into which timorousness and the forced compliance of a race harassed and suppressed throughout two millennia inevitably converts in the face of a disintegrating culture." Translated by NA from Brandes, "Ferdinand Lassalle (Første Afsnit)," 250.

149 See for example Nathansen, *Georg Brandes*, 62–66.

150 Translated by NA from Brandes, "Ferdinand Lassalle (Første Afsnit)," 250–251.

151 Brandes, "M. Goldschmidt," 400–401.

152 Brandes, *Benjamin Disraeli*, 312.

153 See Sutcliffe, *Judaism and Enlightenment*, 103–190; Israel, *Radical Enlighten-ment* (New York: Oxford University Press, 2001), 157–327.

154 Translated by NA from Brandes, "M. Goldschmidt," 400.

155 See Stanislawski, *Zionism and the Fin de Siècle*, 6–18.

156 Henry J. Gibbons suggested the term "transformationist" as a way to charac-terize Brandes' liberal cosmopolitan ideological agenda; see Gibbons, "The reluctant Jew," 74–78. As regards Gibbons' term, it should however be noted that Brandes' belief in an all-inclusive transformation is mainly visible in his early writings, while his later writings present an increasingly pessimistic view on his early ideals.

157 See Sven Møller Kristensen, "Georg Brandes, liberalist and activist," in *The Activist Critic*, ed. Hans Hertel and Sven Møller Kristensen (Copenhagen: Munksgaard, 1980), 9.

158 Ibid.

159 Translated by NA from Brandes, "M. Goldschmidt," 403.

160 See also Brandes, "M. Goldschmidt," 396–398.

161 Cf. Brandes' remark in *Forklaring og Forsvar*: "Equating free-thinkers with atheists is tantamount to deliberate deceit." Translated by NA from Georg Brandes, *Forklaring og Forsvar* (Copenhagen: Gyldendal, 1872), 45.

162 See Georg Brandes, *Levned 1* (Copenhagen: Gyldendal, 1905), 114–117.

163 See Brandes, "Bevægelsen mod Jøderne i Tyskland," 379–380.

164 Translated by NA from Georg Brandes, *Emigrantlitteraturen* (Copenhagen: Gyldendal, 1971), 111–113.

165 Translated by NA from Berthelsen and Egebjerg, "Europa i Danmark, Dan-mark i Europa," 105; see also Skriver, *Europæere i 1800–tallets danske litteratur*, 241–249.

166 Brandes, *Den Franske Æsthetik i Vore Dage*, 52–91.

167 See Berthelsen and Egebjerg, "Europa i Danmark, Danmark i Europa"; Beth Juncker, "Debatten omkring *Emigrantlitteraturen*," in *Den politiske Brandes*, ed. Hans Hertel and Sven Møller Kristensen (Copenhagen: Hans Reitzels For-lag, 1973), 27–66.

168 Translated by NA from Brandes, *Emigrantlitteraturen*, 28.

169 See Brandes, *Emigrantlitteraturen*, 29: "The emigrant is by his very nature op-positional." (Translated by NA.)

170 See Skriver, *Europæere i 1800–tallets danske litteratur*, 245–247.

171 Brandes, *Emigrantlitteraturen*, 99.

172 Brock and Brighouse (eds.), *The Political Philosophy of Cosmopolitanism*, 3. In this context, Ulrich Beck represents so-called strong cosmopolitanism when he, in *The Cosmopolitan Vision* (1–14), states that all forms of national outlook must be overthrown because of their backwardness. In general, however, in cosmopolitanist writings of the last three decades, most scholars variously endorse a balance between the national/particularistic outlook and a cosmopolitan outlook and mindset. Kwame A. Appiah, for instance, projects "cosmopolitan patriotism" as an example of such a balanced contemporary normative stand (Appiah, "Cosmopolitan Patriots," 617–639), while David T. Hansen advocates for a symbiotic relationship between "the local" and "the cosmopolitan" (Hansen, 128). Jocelyn Couture and Kai Nielsen represent a fourth normative stand in Brock and Breckenridge, *The Political Philosophy of Cosmopolitanism*, 191–192, with their notion of "cosmopolitan liberal nationalism."

173 See Beck, *The Cosmopolitan Vision*, 1–14.

174 See Berthelsen and Egebjerg, "Europa i Danmark, Danmark i Europa."

175 See Brandes, *Emigrantlitteraturen*, 111–114.

176 Georg Brandes, *Den romantiske Skole i Tydskland* (Copenhagen: Gyldendal, 1873), 7.

177 Ibid.

178 Brandes, *Den Franske Æsthetik i Vore Dage*, 73–74.

179 Brandes, *Emigrantlitteraturen*, 11.

180 Brandes, *Heinrich Heine*, 6–7.

181 See Larsen, *Professoratet*, 62–76.

182 Cf. Knudsen, *Frigørelsens Vej 1842–77*, 392–393.

183 Cf. Morris-Reich, *The Quest for Jewish Assimilation in Modern Social Science*; Birnbaum, *Geography of Hope*.

184 Simmel, "The Stranger," 182

185 Ibid.

186 Ibid.

187 Amos Morris-Reich, "Three Paradigms of 'The negative Jew:' Identity from Simmel to Zizek" in *Jewish Social Studies*, Vol. 10, Nr. 2 (Indiana University Press, 2004): 179-217.

188 See Birnbaum, *Geography of Hope*; Alexander, *The Dark Side of Modernity*; Morris-Reich, *The Quest for Jewish Assimilation in Modern Social Science*.

189 Ibid.

190 Morris-Reich, *The Quest for Jewish Assimilation in Modern Social Science*; Egbert Klautke, *The Mind of the Nation: Völkerpsychologie in Germany 1851–1955* (New York: Berghahn, 2014).

191 See Elias Bredsdorff, *Henrik Pontoppidan og Georg Brandes. En kritisk undersøgelse af Henrik Pontoppidans forhold til Georg Brandes og Brandes–linjen i dansk åndsliv* (Copenhagen: Gyldendal, 1964), 137–165.

192 See Beck, *The Cosmopolitan Vision*; Derrida, *Cosmopolitanism and Forgiveness*; Bauman, *Modernity and Ambivalence*; Julia Kristeva, *Strangers to Ourselves*; Homi K. Bhabha, "Our Neighbours, Ourselves. Contemporary Reflections on Survival."

193 See Morris–Reich, *The Quest for Jewish Assimilation in Modern Social Sciences*, 117–118.

194 See for example Kristeva, *Strangers to Ourselves*, 6–7: "He readily bears a kind of admiration for those who have welcomed him, for he rates them more often than not above himself, be it financially, politically or socially. At the same time he is quite ready to consider them somewhat narrow-minded. For his scornful hosts lack the perspective he himself has in order to see himself and to see them. The foreigner feels strengthened by the distance that detaches him from the others as it does from himself and gives him the lofty sense not so much of holding the truth but of making it and himself relative while others fall victim to the ruts of monovalency. For they are perhaps owners of things but for the foreigner tends to think he is the only one to have a biography, that is a life made upon of ordeals [...] a life in which acts constitute events because they imply choice, surprises, breaks, adaptions or cunning but neither routine nor rest."

195 Bauman refers to Simmel's essay several more times, for example on pp. 59–60, where he puts forward Simmel's stranger as the basis for his stranger concept.

196 See Kristeva, *Strangers to Ourselves*, 29, 38.

197 Bauman projects the ideal stranger as a role model for "the modern intellectual" on the following pages: Bauman, *Modernity and Ambivalence*, 82–84.

198 See, for example, Beck, *The Cosmopolitan Vision*, 1–14.

199 Ibid.

200 Simmel, "The Stranger," 182.

201 Ibid.

202 Ibid.

203 Simmel, "The Stranger," 181.

204 Simmel, "The Stranger," 182.

205 Bauman, *Modernity and Ambivalence*, 78.

206 Bauman, *Modernity and Ambivalence*, 102–159.

207 Ibid.

208 Simmel, "The Stranger," 182.

209 Simmel, "The Stranger," 184.

210 Ibid.

211 "On the other hand, there is a sort of 'strangeness' in which this very connection on the basis of a general quality embracing the parties is precluded. The relation of the Greeks to the barbarians is a typical example; so are all the cases in which the general characteristics one takes as peculiarly and merely human are disallowed to the other. But here the expression 'the stranger' no longer has any positive meaning. The relation with him is a non-relation; he is not what we have been discussing here: the stranger as a member of the group itself." Simmel, "The Stranger," 184.

212 Ibid.

213 Thus, Simmel writes that "the classical example of this is the history of the European Jews." See Simmel, "The Stranger," 182. He also states that further historical research of this particular type of stranger should focus on Jewish history.

214 Kristeva, *Strangers to Ourselves*, 38.

215 "What do we mean then by cosmopolitan outlook? Global sense, a sense of boundarylessness [...] reflexive awareness of ambivalence in a milieu of blurring differentiations and cultural contradictions. It reveals not just the 'anguish' but also the possibility of shaping one's life and social relations under conditions of cultural mixture. It is simultaneously a sceptical, disillusioned, self-critical outlook." See Beck, *The Cosmopolitan Vision*, 3.

216 See Sorkin, *The Transformation of German Jewry*; Shulamit Volkov, *Jüdisches Leben und Antisemitismus im 19. und 20. Jahrhundert*.

217 See Rosman, *How Jewish is Jewish History*, 115–116.

218 See Stanislawski, *Zionism and the Fin de Siècle*, 1–18.

219 Brandes, *Levned III*, 38–40.

220 Birnbaum, *Geography of Hope*, 1–35.

221 See Volkov, *Jüdisches Leben und Antisemitismus im 19. und 20. Jahrhundert*.

222 See Knudsen, *Frigørelsens Vej 1842–1877*; Kristian Hvidt, *Edvard Brandes. Portræt af en radikal blæksprutte* (Copenhagen: Gyldendal, 1987).

223 Nathansen, *Georg Brandes*, 242–243.

224 Simmel, "The Stranger," 181–182.

225 Simmel, "The Stranger," 182.

226 Brandes, "M. Goldschmidt," 409.

227 Yirmiyahu Yovel (in *The Other Within. The Marranos – Split Identity and Emerging Modernity* (Princeton: Princeton University Press, 2014)) makes an interesting case, however, demonstrating how a similar and vivid culture of Sephardic Jews and *conversos* lived with similar split identities for hundreds of years in Spain and Portugal from the ninth to the sixteenth century.

228 See George Mosse, "Jewish Emancipation – Between Bildung and Respectability," in *The Jewish Response to German Culture – from Enlightenment to the Second World War*, ed. Jehuda Reinharz and Walter Schatzberg (Hanover: University Press of New England, 1985), 1–16.

229 Brandes, "M. Goldschmidt," 402.

230 See Fenger, *Georg Brandes' Læreår*, 120–121, 170; Georg Brandes, *Det Unge Tyskland* (Copenhagen: Gyldendal, 1890), 353–359.

231 Simmel, "The Stranger," 182.

232 See Brandes, *Det unge Tyskland*, 353–359.

233 Karl Gutzkow, *Uriel Acosta. Trauerspiel in Fünf Aufzügen* (North Charleston: CreateSpace Independent Publishing, 2013), 31–33, 78–79.

234 Bredsdorff, *Henrik Pontoppidan og Georg Brandes*, 137–165; Klaus P. Mortensen, *Ironi og Utopi. En bog om Henrik Pontoppidan* (Copenhagen: Gyldendal, 1982), 191–194.

235 Stefanie von Schnurbein, "Literarischer Antisemitismus bei Knut Hamsun und Henrik Pontoppidan: Zwei Varianten mit unterschiedlicher Tendenz," in *European Journal of Scandinavian Studies* 44, no. 1 (2014): 90–102.

236 See Bredsdorff, *Henrik Pontoppidan og Georg Brandes*, 9–165.

237 See Bredsdorff, *Henrik Pontoppidan og Georg Brandes*, 150–163.

238 Ibid.

239 Ibid.

240 Ibid.

241 Henrik Pontoppidan (trans. Naomi Lebowitz), *Lucky Per* (New York: Peter Lang Publishing, 2010), 99–100.

242 Pontoppidan (trans. N. Lebowitz), *Lucky Per*, 135–136.

243 Ibid.

244 Bredsdorff, *Henrik Pontoppidan og Georg Brandes*, 150–163.

245 Pontoppidan (trans. N. Lebowitz), *Lucky Per*, 119.

246 Ibid.

247 Pontoppidan (trans. N. Lebowitz), *Lucky Per*, 136–141.

248 Pontoppidan (trans. N. Lebowitz), *Lucky Per*, 293–299.

249 Pontoppidan (trans. N. Lebowitz), *Lucky Per*, 318.

250 "Nathan kontrasterer farten, foretagsomheden, travlheden og energien i udlandet med danskernes sindighed, sløvhed og tidløse stille ståen. I modsætning til det aktive og revolutionære Europa står Danmark for Nathan som et 'Drømmenes overjordiske rige' – det er 'Torneroses Rige, hvor Tiden stod stille, og hvor Fantasteriets blege Rosenflor og Spekulationens sejge, tornede Stængler lumskelig skjulte det indre Forfald [... Nathan] havde mod til at gennembryde og [...] *sønderhugge det seje Drømmespind, det lodne, forhærdede Puppehylster, hvori Nationens Aand havde indkapslet sig*." Translated by NA from Bredsdorff, *Henrik Pontoppidan og Georg Brandes*, 140.

251 Bredsdorff, *Henrik Pontoppidan og Georg Brandes*, 146.

252 Ibid.

253 Pontoppidan (trans. N. Lebowitz), *Lucky Per*, 329

254 See Klautke, *The Mind of the Nation*, 31–35.

255 Ibid.

256 Ibid.

257 Bredsdorff, *Henrik Pontoppidan og Georg Brandes*, 203–256; Bent Haugaard Jeppesen, *Henrik Pontoppidans Samfundskritik* (Copenhagen: Vinten, 1977), 91–104.

258 Henrik Pontoppidan (trans. Naomi Lebowitz), *Lucky Per*, 376.

259 Ibid.

260 Henrik Pontoppidan (trans. Naomi Lebowitz), *Lucky Per*, 537–538.

261 Ibid.

262 Ibid.

263 See, for example, Nathansen, *Georg Brandes*, 27–38.

264 Translated by NA; see Knudsen, *Frigørelsens Vej 1842–77*, 320.

265 Translated by NA; see Knudsen, *Frigørelsens Vej 1842–77*, 320.

266 Klautke, *The Mind of the Nation*, 12.

267 Ibid.

268 Klautke, *The Mind of the Nation*, 1–4.

269 Joachin Schlör, *Das Ich in der Stadt. Debatten über Judentum und Urbanität, 1822–1938* (Göttingen: Vandenhoeck & Ruprecht, 2005), 349.

270 Ibid.

271 Ibid.

272 Klautke, *The Mind of the Nation*, 19.

273 Klautke, *The Mind of the Nation*, 20–21.

274 Ibid.

275 Rürup, *Emanzipation und Antisemitismus*, 74–94.

276 See Marcel Stoeltzer, "Cultural Difference in the national state: From trouser-selling Jews to unbridled multiculturalism," *Patterns of Prejudice* 42, no. 3 (2008), 250–254.

277 Heinrich von Treitschke, "Unsere Aussichten," in *Der Berliner Antisemitismusstreit*, ed. Walter Boehlich (Frankfurt am Main: Suhrkamp/Insel, 1965), 8–9.

278 Ibid.

279 Geller, *The Other Jewish Question*, 2.

280 Heinrich von Treitschke, "Unsere Aussichten," 8–12.

281 Ibid.

282 Ibid.

283 Stoeltzer, "Cultural Difference in the national state."

284 Klautke, *The Mind of the Nation*, 42–43.

285 Ibid.

286 Klautke, *The Mind of The Nation*, 23–24.

287 Translated from Moritz Lazarus, *Was heisst national?*, (Berlin: Ferd. Dümmlers Verlagsbuchhandlung, 1880), 39.

288 Translated from Lazarus, *Was heisst national?*, 43–44.

289 Simmel, "The Stranger," 181–182.

290 Translated from Lazarus, *Was heisst national?*, 44.

291 Translated from Lazarus, *Was heisst national?*, 45.

292 Klautke, *The Mind of the Nation*, 24–25.

293 Amos Morris-Reich, "Three Paradigms of 'The negative Jew:' Identity from Simmel to Zizek," *Jewish Social Studies* 10, no. 2 (Indiana University Press, 2004): 184–185.

294 Translated from Lazarus, *Was heisst national?*, 27.

295 Morris-Reich, "Three Paradigms of 'The Negative Jew,'" 184–185.

296 See Birnbaum, *Geography of Hope*, 124–125.

297 Shulamit Volkov, *Jüdisches Leben und Antisemitismus.*

298 See Paul Rubow, *Litterære Studier* (Copenhagen: Levin og Munksgaard, 1928); Kristensen, "Aktivisten Georg Brandes," in *Den politiske Georg Brandes*, ed. Hans Hertel and Sven Møller Kristensen (Copenhagen: Hans Reitzels Forlag, 1973), 22–26.

299 Ibid.

300 Jørgen Knudsen, *Symbolet og Manden, 1883–1895*, Vol. 2 (Copenhagen: Gyldendal, 1994), 327–377.

301 Jørgen Stender Clausen's anthologies are good examples of how Brandes continues to combine cosmopolitan practice with idealism in his later writings. See Clausen, *Det nytter ikke at sende hære mod idéer: Georg Brandes' kulturkritik i årene omkring 1. Verdenskrig*; Clausen, *Georg Brandes og Dreyfussaffæren.*

302 Cf. Nathansen, *Georg Brandes*, 100–104; Jørgen Knudsen, *Magt og Afmagt*, Vol. 1, 48–59; Tine Bach, *Exodus*, 207.

303 See Larsen, *Professoratet*, 62–75, 180–191, 220–235, 262–270, 275–283, 313–319, 326–329.

304 Kondrup, *Levned og Tolkninger*, 205.

305 Larsen, *Professoratet*, 130.

306 See Knudsen, *Symbolet og Manden*, 314–323; Brandes, *Levned III*, 28–37.

307 See Rubow, "Georg Brandes' forhold til Taine og Sainte–Beuve," 87–88.

308 Ibid.

309 See Brock and Brighouse, *The Political Philosophy of Cosmopolitanism*, 3–4.

310 See Berthelsen and Egebjerg, "Europa i Danmark, Danmark i Europa," 99–121; Allen, *Icons of Danish Modernity*, 16–124.

311 See Georg Brandes, "Sionismen," in *Samlede Skrifter 11* (Copenhagen: Gyldendal, 1902), 482–486.

312 Ibid.

313 Ibid.

314 See Stefan Zweig, *Verden af i går* (Copenhagen: Gyldendal, 2014), 33. For Herzl's (futuristic) division in the Jewish homeland, see Stanislawski, *Zionism and the Fin de Siècle*, 16–18.

315 See, for example, the articles Brandes wrote in defence of the Romanian Jews: "Jødiske og kristne rumænere" (1901), "Rumænsk Indfødsret" (1901), and "Sionismen" (1901), all in Georg Brandes, *Samlede Skrifter 11* (Copenhagen: Gyldendal, 1902), 456–486.

316 See Brandes, *Verdenskrigen* (Copenhagen: Gyldendal, 1916–17).

317 See Georg Brandes, "Raceteorier," in *Fugleperspektiv* (Copenhagen: Gyldendal, 1913), 167–173.

318 Ibid.

319 Ibid.

320 Ibid.

321 Ibid.

322 See Paul Lawrence Rose, "Renan versus Gobineau: Semitism and Antisemitism, Ancient Races and Modern Liberal Nations," *History of European Ideas* 39, no. 4 (2013): 528–540.

323 See Reinhardt Rürup, "Die Judenfrage der bürgerlichen gesellschaft und die Entstehung des modernes Antisemitismus," in *Emanzipation und Antisemitismus: "Studien zur Judenfrage" der bürgerlichen Gesellschaft* (Göttingen: Vandenhoeck & Ruprecht, 1975), 74–94.

324 Ibid.

325 Ibid.

326 See Jørgen Knudsen, *Symbolet og Manden*, Vol. 2 (Copenhagen: Gyldendal, 1994), 387–389.

327 See, for example, J. C. Heuch, *Dr. G. Brandes' Polemik mod Kristendommen* (Copenhagen: Gyldendal, 1877); Holger Drachmann, "Ostende–Brügge," in *Poetiske Skrifter*, Vol. 6 (Copenhagen: Gyldendal, 1911–12), 241–312; Konrad Simonsen, *Georg Brandes (Jødisk Aand i Danmark)* (Copenhagen: Nationale Forfatteres Forlag, 1913); Harald Nielsen, *Ursupatoren* (Copenhagen: Aschehoug, 1922).

328 See Georg Brandes, "Sagens Genoptagelse" (1903), in Georg Brandes, *Samlede Skrifter 16* (Copenhagen, Gyldendal, 1906), 188.

329 See Brandes, "Sagens Genoptagelse," 190.

330 See Stanislawski, *Zionism and the Fin de Siècle*, 1–19.

331 See Gibbons, "The reluctant Jew," 77–78.

332 See Georg Brandes, "Das neue Judentum," in Henri Nathansen, *Georg Brandes*, 266.

333 Ibid.

334 Translated from Treitschke, "Unsere Aussichten," 9.

335 Fenger, *Georg Brandes' Læreår*, 207–218.

336 See Brandes, "Bevægelsen mod Jøderne i Tyskland," 372–380.

337 Ibid.

338 See, for example, Sorkin, *The Transformation of German Jewry*, 107–123; Morris-Reich, *The Quest for Jewish Assimilation in Modern Social Science*.

339 See Larsen, *Professoratet*, 68–77, 127–132, 220–235, 262–270, 275–283, 313–319, 326–329.

340 See Larsen, *Professoratet*, 313–319.

341 Brandes, "M. Goldschmidt," 400.

342 Brandes, "M. Goldschmidt," 402.

343 Gibbons, "The reluctant Jew," 61.

344 See Brandes, *Samlede Skrifter 9*, 524.

345 Knudsen, *Magt og Afmagt*, Vol. 1, 113–117.

346 Ibid.

347 Ibid.

348 Brandes, "M. Goldschmidt," 404–405; Georg Brandes, "M. Goldschmidt," in *Samlede Skrifter* (1899), 455–456. Apart from the first edition of *Kritiker og Portraiter* in 1870 and the version of "M. Goldschmidt" in *Samlede Skrifter*, Brandes had in 1885 published a second edition of *Kritiker og Portraiter*. However, in this second edition, the essay "M. Goldschmidt" is not included. Still, the second edition of *Kritiker og Portraiter* from 1885 contains "Shakespeare: Kjøbmanden fra Venedig," with the parts about Jewish racial heritage and the trait of flexibility untouched. See Georg Brandes, *Kritik og Portraiter*, 2nd edn (Copenhagen: Gyldendal, 1885), 25–41.

349 See Knudsen, *Magt og Afmagt*, Vol. 1, 101–102.

350 Georg Brandes, *Julius Lange* (Copenhagen: Det Nordiske Forlag, 1898).

351 I have paraphrased this anecdote from Georg Brandes, *Levned I* (Copenhagen: Gyldendal, 1905), 20.

352 Ibid.

353 See, for example, Kondrup, *Levned og Tolkninger*, 90–215.

354 Ibid.

355 Tine Bach has shown how Brandes elsewhere in *Levned* describes how he learned and was used to reciting a Jewish evening prayer. See Bach, *Exodus*, 199. See also Gibbons, "The reluctant Jew," 67. In his biography of Edvard Brandes, Kristian Hvidt writes that as adults the Brandes brothers would visit their parents' house on the same day of the week and eat traditional Jewish dishes, particularly *Cholent*. See Hvidt, *Edvard Brandes*, 243–244.

356 In 1918, Nansen described the family home Brandes grew up in as rather "strong Jewish tinged." See Gibbons, "The reluctant Jew," 57–58. Edmund Gosse, who also visited the Brandes family home and met Brandes' mother, has similarly described the home of Brandes' parents as noticeably Jewish. See Knudsen, *Frigørelsens Vej 1842–77*, 41–42.

357 Brandes wrote an article that was published on 11 November 1901 in *Politiken* about how, for the first time, a "freethinker," Knut Wicksell, had been made a professor at the University of Lund. The article makes a clear analogy with Brandes' situation in Denmark. It catalyzed a petition among the professors at the University of Copenhagen; 40 out of 54 professors signed it, pleading for the appointment of Brandes, before it was handed over to the responsible *Venstre* minister, J. C. Christensen. See Knudsen, *Magt og Afmagt*, Vol. 1, 224–231.

358 Ibid.

359 See Larsen, *Professoratet*, 68–77, 127–132, 220–235, 262–270, 275–283, 313–319, 326–329.

360 See Larsen, *Professoratet*, 19–23.

361 See Knudsen, *I modsigelsernes tegn 1877–83*, 159–166.

362 See Rürup and Nipperdey, "Antisemitismus – Entstehung, Funktion und Geschichte," 95–114.

363 See Kondrup, *Livsværker*, 135–161; Per Dahl, *Om at skrive den danske ånds historie* (Copenhagen: Gyldendal, 1985), 9–25.

364 See Knudsen, *Magt og Afmagt*, Vol. 1, 218–219.

365 See Knudsen, *Magt og Afmagt*, Vol. 1, 101–102.

366 See Knudsen, *Magt og Afmagt*, Vol. 1, 224–229.

367 See Knudsen, *Magt og Afmagt*, Vol. 1, 228–229.

368 Translated by NA from Georg Brandes, *Smaa Romaner fra det Gamle Testamtente* (Copenhagen: Gyldendal, 1914), 157.

369 Georg Brandes, *Breve til Forældrene 1859–71, I: 1859–71* (Copenhagen: Det
Danske Sprog- og Litteraturselskab og C. A. Reitzels Boghandel, 1978); see, for
example, 18–19, 23–24, 30, 35, 40, 64–66, 80.

370 See Brandes, *Symbolet og Manden*, Vol. 2, 381–386.

371 In *Römische Geschichte* (1854–85), Mommsen had described the role of the
Jews in building the Roman Empire as related to a cosmopolitan-influenced
decomposition trait, as Jürgen Malitz details in the article "'Auch ein Wort
über unser Judenthum' Theodor Mommsen und der Berliner Antisemitismusstreit," 148–151. Mommsen portrayed the Jews as playing a particular
minority role in Caesar's vision of the development of the Roman Empire, the
decomposition trait functioning in an innovative and destructive way to shape
the national tradition in a dynamic and cultivating way. As such, according to
Mommsen, the Jews incarnated the cosmopolitan trait of acting as a third party. This characterization of the historical cosmopolitan role of Jews, which for
Mommsen operated as an analogy to how modern Germany should be built,
resembles the way in which Brandes in "M. Goldschmidt," Moritz Lazarus in
Was heisst national?, and Georg Simmel in "Exkurs über den Fremden" framed
Jews as less prejudiced and more objective, ideal strangers. In other words, we
have yet another example of how widespread the topos of the Jewish-related
ideal stranger was in the latter half of the nineteenth century, prior to Simmel's essay. However, in his use of Mommsen's characterization of the Jewish
historical role in nation-building Treitschke had stated that decomposition
was synonymous with the German term *Zersetzung*, as Malitz notes. He thus
synonymized Mommsen's originally positive term with an unambiguously
negative meaning of destruction; as such Treitschke changed the whole perspective on the role of Jews in the ancient shaping of European civilization. As
Jürgen Malitz documents, it is very likely that it was Treitschke's interpretation
of Mommsen's view on the historical role of the Jews in *Römische Geschichte*
that the leading Nazi Hermann Göring decades later referred to when he

spoke of the destructive cosmopolitanism of the Jews that was traceable in every national culture.

372 See Kondrup, *Livsværker*, 142–144; Dahl, *Om at skrive den danske ånds historie*, 15.

373 See Andersen, *Tider og Typer – Goethe II*, 181–262.

374 Translated by Nancy Aaen (NA) from Georg Brandes, "Jobs Bog," *Tilskueren* 10 (1893): 656.

375 See Damian Valdez, *German Philhellenism – The Pathos of Historical Imagination from Winckelmann to Goethe* (New York: Palgrave Macmillian, 2014), 1–56.

376 Ibid.

377 See Susannah Heschel, "Judaism, Islam, and Hellenism: the conflict in Germany over the origins of Kultur," in Jeremy Cohen and Richard I. Cohen, *The Jewish Contributions to Civilization: Reassessing an Idea* (Portland: The Littman Library of Jewish Civilization, 2008), 98–124.

378 Susannah Hechel, "Judaism, Islam, and Hellenism: the conflict in Germany over the origins of Kultur," 101.

379 See Alexander, *The Civil Sphere*, 463.

380 Leonard, *Socrates and the Jews*, 22.

381 See Amos Elon: *The Pity of It All: A Portrayal of the German-Jewish Epoch 1743–1933* (New York: Penguin Books, 2002), 33–64.

382 Ibid.

383 Ibid.

384 Ibid.

385 Ibid.

386 Leonard, *Socrates and the Jews*, 44–47

387 Leonard, *Socrates and the Jews*, 47.

388 See Richard I. Cohen: "'Jewish Contribution to Civilization' and its Implication for Notions of 'Jewish Superiority'," in *The Jewish Contribution to Civilization: Reasssessing an Idea*, ed. Richard I. Cohen (Portland: The Littman Library of Jewish Civilization, 2008), 11–23.

389 Leonard, *Socrates and The Jews*, 73–74.

390 Leonard, *Socrates and The Jews*, 74–75.

391 See also Yirmiyaho Yovel: "Sublimity and Resentment Hegel, Nietzsche, and the Jews," *Jewish Social Studies* 3, no. 3 (1997): 1–25.

392 See Knudsen, *Symbolet og Manden*, Vol. 2, 327–377.

393 See Kristensen, "Aktivisten Georg Brandes," 9–26.

394 Ibid.

395 See Rubow, *Georg Brandes og hans lærere*, 31.

396 See Brandes, *Levned III*, 151.

397 See Jakob Egholm Feldt, *Transnationalism and The Jews* (London: Rowman & Littlefield, 2016), 97.

398 Nietzsche's perception of the genealogical relation between Judaism and Christianity can for example be observed in this passage from the *Vorrede* to *Die Geburt der Tragödie*: "Christentum was von Anfang an wesentlich und gründlich, Ekel und Überdruss des Lebens am Leben, welcher sich unter dem Glauben an ein "anderes" oder "besseres" Leben nur verkleidete, nur versteckte, nur aufputzte. Der Hass auf die „Welt", der Fluch auf die Affekte, die Furcht vor der Schönheit und Sinnlichkeit, ein Jenseits, erfunden, um das Diesseits besser zu verleumden, im Grunde ein Verlangen in's Nicht's, an's Ende, in's Ausruhen, hin zum „Sabbat der Sabbate" – dies Alles dünkte mich, ebenso wie der unbedingte Wille des Christenthums, nur moralische Werthe gelten zu lassen, immer wie die gefährlichste und unheimlichste Form aller möglichen Formen eines „Willens zum Untergang," zum Mindestens ein Zeichen tiefster ERkrankung, Müdigkeit, Missmuthigkeit, Erschöpfung, Verarmung an Leben – denne vor der Moral (in Sonderheit christlichen, das heisst unbedingten Moral) muss das Leben beständig und unvermeidlich Unrecht bekommen, weil Leben etwas essentiell Unmoralisches ist." See Friedrich Nietzsche, *Die Geburt der Tragödie*, 7.

399 See Leonard, *Socrates And The Jews*, 162–176.

400 Simonsen, *Jødisk Aand i Danmark(Georg Brandes)*, 18

401 Kondrup, *Livsværker*, 135–161; Per Dahl, *Om at skrive den danske ånds historie*, 9–25. The fact that Vilhelm Andersen is still celebrated as the founding father of the pedagogy and didactics of literature in a Danish context can be seen, for example, in Thomas Illum Hansen, *Kognitiv Litteraturdidaktik* (Copenhagen: Dansklærerforeningens Forlag, 2011); Nikolaj Elf, *Danskfagets Didaktik. Undersøgelse af danskfagets didaktik* (Forlaget Dansksiden.dk, 2017).

402 Ibid.

403 See Vilhelm Andersen, *Tider og Typer – Goethe II*, 188. Translated by NA from the Danish: "Ingen Kritiker vilde falde paa at kalde Georg Brandes en græsk

Aand. Der er ikke græsk blod i ham [...] af alle græske forfattere er Lukian, en syrer, den eneste, som hans stil har nogen Lighed med."

404 Andersen, *Tider og Typer – Goethe II*, 192–197.

405 Translated by NA from Andersen, *Tider og Typer – Goethe II*, 195–196: "For saa vidt kunne Bjørnstjerne Bjørnson i en artikel i 'Fædrelandet' med nogen Ret frakende ham en 'dansk bevidsthed."

406 Andersen, *Tider og Typer – Goethe II*, 250.

407 Knudsen, *Uovervindelig Taber 1914–1927*, Vol. 1 (Copenhagen: Gyldendal, 2004), 197–199.

408 Henrik Tjørnehøj, *Rigets Bedste Mænd* (Copenhagen: Gyldendal, 1990), 60–61.

409 See Brandes, *Benjamin Disraeli*, 308-313.

410 See Brandes, *Levned III* (Copenhagen: Gyldendal, 1908), 31–32.

411 Ibid.

412 Brandes, *Levned III*, 38–40.

413 Ibid.

414 Brandes, *Levned III*, 38–40.

415 Translated by NA from Brandes, *Levned III*, 38–40.

416 Translated by NA from Georg Brandes, "Jøderne i Finland," in *Samlede Skrifter 18* (Copenhagen: Gyldendal, 1910), 439.

417 See Knudsen, *Symbolet og Manden 1883–95*, Vol. 2, 378–387.

418 Translated by NA from Brandes, *Det Unge Tyskland*, 312; Brandes, *Heinrich Heine*, 29–30.

419 Brandes believes that Hegel was the primary source for Heine's ideal of Hellenism. See Brandes, *Heinrich Heine*, 29–32.

420 Ibid.

421 Ibid.

422 Translated by NA from Brandes, *Sagnet om Jesus*, 50–51.

423 Brandes, *Sagnet om Jesus*, 51: "Maaske var nazaræernes sekt oprindeligt den samme som nasiræerne, i betydning altsaa af indviet eller hellig, fordi de beflittede sig pa et ærbart liv, afholdt sig fra vin, lod haar og skæg voxe."

424 Brandes, *Sagnet om Jesus*, 50–51.

425 Sutcliffe, *Judaism and Enlightenment*, 210–211.

426 Sutcliffe, *Judaism and Enlightenment*, 203–210.

427 Sutcliffe, *Judaism and Enlightenment*, 210–211.

428 Georg Brandes, *Petrus* (Copenhagen: Gyldendal, 1926), 34

429 Georg Brandes, "Jobs Bog," *Tilskueren* 10 (1893): 656.

430 Cohen, "'Jewish Contribuition to Civilization,'" 18–20. For Brandes' references to Graetz, see Brandes, "Kohélet," *Tilskueren* 11 (1894): 820, 836.

431 See Cohen, "'Jewish Contribution to Civilization,'" 18–20. See also Heschel, "Judaism, Islam, and Hellenism: The Conflict in Germany Over the Origins of Kultur," 101–102.

432 Brandes, "Jobs Bog," 661.

433 Brandes, "Jobs Bog," 664–665.

434 Brandes, "Jobs Bog," 664–665.

435 Brandes, "Kohélet," 817–823.

436 Brandes, "Kohélet," 837.

437 Ibid.

438 Brandes, "Kohélet," 827.

439 Brandes, "Kohélet," 829.

440 Brandes, "Jobs Bog," 656.

441 Brandes, *Levned I*, 114–117.

442 See, for example, Paul Rubow, *Georg Brandes' Briller*; Henning Fenger, *Georg Brandes' Læreår*, 123–173 (even in the last sentences of this chapter, Kierkegaard gets the last word); Jørgen Knudsen, *Frigørelsens Vej 1842–1877*, 55–67. See also the influence Kierkegaard (and not Spinoza) is believed to have had on Brandes in this standard encyclopaedical description of Brandes: *Gyldendals Biografi Leksikon*: http://denstoredanske.dk/Dansk_Biografisk_Leksikon/Kunst_og_kultur/Litteratur/Forfatter/Georg_Brandes.

443 See Israel, *Radical Enlightenment*; Steven Nadler, *A Book Forged in Hell – Spinoza's Scandalous Treatise and the Birth of the Secular Age* (Princeton: Princeton University Press, 2011); Willi Goetschel, *Spinoza's Modernity – Mendelssohn, Lessing, and Heine* (Madison: The University of Wisconsin Press, 2004).

444 See, for example, Berthelsen and Egebjerg, "Europa i Danmark, Danmark i Europa."

445 See Brandes, "M. Goldschmidt," 397–408; Brandes, *Benjamin Disraeli*, 308–313; Brandes, *Levned I*, 114–117; Brandes, "Das neue Judentum," 257–266.

446 Timothy Brennan, *Cosmopolitanism Now* (Cambridge (Mass.): Harvard University Press, 1997); Kwame Anthony Appiah, "Cosmopolitan Patriots," *Critical*

Inquiry 23, no. 3 (Spring, 1997): 617–639; Brock and Brighouse, *The Political Philosophy of Cosmopolitanism*; Pollock, Bhabha, Breckenridge, and Chakrabarty, "Cosmopolitanisms"; Beck, *The Cosmopolitan Vision*; Fine, *Cosmopolitanism*; David T. Hansen, "Dewey and Cosmopolitanism," *E&C/ Education & Culture* 25, no. 2 (2009): 126–140; Miller and Ury, "Cosmopolitanism: The End of Jewishness?"

447 Ibid.

448 As mentioned, most of the scholars who have contributed to the blossoming of cosmopolitan literature in the last three decades suggest a balance between a national/particularistic outlook and a cosmopolitan mindset. Kwame A. Appiah, for instance, posits "cosmopolitan patriotism" as an example of such a balanced contemporary normative stand (Appiah, "Cosmopolitan Patriots," 617–639). Jocelyn Couture and Kai Nielsen represent a fourth normative stand in Brock and Breckenridge, *The Political Philosophy of Cosmopolitanism*, 191–192, with their notion of "cosmopolitan liberal nationalism."

449 Pollock, Bhabha, Breckenridge, and Chakrabarty, "Cosmopolitanisms," 578.

450 Kant, "Idea for a Universal History with a Cosmopolitan Purpose," in *Kant's Political Writings*, ed. Hans Reis (Cambridge: Cambridge University Press, 1970), 49.

451 Kant, "Idea for a Universal History with a Cosmopolitan Purpose," 51.

452 Kant, "Idea for a Universal History with a Cosmopolitan Purpose," 49.

453 Kant, "Idea for a Universal History with a Cosmopolitan Purpose," 50–51.

454 See, for example, Feldt, "Forskellige i Fællesskab. Moses Mendelssohn og Frigørelsen"; Leonard, *Socrates and The Jews*, 56–61; Michael Mack, *German Idealism and The Jew*, 23–41.

455 Ibid.

456 Ibid.

457 Ibid.

458 Ibid.

459 Ibid.

460 Kant, "Idea for a Universal History with a Cosmopolitan Purpose," 52.

461 Feldt, "Forskellige i Fællesskab. Moses Mendelssohn og Frigørelsen"; Leonard, *Socrates and The Jews*, 56–61; Michael Mack, *German Idealism and The Jew*, 23–41.

462 Stanislawski, *Zionism and the Fin de Siècle*, 13.

463 Fenger, *Georg Brandes' Lærear*, 38–39.

464 Israel, *Radical Enlightenment*, 11.

465 See Immanuel Kant, "Perpetual Peace. A Philosophical Sketch," in *Kant's Political Writings*, ed. Hans Reis (Cambridge: Cambridge University Press, 1970), 100–102.

466 Brandes, *Emigrantlitteraturen*, 16, 21.

467 Translated by NA from Brandes, "M. Goldschmidt," 401.

468 Brandes, *Levned I*, 114–117.

469 See Israel, *Radical Enlightenment*, 159–327.

470 Schwartz, *The First Modern Jew*, 15–32.

471 Sutcliffe, *Judaism and Enlightenment*, 133–137.

472 Israel, *Radical Enlightenment*, 160–173.

473 Schwartz, *The First Modern Jew*, 28–30.

474 Ibid.

475 In this context, Yuri Slezkine's *The Jewish Century* (2006) could also be mentioned.

476 Sutcliffe, *Judaism and Enlightenment*, 121–122; Nadler, *A Book Forged In Hell*, 61–66, 108–112.

477 The very first works containing eternal Jew readings of Spinoza, for example Wachter's book, laid the ground for this view of modernity as Jewish-based, since they position the kabbalah as a major influence; however, the kabbalah is only mentioned once in the *Tractatus*, and Spinoza writes negatively about it. See Spinoza, *Theologisch-politische Abhandlung*, chapter 9, 113–124. See also Schwartz, *The First Modern Jew*, 28–32.

478 Fenger, *Georg Brandes' Lærear*, 80, 120–121, 131–143, 169–170.

479 Fenger, *Georg Brandes' Lærear*, 120–121, 170.

480 Fenger, *Georg Brandes' Lærear*, 80, 120–121, 131–143, 169–170.

481 Schwartz, *The First Modern Jew*, 72.

482 See Israel, *Radical Enlightenment*, 13.

483 Fenger, *Georg Brandes' Lærear*, 120–121, 170.

484 Sorkin, *The Transformation of German Jewry*, 140–155.

485 Fenger, *Georg Brandes' Lærear*, 120–121, 170.

486 "It is difficult to say anything pleasant about Auerbach except that he was probably a good human being. [...] His work can in no way be compared to the masculine art of Gottfried Keller. In his Jewish pseudo–historical novels, there is a sickly humanism and tolerance, with which even the most passionate admirer of Lessing and Lessing's Nathan will have difficulties. [...] Brandes' admiration should be understood on the basis of the historical context – and the racial kinship." Translated from Fenger, *Georg Brandes' Læreår*, 120–121.

487 See Schwartz, *The First Modern Jew*, 55–79; Skolnik, *Jewish Cultural Memory and the German Historical Novel*, 23–44.

488 Schwartz, *The First Modern Jew*, 72.

489 See Schwartz, *The First Modern Jew*, 55–79; Skolnik, *Jewish Cultural Memory and the German Historical Novel*, 23–44.

490 Nadler, *A Book Forged In Hell*, 108–112.

491 Translated from Berthold Auerbach, *Spinoza – Romanbiografie* (Berlin: Europäischer Literaturverlag, 2014), 84.

492 Translated from Auerbach, *Spinoza*, 236.

493 Skolnik, *Jewish Cultural Memory and the German Historical Novel*, 23–44.

494 Schwartz, *The First Modern Jew*, 72–73.

495 Auerbach, *Spinoza*, 256–259.

496 Ibid.

497 David Biale, *Not In The Heavens: The Tradition of Jewish Secular Thought* (Princeton: Princeton University Press, 2011), 1–14.

498 Leonard, *Socrates and The Jews*, 1–104, 139–176.

499 See for example Brennan, *Cosmopolitanism Now*; Brock and Brighouse, *The Political Philosophy of Cosmopolitanism*; Beck, *The Cosmopolitan Vision*; Fine, *Cosmopolitanism*.

500 Ibid.

501 Spinoza, *Theologisch-politisch Abhandlung*, chapter 17, 179–196.

502 Translated by NA from Brandes, *Benjamin Disraeli*, 311–312.

503 See Brandes, *Jobs Bog*, 656.

504 See Brandes, *Jobs Bog*, 664–665.

505 See Brandes, *Jobs Bog*, 661

506 Translated by NA from Brandes, *Jobs Bog*, 661.

507 Translated by NA from Brandes, *Jobs Bog*, 662.

508 Translated by NA from Brandes, *Jobs Bog*, 662.

509 Brandes, *Kohélet*, 827–828.

510 As regards the influence of Nietzche on Brandes from the late 1880s and on-wards, the first lines of the following quotation could also viewed as a reaction to Nietzsche's point that the Christian idealization of suffering and compassion originally stems from Judaism.

511 Brandes, *Kohélet*, 828.

512 Brandes, *Kohélet*, 828–829.

513 Brandes, *Kohélet*, 829–830.

514 Brandes, *Kohélet*, 837.

515 Brandes, *Smaa Romaner fra Det Gamle Testamente*, 163–164.

516 Brandes, *Sagnet om Jesus*, 14–15.

517 Miller and Ury, "Cosmopolitanism: The End of Jewishness?", 347.

518 Larsen, *Professoratet*, 232–233.

519 Brandes, "Das neue Judentum," in Nathansen, *Georg Brandes*, 257–266.

520 Brandes, "Das neue Judentum," 259.

521 Brandes, "Das neue Judentum," 258.

522 Brandes, "Das neue Judentum," 266.

523 See Georg Brandes, "M. Goldschmidt," in *Kritikerog Portraiter* (Copenhagen: Gyldendal, 1870), 401; Brandes, *Levned III* (Copenhagen: Gyldendal, 1908), 308.

524 Miller and Ury, "Cosmopolitanism: The End of Jewishness?"

525 Ibid.

526 Rosman, *How Jewish is Jewish History*, 126.

527 In *Modernity and the Holocaust*, Bauman defines "sliminess" thus: "As a matter of fact, the explosion of modern scientific method and the powerful strides towards the rationalization of daily life in the early years of modern history coincided with the most fierce and vicious episode of witch-hunting in history. [...] It was, on the other hand, most intimately related to the intensity of anxi-eties and tensions provoked or generated by the collapse of the ancient régime and the advent of modern order. The old securities disappeared [...]. Age-long distinctions were ignored, safe distances shrank, strangers emerged from their reserves and moved next door, secure identities lost durability and conviction. Whatever remained of old boundaries had to be built around new identities – this time, moreover, under conditions of universal movement and accelerating

change. [...] I propose that the conceptual Jew has been historically construed as the universal 'viscosity' of the Western world. He has been located astride virtually every barricade erected by the successive conflicts that tore apart the Western society at its various stages and in various dimensions. The very fact that the conceptual Jew straddled so many different barricades, built on so many, ostensibly unrelated, front lines, endowed his sliminess with the elsewhere unknown, exorbitant intensity. His was a multi-dimensional unclarity and the very multi-dimensionality was an extra cognitive incongruence unencountered in all other [...] 'viscous' categories spawned by boundary conflicts." See Zygmunt Bauman, *Modernity and the Holocaust* (Cornell University Press: London, 1989), 40–41.

528 See Daniel Boyarin and Jonathan Boyarin, "Diaspora: Generation and the Ground of Jewish Identity," *Critical Inquiry* 19 (1993): 693–725.

529 See Rosman, *How Jewish is Jewish History*, 127.

530 Jordheim, "Against Periodization", 159.

531 See Beck, *The Cosmopolitan Vision*, 73–74.

532 See Beck, *The Cosmopolitan Vision*, 1–5.

533 See, for example, Fine, *Cosmopolitanism*, 6–14; Victor Roudometof, "Transnationalism, Cosmopolitanism, and Glocalization," *Current Sociology* 53 no. 1 (January 2005): 116–117.

534 Fine, *Cosmopolitanism*, 6–14.

535 Beck, *The Cosmopolitan Vision*, 1–14.

536 See Brock and Brighouse, *The Political Philosophy of Cosmopolitanism*, 3.

537 See Karl Marx, "Speech at Anniversary of People's Paper" in Karl Marx & Friedrich Engels, *Selected Works,* Vol. 1 (Moscow: Progress Publishers, 1969), p. 500

538 See, for example, Roudometof, "Transnationalism, Cosmopolitanism, and Glocalization," 113–135.

539 See Derrida, *Cosmopolitanism and Forgiveness*, 18–23; Beck, *Cosmopolitan Vision*, 9, 20, 46–47; Fine, *Cosmopolitanism*, ix–xvii, 4, 22–38; Mcmurran, "The New Cosmopolitanism and the Eighteenth Century," 23–27.

540 Fine, *Cosmopolitanism*, 4.

541 Kant, "Idea for a Universal History with a Cosmopolitan Purpose," 52.

542 Sheldon Pollock, Homi K Bhbaha, Carol A. Breckenridge, and Dipesh Chakrabarty, "Cosmopolitanisms," 585–586.

543 Beck, *The Cosmopolitan Vision*, 1.

544 Beck, *The Cosmopolitan Vision*, 9–10, 45–46, 128, 167–168.

545 Miller and Ury, "Cosmopolitanism: The End of Jewishness?"

546 See Bauman, *Modernity and Ambivalence*, 82–84.

547 In a comment on this genre's importance, Richard Kämmerling writes in *Die Welt* that "Er bietet dem Leser die Chance, sich in seiner Fremde zu Hause zu fühlen." See https://www.welt.de/kultur/literarischewelt/article151957006/Man-sollte-uns-zwingen-den-Fluechtlingen-zuzuhoeren.html.

548 Firstly, on page 4, Derrida writes that the "cities of refuge" will be inhabited by all types of migrants, and thus all migrants will come to describe the more progressive civilization of these cities: "Whether it be the foreigner in general, the immigrant, the exiled, the deported, the stateless or the displaced person [...], we would ask these cities of refuge to reorient the politics of the state." However, on page 6, he modifies the definition of the inhabitants so that now the rather progressive migrants and refugees are mainly intellectuals, journalists, and artists: "the victims of these are innumerable and nearly always anonymous but increasingly, they are what one refers to as intellectuals, scholars, journalists, and writers – men and women capable of speaking out [...] – in a public domain that the new powers of communication render increasingly formidable." See Derrida, *Cosmopolitanism and Forgiveness*, 4–6.

549 Ibid.

550 Derrida, *Cosmopolitanism and Forgiveness*, 23.

551 See Derrida, *Cosmopolitanism and Forgiveness*, 4–5.

552 Bhabha, "Our Neighbours, Ourselves," 2–3.

553 Ibid.

554 Inger Hammar, "From Fredrika Bremer to Ellen Key: Calling, Gender and the Emancipation Debate in Sweden, c. 1830-1900" in *Gender and Vocation: Women, Religion, and Social Change in the Nordic Countries, 1830-1940*, ed. By Pirjo Markkola (Helsinki: Finnish Literary Society, 2000), 58.

555 See Biale, *Not in the Heavens*, 16–17.

556 At one point, Graetz writes to Marx: "Its author is a rude realist in a world of fantasies turned towards the heavens, who had the courage to say outright that in a certain sense this world should be more important than that doubtful other world and who nineteen hundred years ago already preached the rehabilitation of the flesh." Biale, *Not in the Heavens*, 17.

557 See Kant, "Idea for a Universal History with a Cosmopolitan Purpose," 45.

558 Georg Brandes, "Jobs Bog," 656.

559 Brandes, "Shakespeare: 'Kjøbmanden i Venedig," 119–120.

560 Brandes, "M. Goldschmidt," 409.

561 Brandes, *Benjamin Disraeli*, 311–312.

562 Brandes, "Ferdinand Lassalle (Første Afsnit)," 250–251.

563 Brandes, "M. Goldschmidt," 400–401.

564 Brandes, *Benjamin Disraeli*, 312.

565 Brandes, "M. Goldschmidt," 400.

566 Brandes, *Emigrantlitteraturen*, 111–113.

567 Brandes, *Emigrantlitteraturen*, 28.

568 Brandes, *Emigrantlitteraturen*, 99.

569 Brandes, *Den romantiske Skole i Tydskland*, 7.

570 Brandes, *Den Franske Æsthetik i Vore Dage*, 73–74.

571 Brandes, *Emigrantlitteraturen*, 11.

572 Brandes, *Heinrich Heine*, 6–7

573 Brandes, *Levned III*, 38–40.

574 See Georg Brandes, "Jøderne i Finland," 439.

575 See Brandes, *Det Unge Tyskland*, 312; Brandes, *Heinrich Heine*, 29–30.

576 Brandes, *Sagnet om Jesus*, 50–51.

577 Brandes, "Jobs Bog," 656.

578 Brandes, "Jobs Bog," 661.

579 Brandes, "Kohélet," 827–828.

580 Brandes, "Kohelet," 829–830.

581 Brandes, *Levned*, 114–118.

582 Brandes, "Jobs Bog," 662.

583 Brandes, "Kohélet," 828–829

584 Brandes, *Smaa Romaner fra Det Gamle Testamente*, 163–164.

585 Moritz Lazarus, *Was heisst national?*, (Berlin: Ferd. Dümmlers Verlagsbuch-handlung, 1880), 39.

586 Lazarus, *Was heisst national?*, 43–44.

587 Lazarus, *Was heisst national?*, 44.

588 Lazarus, *Was heisst national?*, 45.

589 Lazarus, *Was heisst national?*, 27.

590 Heinrich von Treitschke, "Unsere Aussichten," 9.

591 See Berthold Auerbach, *Spinoza – Romanbiografie* (Berlin: Europäischer Literaturverlag, 2014), 84.

592 Auerbach, *Spinoza*, 236.

Index of Names

References to Georg Brandes are omitted, as well as references
to fictitious and Biblical names